Counterproductive

From "Life," 1913.

Efficiency Crank: Young man, are you aware that you employed fifteen unnecessary motions in delivering that kiss?

Counterproductive

Time Management in the Knowledge Economy

MELISSA GREGG

DUKE UNIVERSITY PRESS

DURHAM AND LONDON

2018

Designed by Matthew Tauch
Typeset in Minion Pro and The Sans C4s
by Copperline Books

Library of Congress Cataloging-in-Publication Data
Names: Gregg, Melissa, [date] author.
Title: Counterproductive : time management in the
knowledge economy / Melissa Gregg.
Description: Durham : Duke University Press, 2018. |
Includes bibliographical references and index.
Identifiers: LCCN 2018035549 (print)
LCCN 2018044222 (ebook)
ISBN 9781478002390 (ebook)
ISBN 9781478000716 (hardcover : alk. paper)
ISBN 9781478000907 (pbk. : alk. paper)
Subjects: LCSH: Time management. | Labor productivity. |
Performance standards. | Mindfulness (Psychology) | Success
in business—Psychological aspects.
Classification: LCC HD69.T54 (ebook) |
LCC HD69.T54 G74 2018 (print) | DDC 658.4/093—dc23
LC record available at https://lccn.loc.gov/2018035549

Cover art: Richard Ibghy and Marilou Lemmens,
Output Index (1848–1957), from the series, *Each Number
Equals One Inhalation and One Exhalation*, 2016–2017.

Frontispiece: Cartoon reproduced in Mark Sullivan,
*Our Times: The United States 1900–1925, Part IV,
The War Begins 1909–1914* (New York: Charles Scribner's
Sons, 1932), 87.

FOR MY FATHER, who showed me the value of perseverance

in work and the freedom to be gained from building

a world on one's own terms

Contents

Preface

I can't remember when I started doing it. Every time I visit a second-hand bookstore, I head to the business section to look for self-help manuals. The particular style I like is addressed to wannabe executives struggling to get their act together. The frank titles and bold fonts cut to the chase: Getting Things Done. Stress and the Manager. Leave the Office Earlier. How to Get Control of Your Time and Your Life. The melodrama of corporate careers, life-job conflicts, and endless bureaucratic bloat transpired in an entertaining yet poignant way. Initially, the books provided solutions to a world of work that I barely knew. I had not personally experienced many of the issues that were commonplace in the authors' stories, which were based on the anxieties that so many others apparently faced. I read to overcome my own lack of exposure to the culture of office life. Perhaps this curiosity came from growing up in an extremely remote place, with no real work culture to speak of, such that the idea of an organizational career seemed completely strange. And yet, over the years that my purchasing practice grew in to the text you are now reading, the dilemmas recounted in my time management guides became increasingly—indeed, painfully—familiar.

When I started buying used self-help books, it seemed nothing more than a perverse side hobby. One day I might have a chance to apply my literary training to these works and write about time management as a genre, I figured. The formulaic advice imparted by productivity gurus fascinated me, especially given how often they simply repackage already well-known tips. If the point of the books is to impart the secrets of professional success, how secret can they be? I wondered. How does this insatiable industry for productivity continue trading on essentially unchanging insights? I concluded that the function of the books has to be something other than purely practical or we would never need so many versions of the same advice. The consolation readers find in the idea of productivity is the real basis of my interest: the pleasure entertained in the fantasy that time can be managed.

Time management manuals bear all the hallmarks of the definition of genre that I learned from Graeme Turner, among other scholars of popular culture. A genre is a predictable narrative that provides satisfying imaginary resolutions to persistent social contradictions. Like the fairy-tales from which they typically emerge, genres have the function of acknowledging what is unacceptable or difficult about the organization of a world, only to conclude with an enlightened reassertion of the status quo. The implications of this principle for the politics of contemporary labor form the substance of my analysis in this book. Delivering productivity pedagogy to isolated readers, time management genres have assisted in the dissolution of collective action against the structural transformations to knowledge work over many decades. Their optimistic formulas simulate a structure for "immaterial" workloads—the unquantifiable labors that mid-rank professionals perform to maintain ongoing employment. Productivity instruction is the hokey Band-Aid covering much deeper problems that affect the way work is arranged in the present. And it is here that I must mention another guiding factor in this book's development: the discovery of self-help guides in my mother's library after she died of cancer.

Sandra Gregg (formerly De Soza) was a teacher, a first-generation university graduate from a conservative working-class family. She had few immediate role models for managing a career that involved commuting between an island home on a sheep farm and a job teaching high school girls in the city. The fact that self-development books appeared on her shelf seemed proof to me that a degree of stress attended her characteristically graceful composure for an unknown amount of time. I will always wonder whether work-related anxiety contributed to her persistent illness and whether a different way to organize her schedule would have helped.

As I have come to reflect on this project, the trauma of unexpected death, my acquisitive practice, and the topic of time management appear to be intricately linked. I now realize that this book is a culmination of many densely buried habits of coping with the disruptive change that my mother's passing precipitated. I expressed some of these suspicions in a blog post following the first complete draft of the manuscript. I wrote to process the surprising outpouring of emotion that came over me when I submitted the book to my patient editor. It was not the typical relief of getting an overdue deadline off my back. Instead it was a vast wave of grief that cascaded out of my body as I meditated alone one evening. In the concluding parts of this book, I explore some of the reasons that this experience of purging and loss may have arrived when I was also extremely happy to have laid something important to rest. The actual blog post I include as a postscript.

I   Theory

Introduction

The Productivity Imperative

Counterproductive explores how productivity emerged as a way to think about workplace performance at the turn of the twentieth century and its ongoing consequences for the administration of labor today. This history of time management—in theory and in practice—offers an account of the philosophical underpinnings for productivity, a reappraisal of its original premises, and a set of provocations regarding its ongoing relevance in the modern workplace. At a macro level, productivity is the principal metric used in domestic economic modeling and forecasts for enterprise efficiency. But as my previous research has shown, for the many workers involved in information and communication services, productivity is also experienced as an archly personal, everyday concern.[1] A dwindling supply of secure, predictable jobs, combined with a cutthroat job market for heavily indebted college graduates, creates pressure to prove one's ongoing value. For the generations making a living in the shadow of the Organization, the productivity imperative is an intimate interpellation.[2] It is the cumulative effect of corporate cost-cutting measures that urge employees to "do more with less" and "work smarter, not harder."[3]

A significant contradiction exists in the aspiration to be productive when statistics reflect a decline in salaried compensation relative to corporate earnings. According to the McKinsey Institute, the present generation of workers has little hope of achieving the level of wealth of their parents.[4] In the United States, vast inequalities persist between workers within and across states, split between low-wage service work and highly compensated technical trades.[5] The outsourcing of "mental" as much as "manual" labor involves evacuating middle-class jobs to the lowest global bidder.[6] Given these circumstances, it seems timely to ask: to what end do we need to be productive—for our own good or for our managers'? Who are our bosses, anyway, in a world of decentralized, algorithmic labor? Is productivity even the right measure for work when jobs with discrete, measurable outputs may be in decline?

These questions, while worthy of analysis in their own right, arise from a set of unresolved issues that linger from my previous book, *Work's Intimacy*, for which *Counterproductive* may stand as a prequel. Both books seek a language to explain why apparently privileged people work as often and as hard as they do.[7] My earlier analysis found that information professionals derive a compelling degree of pleasure from the performance of productivity, at times to the detriment of other personal or social interests. The current book is prompted by this historical curiosity, in which workers learn to "do what they love" in the service of others' profit.[8] I want to provide a backstory for today's heady narratives of passion exercised through work.

To do this, I focus on one resilient trait. *Counterproductive* shows how time mastery became a defining quality of professionals over an extended historical period, remaining constant through successive waves of managerial discourse.[9] The imposition of temporal regimes through efficiency engineering directed the affective intensity of labor accomplishment in two ways: first, toward heroic individual feats for external measurement, and later, toward inwardly generated methods of self-scrutiny and enhancement. This gradual adjustment to productivity as common sense was a necessary reconfiguration of attitudes toward self and work performance. It was the principal means by which management regimes upended the default assumption of labor politics—namely, that solidarity and power are formed through the collective imposition of work limits.

From the earliest instances of time management in the factory to the software that facilitates disparate schedules today, the following chapters show how the productivity imperative separated workers from one another by assuming a logical order of privilege. Valuable jobs became concentrated at the top of the organizational hierarchy, accruing ever greater status, while tasks deemed trivial were delegated or outsourced to subordinates. Productivity logic thus sanctions those whose labor is regarded as vital in advancing the spirit of enterprise and justifies the ability to offload mundane matters to others. This is the way in which we can say that productivity is hegemonic in the modern workplace: efficiency thinking normalizes asociality and asymmetry in the guise of appropriate professional conduct. To overcome this way of organizing labor requires a fundamental reckoning with the legacy of the corporate firm and the practices inherited from industrialization.

As we will see, much of this history is gendered. In the Fordist era, the executive-secretary was the standard delegation couplet, part of a comprehensive sexual contract that required women's poorly compensated participation.[10] In feminism's aftermath, contemporary productivity technologies displace the ongoing trauma arising from the death of the secretary.[11] Today's startups openly celebrate the delegation dynamic and the beauty of software-led servitude: "By far our most common service," says Ted Roden of the task-harvesting website Fancy Hands, "is making phone calls for people. Calling a restaurant, for example, to change a reservation that was really hard to get in the first place—that's the sort of thing that most of us would like to hand off to someone else, but until now couldn't find anyone willing to do it."[12] The gradual retreat of the office secretary in the service of others' productivity is here offset by technologies that continue the same tradition of entitled delegation. The digital personal assistant—the TaskRabbit, the Uber driver, and the Turk worker—is the technical means by which class privilege can be maintained despite widespread occupational insecurity.[13] For an elite demographic of professionals, technology provides both the *techniques* (skills) and the *technics* (infrastructure) that enable the *practice* of productivity.[14] Digital platforms offer a system for interchangeable tasks and a simulated management function that offsets the need to identify work limits. This process is captured in the tagline for the popular productivity package Evernote, whose premium upgrade "keeps your progress predictable, even when the workday isn't."[15] Technology's dependable role is likewise evident in innovations such as Humin, an app that its website claims "remembers all the tiny details about how and where you met someone"—much like an old-school secretary. In each case, a device running a program ensures elegance in social encounters, especially when status and credibility are at stake.

For its middle-class users, productivity software offers a reassuring if topical salve for a period of perceived ontological volatility. Time management tools are material and psychological support for jobs and careers that are felt to be unstable, improvised, and forever running at a frantic pace. Efforts to control time are a way to cope with this condition of so-called *precarity*, which many scholars consider the defining character of our contemporary moment.[16] By focusing on genres of time management, my analysis continues the work of critics such as Lauren Berlant, especially the textual examples she reads as symptoms of the impasse that post-Fordism represents to notions of "the good life."[17] The very prospect of a salaried lifestyle is just one aspect of the broader paradigm of social security institutionalized, albeit briefly, in the postwar settlement. Paying attention to productivity technologies, and the social practice of delegation in particular, we can see that insecure work seems pervasive now only because it is experienced by growing numbers of workers whose time was once managed by others.[18] For the many partially employed gig workers, contract staff, and laborers who make a living at the will of suppliers, contingency has always been the lived condition of employment. These qualifications are essential to adequately describe the stakes of a globally mediated and persistently racialized division of labor today.[19]

In the case of the salaried workers who are my primary focus, devolved hierarchies, mobile technology and the push for more flexible working hours mean that time is experienced differently than the iconic 9–5 regime.[20] The fetish for collaboration in large and small organizations renders working days subject to individual calendars and dispositions. Schedules become battle zones of alignment between distributed peers in teams, adding a layer of coordination to what had previously been taken-for-granted office presence.[21] This decentralized professional milieu is less a matter of increasing busyness among workers as it is the logistical nightmare of achieving synchronicity. In the words of Judy Wajcman, this is a problem not of time but of *timing*.[22] Wajcman's empirical evidence demonstrates that time pressure results from multiple converging elements. Among the relevant factors, she lists an increase in the *volume* of work expected of employees; an increase in *temporal*

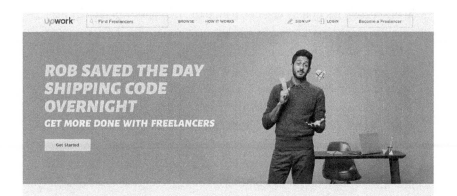

FIGURE I.1 Digital platforms for gig work trade on an idea of productivity that normalizes delegation as the marker of professional success.

disorganization as worker and workplace lose their innate proximity; and the phenomenon of *temporal density.* The latter is the intensification of job function when multitasking and moving between different tasks becomes ingrained.[23] The psychological toll of windows, tabs and feeds filtering through devices, on top of the already hectic pace of meeting-heavy corporate cultures, creates a feeling of perennial context switch. Today's productivity performances are therefore characterized by the porousness of work's physical and temporal architectures, exacerbated by new technologies and platforms. Subsequent chapters reveal how previous examples of efficiency engineering also reflect their own particular socioeconomic and technological circumstances.

There are challenges in identifying an accurate or appropriate class subject for the user of productivity tools. This is not a conceptual quibble; nor is it an apology for neglecting to incorporate user studies as part of my method in later chapters. The changing manifestation of class identity is precisely the impetus for my broader project. Along with a number of recent scholars, I maintain that one's relationship to time is a primary means by which power is experienced. Temporal sovereignty—"the ability to choose how you allocate your time," according to Wajcman—is a historically specific form of freedom.[24] And as Sarah Sharma illustrates, in the current geography of labor, temporal awareness is politically nec-essary to recognize "how one's management of time has the potential to further diminish the time of others."[25] My specific approach builds on these insights to suggest that the activity of time management is a way to displace anxiety about a much larger concern than mere productivity. The bigger issue that aestheticized activity avoids is the sense that we may have reached the end of a certain kind of salaried worker, whose experience of time on the terms of the Organization served as an endur-ing index of modernity. Efforts to achieve productivity are in this sense prompted by nostalgia for a time that a clock or a stopwatch *could* deter-mine and define our orientation to a job. The metrics that would replace this form of solace regarding work's completion, as much as its victories, continue to evade us. *Counterproductive* therefore conveys the pointless-ness of the quest for productivity in today's workplaces, given the general inability of labor activists to articulate an effective "chronopolitics."[26]

Understanding the futility of salaried productivity in a world of 1 percent profiteers is a vital perspective for labor activists and scholars to grasp. This realization matters regardless of whether we are in fact witnessing a decline in the number of ongoing salaried jobs, which is much debated and generally difficult to assess in a dynamic global econ-omy. It also explains why the practice of productivity is not limited to knowledge workers, even though time-management techniques are best understood within the confines of a very particular history of white-collar affect.[27] Productivity concerns effectively mediate the sense of ap-prehension that Richard Sennett ascribes to all work cultures "empha-sizing constant risk," in which "past experience seems no guide to the present."[28] *Counterproductive* approaches these modern maladies by way of a legacy story, a reenactment of the discursive influences that shaped professional subjectivity in the period of history defined by the factory and the firm. The chapters demonstrate how, over the course of many decades, productivity accrued virtue as a framework for living ethically through work.[29] Such a comforting equation requires detailed interro-gation in light of the empirical details of inequality outlined earlier. In devising a new take on productivity practices, I join other critics and thinkers engaged in the unpopular task of arguing that productivity is a unit of measure—at best, a self-illuminating practice—rather than a calling.[30]

The moral appeal of productivity as it is performed by a specific and influential group of knowledge professionals rests on the term's ability to accommodate a post-secular belief system to guide the expenditure of time and effort. By post-secular, I mean that productivity has a motivational ethos that surpasses, without requiring adherence to, any one cultural belief system or edict. Productivity's capacity to propel *activity* without recourse to any framework of philosophical *purpose* marks its present dominant form. While it may be tempting to read productivity as the secular replacement for the original spirit of capitalism, such a reading would imply that there are other spiritual traditions that continue to be welcome in addition to the quest for productivity in labor. The implication of my argument is that, in the West, this has not been the case for some decades. The reason our leaders struggle to account for terrorism, for example, is that the sacred motivations of nonproductive subjects pose the most inconceivable threat to the Euro-American way of life.

Max Weber's original reading of Protestantism attributed religious devotion to the work ethic. Adherence to duty inspired sacred favor through material wealth, reinforcing the sense of one's chosen status.[31] As contemporary employers seek to motivate workers from diverse cultural backgrounds, this perspective requires revision. In the current context, productivity is an accommodating signifier that fills the spiritual void of profit-driven corporate culture, generating a self-affirming logic for action. Productivity succeeds as an inclusive if myopic belief structure at a time that workplaces are challenged to celebrate a variety of values without privileging any ideology in particular. In the chapters that follow, we will see how the adoption of popular efficiency techniques, tools, and apps avoids difficult questions of meaning and purpose by emphasizing activity *in and of itself.* The aim of this book is to trace the genealogy of these time-management efforts, both in and outside the office, to understand how this work-centric worldview became possible. My further intention, given the exhausting amount of purposeless activity apparently taking place,[32] is to ask how practices of professionalism can be reimagined to better situate our labor in relation to cause and consequence.[33]

Also guiding this account is the observation that the productivity ideal informing both information technology (IT) and workplace design trades on a model of work that is more than a hundred years old. Identifying the origins of time-management tenets reveals how many of the discourses of efficiency inherited from previous eras are ill suited to a world revolutionized by mobile and digital platforms. Scientific management eliminated wasted motion to drive production in the factory and the office at a time that people worked in fixed hours and locations, with measurable inputs and outputs. In today's distributed work worlds, mobile devices turn any location into a potential workplace. What we count as work has also broadened to incorporate the logistical, administrative, and social aspects that accompany the formal demands of most jobs. My analysis, as a scholar of gender and queer life, begins with the observation that the dawn of scientific management was a time of restricted workforce participation and, thus, comparatively simplistic theories of labor composition. Pioneering productivity studies focused on the repetitive manual labor of young, often migrant workers, many of whom were poor women. Assumptions typical of the era established class, gender, and ethnic biases that continue in management theory and practice today. As I will show, the ideas of productivity developed in earlier moments of efficiency measurement hold little credibility in light of findings that suggest coercion in key experiments. Maintaining allegiance to compromised research is not just bad habit. It is symbolic of larger issues affecting the authority of management as a discipline.[34]

Given my background in gender and cultural inquiry, I feel a sense of urgency to redress these issues, especially because of the continuing lack of diversity at the senior level in business schools and the combined effect of STEM and management degrees that appear largely bereft of feminist thought.[35] This critical absence has significant knock-on effects in the practical world of business, where the diversity industry often floats free of post-structuralist theory or complex philosophies power. I will never forget sitting on a conference call at Intel in 2016 listening to the diversity team explain "intersectionality" to management. A century after the first studies of manufacturing targeted minority workers we are only beginning to see the language of corporate America reflecting the subjectivities on which it has relied for its success. In this book, as in other writing, I try to apply critical theories of gender and management to practical questions in real workplaces, including my own.[36]

This book consists of three parts. Part I, "Theory," tackles the legacy of time-management methods introduced by turn-of-the-twentieth-century progressivists to optimize work in the office and factory. Chapter 1 considers the personalities and principles that mark the emergence of time management as a *science*, in the spirit of feminist science and technology studies. Specifically, I note the influence of time-and-motion study in ushering forth the focus on individual performance that productivity regimes continue today. This early work, pioneered by the human factors engineer Lillian Gilbreth, anticipated the link between productivity and athleticism as a compelling vision of workplace accomplishment. As we will see, Gilbreth's articulation of individual outputs with the moral stimulus of self-improvement is the framework through which management regimes encouraged workers to plan and progress their careers for decades. Because Lillian Gilbreth was the wife of the more publicly known management consultant Frank Gilbreth, her position as a founder of human factors engineering and workplace psychology is often overlooked in conventional academic accounts. A growing volume of research documents the substantial contribution made by writers such as Lillian Gilbreth, Ellen Richards, and Christine Frederick in the longer story of scientific management, despite social attitudes that prevented them from being recognized at the time.[37] This history is one of the most exciting discoveries unveiled in the course of my research.

Along with their male peers, these bold and enterprising women used the latest labor-saving theories to advocate for the efficient expenditure of time in work, although their interest was the domestic labor performed by women. Home economists of this generation predate feminist critics who note women's absence in both Marxist and historical accounts and precipitated efforts to compensate domestic activity.[38] Their writing actively promoted housewifery as a noble calling for middle-class women, even if their own lived example failed to follow these recommendations.

Sharing the skills to create orderly routine amid a range of tasks and distractions, this productivity advice tailored to the domestic sphere finds new relevance today as more people find themselves working from home, dealing with constant interruptions from attention-seeking technologies and contending with the ongoing effects of what in my previous book I termed "presence bleed." Turning to the era of home economics, the movement Ellen Richards described as "the art of right living,"[39] allows us to see that the productive lifestyle facilitated by software services and "smart home" devices today is hardly novel. It is instead an extension of issues first encountered by women in the margins of industrialization.

Domestic science visionaries also advanced the same principle of productivity that has held for more than a century: a covert reliance on delegated labor both in and outside the home. Engaging with time management's precursors, the women running *home* enterprises in the interests of greater efficiency, troubles our assumptions about who the first managers actually were. This different take on the history of management allows us to see that "the servant question" that pervaded discussions in polite New England society continues to define the ethical terrain of workplace relations in the present. Today's productivity apps reinscribe the hierarchy of superiority instituted by the female head of the home enterprise. For every TaskRabbit user empowered by outsourcing odd jobs today, connection to this larger history is needed to understand how routine work takes noticeably gendered and racialized forms.[40]

Part I also consults original materials and archives to uncover the gendered dynamics that allowed an overriding paternalism to color early initiatives in management theory. A selective rendering of workplace sites and participants, coupled with a pervasive blindness to power dynamics, marked a founding flaw in the documents that established the premise of productivity in academic discourse. Yet subsequent iterations of management thought left these unhelpful first principles in place. The further contribution of this opening chapter is to note that in the shift from the home to the firm, the operating assumption driving efficiency reform in labor switched from spiritual motivations to the pursuit of profit.

Part II, "Practice," provides an analysis of time-management techniques in two popular formats: the self-help book and the mobile app. Appraisal of productivity techniques in both written and digital form shows how time management became a way of life for knowledge professionals seeking affective security amid job volatility. The spike in time-management manuals published in the 1970s and 1990s, and the boom in productivity IT more recently, reflects distinct generational experiences of white-collar affect.[41] It is hardly incidental that productivity pressures rise in tandem with various economic downturns; the point of comparing the two periods of time-management practice is to note the amount of repetition in advice offered to readers and users. The mantras of time-management gurus espoused in manuals and later engineered into software have few empirical bases, even if they offer a kind of consolation at the level of aesthetics, as we will see. Such performative processes are the crucial foundation for productivity as a post-secular activity absent content. To the extent that time management manifests as a distinct genre, the chapters in part II illustrate that there is something structurally predictable in how we are asked to negotiate the changing expectations of knowledge work. My reading reinforces how time-management instruction and adherence have become a necessary form of immaterial labor in an information economy, training workers to embrace their flexibility.

Comparing textual pedagogies of time management with the software services available in app form today establishes the formidable role of self-help genres in the adoption of management common sense. The power of casual citation and mimicry in fashioning authority for time-management techniques gives productivity thinking a necessary cultural weight, confirming its function as "mythology."[42] This is not to discount the material usefulness of time-management training for readers coping with workplace deficiencies of various kinds. In each chapter, I delight in introducing examples that have proved both fun and practical at different times. As in any genre, the degree of predictability that haunts the narratives of these texts provides its own pleasure in the satisfying resolution of lived contradictions.[43] The overriding intent of this middle section of the book is to show that these highly successful popular genres of time management were crucial in encouraging a personalized relationship to efficiency, continuing the initial work of scientific management's prophets and forebears.

Both chapters in part II draw from the writing of the philosopher Peter Sloterdijk to explain the biopolitical turn that sutures career aspiration to self-management. In *You Must Change Your Life* (2013), Sloterdijk elaborates on the words of Rainer Maria Rilke to produce a theory of the Western individual understood as a practicing subject. The notion of "anthropotechnics" explains the popular tendency throughout history for individuals to engage in various forms of asceticism to improve themselves.[44] Sloterdijk's detailed account of disciplinary regimes and habits is intended to critique the reification of religious practice and thus extends to more secular forms of self-restraint, denial, and training. (A key example is sports.) All of these initiatives are framed in his reading as a response to the feeling of "vertical tension": an awareness of the self within oneself that is haunting one's present insufficiencies. Vertical tension is the perception that there is always something more that one is capable of, a level of self-competence that is not yet achieved and liberated, a degree of excess capacity or potential that can be tapped with the right level of focus. My counter-narrative of management theory over the past century uses this idea to explain how neoliberalism's individualizing discourses enacted a convenient marriage between career ambition and notions of self-worth. Productivity theory traded on our vulnerabilities as practicing subjects, our sense that there may always be more that we can do to prove our contribution and value. In an age of precarity, it is unsurprising that the audience for these feats becomes the potential employer. The capitalist hijacking of self-formation fully exploits our admirable quality of desiring accomplishment, fanning a quest for victories that will never be satisfied or exhausted.

Sloterdijk's practicing individual displays aspects of the self-governing behavior that is customarily attributed to Michel Foucault and Nikolas Rose in their writing on subjectification.[45] Adding a spiritual dimension to these economic and medical diagnoses, Sloterdijk's poetic theory is attractive for highlighting the inner motivation and drive in individuals' efforts to self-realize. Sloterdijk expresses the quest for enhanced efficiency and performance in terms of athleticism. Even colloquially, it is axiomatic that any result can be improved on with a dedicated commitment to training. There is something positive and affirming about this process of goal identification for individuals that typical diagnoses of neoliberalism routinely ignore. In the case of employees, my sense is that this is part of the pleasure of work and its intimacies that I discovered in countless interviews. I have found no better explanation of productivity as it manifests in the work settings of today's information professional than Sloterdijk's concept of athleticism. It is the primary model for career advancement in organizations that foster individual feats of heroism as the hallmarks of success.[46]

Sloterdijk writes, "The athlete is meant to want something that is not entirely impossible, but fairly improbable: an unbroken series of victories."[47] The analogy to career progression is clearest when we consider how workers are expected to maintain an unbroken series of appointments that demonstrate ever more profound skills and achievements. So while productivity is not in itself a damaging aim for workers, deep analysis of time-management self-help reveals how striving for personal greatness normalizes the asociality of professional aspiration. In the resource-depleted organization, the ultimate effect of career-oriented athleticism is to render all colleagues competitors.[48]

Part III, "Anthropotechnics," brings together my interest in productivity platitudes and Sloterdijk's philosophy to examine the infatuation with mindfulness taking hold in technology and corporate cultures in recent years. Mindfulness practices mobilize aspects of previous time-management methods that create awareness and attention to a broader purpose for one's work. In doing so, mindfulness provides a sanctioned mode of disengagement from the social, a defense against the ceaseless expectation of productivity. The sheer popularity of mindfulness in relation to other technology trends—indeed, the extent to which mindfulness programs have become commonplace within tech companies themselves[49]—points to a desire for *time out* from the non-stop pace of constantly connected work lives. This concern for the belabored self relates to developments in health and wellness services in the workplace as much as it reflects the focus on resilience in activist communities.[50] In the very week that I am revising this manuscript, for example, Intel employees have been invited to join a series of lunchtime webinars to learn the basics of mindful meditation (which I did).

If we adapt the sociological lens of time scholars such as Eviatar Zerubavel,[51] the turn to mindfulness can be seen as a response to the decline in collective opportunities to experience ritual in the workplace. As performed by Silicon Valley personalities, already famous for rejecting the temporality of the buttoned-up office, mindfulness continues an established tradition of finding enlightenment in alternative cultures that smooth the way for more stimulating business transactions.[52]

In contrast, my account of the mindfulness movement explicitly links the desire for self-care through time out with previous versions of labor politics. I suggest that the selfless qualities of meditation have the capacity to refashion a different relationship to time from the one enshrined in the organizational form. The ultimate question raised in chapter 4 is whether an emerging practice of mindful labor can introduce ethics to the pursuit of productivity once the pact between time and self-sovereignty is suspended. Mindful labor may prove the best means currently available to reinsert collegiality and other-oriented concern into the conversation about work futures.

Mindfulness and wellness initiatives are an important opportunity in the broader history of productivity that this book outlines. They introduce the prospect that our dominant attitude toward time could depart from one of possessive individualism to something much more lateral, even collective, in the interests of sustainable livelihoods. In the conclusion of the book I explore alternatives to productivity as a mode of conduct for personal and professional achievement, drawing on my latest research investigating new enterprise activity. The examples chosen shift the typical focus of work from the model of competitive, linear athleticism to something less heroic, even ephemeral. My case studies feature collectives that gather outside the office clock and calendar, experimenting with new forms of collaboration beyond the enterprise. In these "productive atmospheres," workers are developing social worlds that make a virtue of contingency, building communities of support to withstand the anonymizing effects of the job market.

Counterproductive aims to decenter the "individual contributor" as the pinnacle of workplace agency. This objective is inspired by Kathi Weeks and other writers who are developing feminist interpretations of autonomism and workerist principles.[53] In so many debates about the future of work today, we remain trapped in a paranoid register of loss and nostalgia, buoyed by nightmare scenarios of robots and algorithms stealing whatever secure jobs remain. Leaving aside the complexities of this technological transition, in which machine-assisted work will still require our consent and training, this book aims at a different target. Versed in the knowledge of management theories that consistently have exacerbated individual fears throughout history, we must now move the conversation about work from the angst of careers to the cultivation of atmospheres. Understanding the social conditions of our labor not only better reflects the nature of privilege and exploitation—our dependence on one another as we seek freedom from and within work—but it also recognizes the material consequences of our chosen livelihoods on a finite planet.

My concluding provocations therefore offer a set of recommendations for *post-work* productivity. These principles invite a new attitude toward technology and workplace design: a toolbox with which we can begin to construct durable work worlds in and adjacent to the compromised institutions of labor and its politics. As someone who has regularly moved the location of my professional practice in the search for an accommodating environment, I do not mean for this book to serve as an abstract account of the problem of productivity. I seek fellow travelers interested in developing counterproductive gestures within and outside the organizational forms we inherit, to realize more liberating, cooperative, even selfless experiences. Right now, mindfulness techniques of personal care provide small comfort for the trauma of productivity, a pause button for the drama of days with too much To Do. But placed in the context of a hostile political culture and the malaise that accompanies looming environmental threat, mindfulness may prove pivotal in recognizing the degree of reactivity that attends our public conversations as much as our everyday work. Consumer-led software innovation, coupled with other attributes of a sharing economy, provides a nascent infrastructure for a renewed sense of perspective and solidarity in the wake of the bureaucratic organization. For the good of the planet and our health, this generation's labor movement has no choice but to be collective in mind and spirit.

METHOD

I should admit that I draw heavily on Sloterdijk's *You Must Change Your Life* as both a generative model and an act of homage. I encountered the text at a time of profound personal transition, having left my home in Australian academia for the unknown world of American high tech. I found solace in the book's message, which helped me understand why I so regularly seek new horizons for my thinking and writing. It gave me comfort to know that my serial attraction to transformation and self-realization has precedent dating back thousands of years. That said, Sloterdijk's characteristically confident missive had little to offer when I faced the realization that few colleagues from my previous life seemed destined to join me on this journey. Having moved my work to an industry audience, I struggle to maintain connection with close academic colleagues and friends whose personal productivity pressures leave little time for an e-mail or a Skype date. Feeling overwhelmed by a new job and a new country while writing this book exacerbated what were already unhelpful habits of stress accumulation, angst internalization, and social avoidance. While I have often been described as "productive" (a word I never took as a compliment), the fact that my health suffered in my new location left me feeling lost and without bearings. All of my usual metrics for workplace performance and inclusion seemed lacking, and I did not know where to find them. The irony of this experience continues to plague me, given the motivations uncovered by reflecting on my past and my mother's illness.

For Sloterdijk, anthropotechnics is an other-oriented ethics. It welcomes and celebrates a diversity of ascetic practices as long as these efforts advance the shared project of planetary survival, or "co-immunity." Emerging from his Spheres trilogy,[54] the concept of co-immunity provides a connection among "bubbles," the psychological and spatial support structures individuals develop as protection from the traumatic contaminants of the outside world. In the best possible light, I view productivity practices as so many variations of this need for personal insulation. Productivity genres summon a membrane of protection against the aggressive climate of a capitalist economy and the private worries of an interior world. In the bubble of personal productivity, the practicing subject finds a more accommodating environment than the formal genres of management surveillance. Productive atmospheres enable self-propelling support systems that may prove more sustainable than previous identities forged through labor. These are the best intentions we can bestow on the examples of co-immunity illustrated in this book.

Adopting this framework has limitations, however. Taken literally, there is no guarantee that elite workers concentrated in particular neighborhoods will offer sanctuary to those whose unproductive lifestyles prove questionable. In *Chaos Monkeys* (2016), his caustic account of life at Facebook and Twitter, Antonio Garcia Martinez captures the zeitgeist of modern-day San Francisco when he writes that Californians will "step right over a homeless person on their way to a mindfulness yoga class":

> It's a society in which all men and women live in their own self-contained bubble, unattached to traditional anchors like family or religion, and largely unperturbed by outside social forces like income inequality or the Syrian Civil War. . . . Ultimately, the Valley attitude is an empowered anomie turbocharged by selfishness, respecting some nominal "feel-good" principles of progress or collective technological striving, but in truth pursuing a continual self-development refracted through the capitalist prism: hippies with a capitalization table and a vesting schedule.[55]

Like the world-changing rhetoric of so many startup entrepreneurs, productivity always risks being a solipsistic performance, a belief structure premised on individual sovereignty. It assumes that both time and one's self can be known and conquered through the exercise of determined will. This is why productivity has become such an accommodating capsule for contemporary notions of freedom: being productive, we embrace a pressing sense of responsibility to carry out tasks that appear obvious and necessary in a broader catalogue of things that always need doing. The effect of this circularity is to obviate the need for frank conversations about morality or virtue, which can be related only to the distribution of work and of wealth at a time of growing inequality.[56]

The simultaneous discipline and arrogance involved in the quest to master time is fallibly human. It is not incidental that the productivity imperative holds prominence as we enter an era some are calling "platform capitalism"—that is, an economy and a society increasingly built by software engineers.[57] Time management's delegation dynamic appeals to the programmer mind set, which, after all, continues to trade on the language of masters and slaves in delivering the infrastructures of command and control. But productivity has shaped professional subjectivity in each period of capitalist enterprise. When we covet productivity in the present, we rarely consider its relationship to the manifold conditions that transformed work and home over the course of a century. Among these, a partial list would mention the decline in domestic servants, the shrinking size of families, the persistent presence of women in paid work across every class bracket, the character and location of housing, increased life expectancy, the passions of religious belief, the availability of information, education and communication media, and the growth in cheap and powerful computation devices. Together, these and many other developments have placed greater expectations on individuals to navigate their own course through life as secular organizations retreat from the obligation of resource provision. I crave more substantial encounters among anthropology, history, information and computer sciences, design, engineering, management, and gender and cultural studies to account for these manifold developments. Of course, the very forces of productivity that I explore here are some of the most prominent obstacles that prevent such writing from occurring.

My earlier study of information professionals made a feature of sharing participants' experiences in their own words. In *Work's Intimacy*, I deliberately wanted the workers to speak for themselves. In situ interviews were critical for revealing just how fraught the vocabulary for social contribution through work had become. In the late 2000s, employees felt torn between the competing pleasures and constraints of digitally mediated jobs. Their legitimate gratitude for workplace flexibility assisted by mobile devices made them feel lucky to work wherever they could. At the same time, the very character of work, and what productive labor actually meant to them, remained largely unexamined. This left a fair proportion of study participants unable to "count" as "work" the growing habits of checking email, anticipating contact, and using personal time to catch up on tasks left aside in the service of other, presumably more urgent duties. At this juncture, maintaining a reliable, responsive, available, and competent professional persona was considered a necessary evil, despite the damage this might have wrought to health, families, and friends. For this book, I consult the past, and some distinctly unfashionable artifacts, to track the origins of the discursive formations routinely invoked in my previous project. I always suspected a degree of repetition would become apparent in the common neuroses arising around productivity; indeed, I saw value in sharing this simple observation, imagining it might be empowering for workers to feel less lonely in their encounter with intensifying workloads.

The consistent interest in productivity techniques I have found in popular culture over the course of many decades shows that optimizing output is hardly a recent concern. Nor is productivity solely the domain of managers at the forefront of economics and industry. Our ability to organize ourselves and our work is a chronic source of professional anxiety. From the materials assembled in this book, we can note that it is a burden carried especially by workers with little power in organizational hierarchies and whose jobs lack clearly measurable outputs. While these findings and methods map on to my disciplinary training in gender and cultural studies, English literature, and sociology, I am also excited that this work has led me to new audiences in science and technology studies, critical management studies, feminist media studies and software studies. These hybrid conversations are only going to be more necessary as our work and home lives become algorithmically mediated. By placing scientific management and its myths of origin under scrutiny, we can question the functions served by productivity's self-perfecting impulse when the social, material, and spiritual rewards for labor are no longer so obvious—not least because of the same processes of software engineering that give rise to the dawning data economy. My hope is that this book offers a more accurate and beneficial discussion of work in the past *and* present so that employees of the future may not only understand the true value of their many contributions but, in so doing, entertain a broader set of options for making a life around a living.

1 A Brief History of Time Management

This history of time management begins with the experience of women in the home prior to industrialization. As is the case for many disciplines, the origins of scientific management are typically attributed to great men, in particular, the Taylorites auditing the assembly lines of capitalist industry. But considering the homes these men left behind every day is one way to appreciate the popular purchase of productivity methods as they emerged in tandem with formal business registers. This chapter unseats the commanding position of Frederick Winslow Taylor in the mythology of workplace timekeeping, offering a feminist account of the milieu that contributed to the enshrining of productivity principles in management lore. While Taylor is often regarded as the figurehead of scientific management, each section of this chapter will highlight women's vital role in the variations of efficiency engineering. The point of this exercise is not simply to correct the historical record; it is also to show that the commercialization of intimate space is not a recent phenomenon. My analysis illustrates that productivity practices have hardly changed in a century of application in the domestic realm. What has changed, albeit slowly, is the conception of work, whereby some tasks have become more important and worthy of measure in the market economy. The recent uptick in services that have long been concentrated or delegated within the household shows the permeability of this boundary. Airbnb, TaskRabbit, Thumbtack, and Etsy are just the most recent examples of the diverse assets and human resources that constitute domestic enterprise.

Time-management principles became mainstream in the home at the same time that they entered the factory not least because the men and women discussing the ideas in forums such as Manhattan's Efficiency Society socialized in private settings as much as at salubrious downtown hotels. From the beginning, scientific management was a front advanced jointly in the public and private spheres. This is the lasting influence of time-and-motion experts Frank and Lillian Gilbreth, the married couple who epitomized their trade by adopting Gantt charts to run a household of twelve children. Contemporary theories of work often imply that market logic only recently came to intrude on the sanctity of the family.[1] Turning to history, we can see that this is a nostalgic view. Following the evidence presented in this chapter, we may even observe that it is women's experiences as homemakers at the turn of the twentieth century that anticipate many of the issues afflicting today's distributed workplaces in the quest for greater productivity.

Guidebooks for nineteenth-century housewives addressed a range of time-management problems, including how to cope with constant interruption and distraction, the neediness of others—whether husbands, children, or staff—and the challenge of juggling competing tasks. The diversity of women's household labor and its untrammeled reach across time and space led to the debilitating effects of what we now call "context switch," where reactive responses and constant "firefighting" wither the day away. In domestic handbooks, authors such as Catharine Beecher accorded structure to repetitive duties, touting incentive schemes and time-based competitions typical of today's gamification techniques. Given the relative absence of women from the paid work world at the time of management theory's establishment, these formative productivity practices rarely grace business school curricula. Active discrimination and moral surveillance erased women's intellectual contribution to productivity theory in keeping with the broader social imperative to confine their work to particular industries and domestic settings.

The expanding interest in scientific management and efficiency principles in the early 1900s included a significant agenda for organizing women's work in the home. The efficiency proselytizers Harrington Emerson and Frank Gilbreth each provide an epigraph for the domestic science celebrity Christine Frederick's *Household Engineering* (1915), acknowledging housewifery as demanding the highest acumen and skill. "Housekeeping is not only the oldest, most fundamental and complex of all professions," writes Emerson, "but modern success in it is more difficult to attain than success in factory, warehouse, transportation or shop, because it must be attained by women working alone, and with many purposes." Gilbreth is similarly effusive: "Nothing is more worth while than bringing efficiency into the home. When housekeeping becomes a science, as well as an art, when it is based on measurement—then it becomes worthy of the best brains and highest endeavor."[2]

Middle-class women such as Frederick and Frank Gilbreth's wife and collaborator, Lillian, mixed progressivist principles, professional ambition, and patriotic duty in appealing to readers who were otherwise being tempted by new kinds of market-based employment. To encourage more women to remain in charge of the home front, Frederick and Gilbreth addressed U.S. homemakers as expert managers.[3] In addition to the capacities they enumerated and encouraged in homemakers themselves, time-management techniques and delegation skills became part of a suite of strategies designed to formalize domestic service and attract a better quality of candidate for routine labors. As we will see, over the course of subsequent decades, the employment of time for specific duties gave middle-class women a sense of agency within, if not freedom from, home-based work. The solution to productivity pressures within the home often rested on outsourcing trivial tasks to others. This advice reflected the personal lives of Frederick and Gilbreth, who each employed secretaries to maintain their writing output. In Gilbreth's case, a cadre of support staff helped raise her large family even before the untimely death of husband Frank.

DOMESTIC SCIENCE: MANAGING THE HOME ENTERPRISE

Home economics began as a civic movement prior to its transformation to a state-sanctioned science suited to formal instruction in schools.[4] Its emergence at the turn of the twentieth century coincided with a series of social changes that included the growing recognition of women's right to education, the reformist spirit of progressivism, and the rise of scientific authority. The pioneer of home economics, Ellen Richards, was a trained chemist and the first female graduate of the Massachusetts Institute of Technology. Her technical acumen, evident in works such as *The Chemistry of Cooking and Cleaning* (1882), found suitable application in domestic settings that were coming to be understood in terms of health and hygiene.[5] Richards's preferred term for home economics was "euthenics," which she envisaged as a sister discipline to eugenics: "Where eugenics bred the perfect individual, euthenics would supply the ideal environment."[6] Richards's book *The Art of Right Living* (1904) reflects this optimism in chapters devoted to "the factors that make up the efficient individual," including nutrition, physical motion, eating, sleep, amusement, exercise, pleasure, aim or purpose, environment, and health. Her goal for the home economics movement was to ensure "the freedom of the home from the dominance of things and their due subordination to ideals." This ability to triumph over "things" and focus on the right way of living is key to the efficiency thinking that would mark not only household management, but also reams of popular time-management instruction in the decades to come.

In the United States, the mid-1800s had already seen considerable attention paid to women's roles, as increased manufacturing and the growing availability of consumer goods moved previously self-sufficient home-based textiles, arts, and crafts to factories. Households were required to take on different functions, and the home became a site for spiritual and lifestyle practices, particularly in influential New England families who set the tone for appropriate social and economic convention. Domestic advice emerged as a genre of publishing in the 1830s. Much of the early literature illustrated practical steps for women to make a virtue of themselves and their residences. Women's position as heads of households entailed modeling an appropriate balance of self-denial and self-sacrifice in the business of sustaining life for others. The "cult of domesticity," as it became known, granted women a privileged place in society by encouraging them to embody the values of the nation—specifically, Christianity. Commenting on the importance of domestic manuals, Sarah Leavitt notes the significance of Evangelical Protestantism to middle-class life in the mid-nineteenth century: "Advisors saw instructions on the arrangement of the furniture and the types of wood used in the parlor not only as aesthetic concerns, but as symbols of honesty, faith, and good judgment."[7] Through her taste and frugality, the home manager showed competence and spiritual devotion in equal measure. Demonstrating the proper use of time epitomized this general tendency.

The American Woman's Home (1869), by Catharine Beecher and her novelist sister, Harriet Beecher Stowe, is a hallmark of the period. The talented pair hoped the book would "elevate both the honor and the remuneration of all employments that sustain the many difficult and varied duties of the family state, and thus to render each department of woman's profession as much desired and respected as are the most honored professions of men."[8] The co-authored text updated Catharine Beecher's earlier *Treatise on Domestic Economy, for the Use of Young Ladies at Home, and at School* (1841) to include insights from her experience as principal of the Hartford Female Seminary. Tailoring its advice to suit the changed circumstances affecting women following the Civil War, the manual was affordable enough for middle-class families to purchase and benefited from adoption on a growing number of vocational courses available to women.

Beecher and Beecher Stowe's guide, like Richards's, expresses the need for a life of ideals. These overriding goals provide a sense of purpose to determine which tasks matter in the exercise of daily duty. Section XXVII, "Habits of System and Order," offers the clearest instance of time-management instruction of this kind. Considering all the habits vital for success in the home enterprise, Beecher and Beecher Stowe write, none surpasses the virtue of rising early. Solitary moments at the beginning of the day provide respite and reflection away from the concerns of others. This process is crucial for assessing the right order of duties, such that

> where a woman lacks either the health or the energy to secure a period for devotional duties before breakfast, let her select that hour of the day in which she will be least liable to interruption, and let her then seek strength and wisdom from the only true Source. At this time, let her take a pen, and make a list of all the things which she considers duties. Then, let calculation be made, whether there be time enough, in the day or the week, for all these duties. If there be not, let the least important be stricken from the list, as not being duties and therefore to be omitted. In doing this, let a woman remember that, though "what we shall eat, and what we shall drink, and wherewithal we shall be clothed," are matters requiring due attention, they are very apt to obtain a wrong relative importance, while intellectual, social, and moral interests receive too little regard.[9]

This passage captures many of the persistent features of time-management practice that define the productivity genre. The emphasis on solitary reflection, taken in deliberate retreat from others' disruption, is necessary for calculating the merits of various activities in relation to a greater cause. Making a list of all the things that are considered part of her work allows the home manager to consider competing matters in relation to a larger value system. Importantly, she is encouraged to prioritize utilitarian functions in relation to intellectual, social, and moral interests. There is a broader perspective to maintain in this God-fearing era; the domestic duty housewives perform is a grave and sacred calling.

Preserving "good temper in the housekeeper" involves coming to terms with the inevitability of interruption. The lady should "calculate on having her best-arranged plans interfered with very often; and to be in such a state of preparation that the evil will not come unawares."[10] Feminine qualities of cheer and diminutive care come to the fore in these passages. The Christian homemaker must acquire the disposition and discipline that will allow her to accommodate the demands of others willingly and with good grace. In this vision, time management is not a heroic art. There is no evident assumption that the housewife has the power to actually control her fortunes. Practicing domestic economy is a matter of creating a resilient structure that ensures refined calm in service to others and, above all, to God.

Racial and cultural superiority are two ideals the contemporary reader finds evident in Beecher and Beecher Stowe's manual. The Christian family state is "the aptest earthly illustration of the heavenly kingdom, and in it woman is its chief minister."[11] The homemaker provides "the training of our race to the highest possible intelligence, virtue, and happiness, by means of the self-sacrificing labours of the wise and good."[12] The righteousness of religious calling accords with hierarchical assumptions of cultural reproduction, a perspective that, in gesturing toward the ultimate purpose of moral engineering, has significant consequences. Through the superiority of her sex and race, the middle-class woman holds a position at the pinnacle of the household enterprise that is unchallenged in these works. The inevitable whiteness of progressive ideals enshrines an estimation of labor in league with the Darwinian spirit of the times.

The hierarchical organization of domestic economy underwrites the sisters' attempt to discuss "The Servant Problem," a complex popular debate in which American women struggled, in contrast to their British peers, to adopt an appropriate attitude toward hiring domestic help. "In England, the class who go to service *are* a class, and service is a profession," Beecher and Beecher Stowe write.[13] The New World posed problems of acculturation to meet new egalitarian attitudes. Beecher and Beecher Stowe wonder why the well-bred "girls of New England" preferred to work in the factory or the office rather than service the needs of residences in the local community. Exercising their right to access paid work, American women "left the whole business of domestic service to a foreign population; and they did it mainly because they would not take positions in families as an inferior labouring-class by the side of others of their own age who assumed as their prerogative to live without labor."[14] The servant *problem*, in essence, was that working as a subordinate to one's own kind went against cherished ideals of American liberty. Even domestic help arriving from foreign countries believed in these ideals, which made the girls difficult to discipline. In America, "the general character of society" made servants "cumbrous and difficult to manage."[15] Formalized instruction, issued by the woman in charge of the house, provided the best means to avoid trouble.

The American Woman's Home instigates a protracted social effort to affirm the respectability of housework by according it scientific and philosophical consequence in addition to religious calling. Women who fail to adopt "the systematic employment of time," according to Beecher and Beecher Stowe, "are rather driven along by the daily occurrences of life; so that, instead of being the intelligent regulators of their own time, they are the mere sport of circumstances."[16] Women's particular responsibility for time management is a test of character achieved through force of will and right habit. In this view, "There is nothing which so distinctly marks the difference between weak and strong minds as the question, whether they control circumstances or circumstances control them."[17] The Beecher and Beecher Stowe tome deftly maneuvers among established customs, religious beliefs, and the increasingly secular movements of science and management. Other publications in the art of household management, such as the Lippincott's Home Manuals series, use diagrams to illustrate the appropriate chain of command in domestic duties. Lydia Ray Balderston's *Housewifery: A Manual and Text Book of Practical Housekeeping*

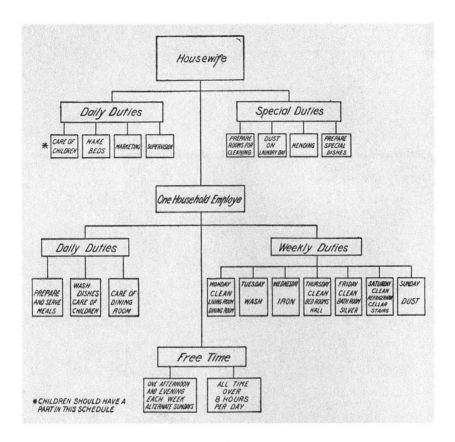

FIGURE 1.1 An organization chart from the 1920s showing the housewife at the pinnacle of the domestic enterprise. In Lydia Ray Balderston, *Housewifery: A Manual and Textbook of Practical Housekeeping* (Philadelphia: Lippincott, 1919), 16–17.

(1919) draws on expertise gained while teaching housewifery and laundering at Columbia University and includes a version of the corporate organizational chart.

In these visions of capital, housewifery is a business run by a lady boss.[18] The housewife's time is privileged and relieved by a host of daily and weekly duties delegated to others. At every opportunity, the woman of the household is encouraged to eliminate useless motions and enjoy increased "happiness minutes" within the family.[19] Balderston's text shares tips for designing a home and arranging furniture to minimize motions and footsteps, from shortening the reach between benches and

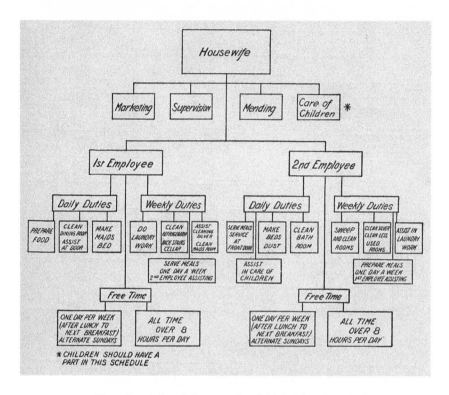

FIGURE 1.2 Key tasks are identified, assigned, and delegated, with units of activity expanding as help is available.

sinks in kitchens to reducing the number of arm gestures involved in making beds. Such materials prove the extent to which women's work was finding equivalence with the productivity principles guiding task work in the public, market economy.

Christine Frederick remains the best-known U.S. time-management expert of this period due to a series of magazine articles ultimately published as a book, *The New Housekeeping* (1912).[20] Frederick got her break writing approachable synopses of scientific-management principles as household editor for the *Ladies' Home Journal* in 1912. Adopting the chit-chat anecdotal style that would characterize time-management gurus for decades hence, Frederick used the setup of a conversation with her husband and his friends "the efficiency engineers" as the pretext to introduce her book *Household Engineering* (1915), which the Home Economics Association of America would publish in at least five imprints between 1915 and 1923.[21] Frederick's tips to housewives endorsed strictures such as grouping together food supplies, saving steps between stations, adopting the correct height for surfaces and sinks, sitting for certain tasks, ensuring adequate lighting and ventilation, even recommendations for the most effective floor surfaces. *Household Engineering* pays close attention to the possibilities of optimizing time and minimizing distractions:

> Plan definitely when you want tradespeople to call and insist that they do not call at other times. The special shelf near the kitchen or rear door on which supplies may be laid has been spoken of. Give orders that bundles, articles, etc., shall be left here with as little interruption as possible. Keep a supply of change in the kitchen. Running upstairs to a pocketbook, even once a day every day in the week, runs into enough time in a year to read several best sellers![22]

Far from encouraging interaction with house callers, efficiency logic encourages the housewife to seize her role as a manager, tasked with informing outsiders of appropriate behavior.

> *Today the woman in the home is called upon to be an executive as well as a manual laborer.* Just to be a good worker and keep on working until you drop is not sufficient — or efficient either. The more planning, the more brains, the more management, a woman puts into her housework, the less friction and the less nervous energy she will have to expend. Housework above any other must be followed on the schedule plan so that a woman will know what she must do, how long it takes her to do it, and when she can get through and do something else.[23]

For Frederick, the application of scientific management would "dignify housework and attract a better class of girls" to perform it.[24] Her advice manuals offered ideal times, in minutes, for housewives to perform regular tasks. This process created an incentive structure for routine labor such as laundry, cooking, and cleaning. Every effort was made to encourage women's creativity through labor. The following passage conveys Frederick's aim to bring modern professionalism to the sacred duty previously accorded to housework by the likes of Beecher:

> Many women still persist in thinking that by timing themselves they are holding a kind of whip of drudgery over themselves. On the contrary, no one factor makes a piece of work more interesting than that of timing it, and if possible, lessening this time in future work. Instead of making a task drudgery, the timing acts as a stimulus to do the work more efficiently and "beat the record" of a previous effort.[25]

In this passage, we can already see an idea of athletic performance in labor coming to the fore.

As her profile developed, Frederick instituted a model kitchen in her home to test samples sent to her by companies seeking female consumers. A similar progression took place with the untimely passing of Frank Gilbreth, as Lillian transformed her industry expertise to the home and even the personal hygiene concerns of women. The Gilbreth Management Desk is one remarkable legacy from this era—a prototype commissioned by IBM for the Century of Progress exhibition in Chicago in 1933. Sadly never built for purchase, the desk promised to solve "household problems concerning Children, Clothing, Education, Finance and Maintenance, Food, Health and Medical Care, House Cleaning, Laundry, Recreation and Culture, Servants, Social Affairs and many other subjects."[26] The model desk is yet more evidence that efficiency, multitasking, and organizational expertise enacted by women in the home covered a wealth of personal and public roles.

Both Frederick and Gilbreth inhabited a contradiction in recommending that their largely female readers adopt time management principles to satisfy ambition and intellect. Neither writer followed her own advice to pursue homemaking as a profession and instead enjoyed a substantial degree of recognition and career legitimacy outside the home.[27] The freedom these productivity experts enjoyed to pursue fulfilling work was made possible by a flank of staff: in Gilbreth's case, up to seven full-time assistants and a live-in mother-in-law supplemented her capacity to raise a dozen children. Frederick, meanwhile, enjoyed the luxury of a secretary to type out columns and respond to considerable amounts of fan mail. Her biographer Janice Williams Rutherford notes, "The volume of her writing and the need for staff suggest that, in her own home, she delegated and supervised much of the work she urged other women to find fulfilling."[28]

Domestic advice manuals from the 1910s onward mark a gradual shift from religious devotion and duty directed to the needs of others to ideas of efficiency based on self-improvement and individual accomplishment. Frederick's maxim *"that women master their work, instead of letting their work master them"* comes with some durable additional advice:

> The end and aim of home efficiency is not a perfect system of work, or scientific scheduling, or ideal cleanliness and order; it is the personal happiness, health, and progress of the family in the home. The work, the science, the system, the schedule are but some of the means to that end, not the end itself. . . . I would feel very badly about it if my earnest plea for a more efficient attitude of mind should result in nothing else but increased slavish devotion to work.[29]

Frederick's upbeat style marks a turn toward the streamlined and pragmatic techniques of productivity coaching that would appear in the do-it-yourself texts for business instruction decades later. "Make out a schedule of your present plan of work," she urged. "Study to see where it can be improved. Try the new schedule two weeks. Revise and try another two weeks, and report."[30] Here begins a process of training oneself to identify typical causes for interruptions and institute a system to take care of such issues without encroaching on a prioritized schedule. We will see this system replicated many times in coming chapters.

These early documents of efficiency and labor enhancement prove that the science of management was not limited to the factory or the office at the turn of the twentieth century; productivity was also the principal logic of the household. Women's work as domestic managers is not commonly considered in the history of management theory, even though it shows all of the same qualities of the burgeoning science and likely was practiced by as many qualified practitioners. As a result of these writers, homemakers in the early 1900s would start to count their steps, keep records of the speed of chores, remodel their kitchens to reduce wasted motions, and organize their staff and families with the assistance of Gantt charts. Such tips and directives advanced the same "Principles of Scientific Management" famously outlined by Taylor in his lectures at Harvard Business School,[31] but the domestic focus and female audience for these writers kept their work comparatively unknown. Knowledge of this history is important to correct the notion that intimate and domestic life have only recently been commercialized following a period of sanctity that the Fordist sexual contract helped to enshrine. The domestic science movement that flourished in the United States in the twentieth century is an extension and further classification of management techniques that were already well under way following the Civil War. To appreciate this background, and acknowledge women's role as managers and efficiency engineers, requires attention to the ongoing role of the domestic enterprise in securing the economic and affective well-being of the nation. The equally foundational role that women played in establishing factory- and office-based measures for productivity is the focus of the next section.

THE CINEMATIC ORIGINS OF PRODUCTIVITY

Lillian Gilbreth is typically remembered as the wife of Frank, the time-and-motion expert immortalized in the book and film *Cheaper by the Dozen*. The story came to prominence following an enterprising memoir by two of the couple's children, Frank B. Gilbreth Jr. and Ernestine Gilbreth Carey, whose popular tale continued a family tradition of self-promotion. The book and subsequent film (first released in 1950) each do Lillian a major disservice. Her career is not mentioned, apparently in the interests of entertainment, leaving the impression that she was a stay-at-home mother. At the time of her death in 1972, Lillian Gilbreth had been recognized as the first woman to be appointed to the National Academy of Engineering, among many other firsts in a prolific consultancy career. She was Honorary Member Number One of the Society of Women Engineers on its foundation in 1950, and served five presidents in a range of civic and labor-focused roles. Following a life of tireless initiative in business and education, Gilbreth retired only at age ninety. Her absence from histories of management theory as anything other than a wifely appendage is emblematic of a time that the intellectual contribution of a female partner could be removed from the historical record by ignorance as much as by design. Publishers initially demanded that Lillian Gilbreth disguise her contribution to Frank's business by using only the initials of her first name. These directives and strategic omissions can no longer be tolerated. Jane Lancaster's detailed biography makes a strong case that the bulk of Frank Gilbreth's work on fatigue and motion study was written with or entirely by Lillian. This perspective only gains credibility when pondering the remarkable output that continued as Lillian learned to support a large family singlehandedly following Frank's early death.

At the turn of the twentieth century, the Gilbreths were part of an active group of New York intellectuals from a range of industries, universities, and research institutions who shared the hope that science could advance perfectibility in industry. As newlyweds, the Gilbreths saw benefits in associating with the more famous workplace consultant Frederick Taylor, who advocated using a stopwatch to time workers in the completion of tasks. Taylor's method for improving industrial output hinged on the projected rate of an "ideal man" against whom all others would be judged.[32] The Gilbreths, while careful to distinguish their own "time-and-motion" technique from Taylor's, nonetheless gained profile partly by standing in for Taylor when his schedule could not accommodate all invitations. The alliance was evident as early as July 1910, when Taylor mentioned Lillian's work at a conference keynote address in Britain. At the time, this was an unprecedented acknowledgment of a female thinker's influence on industrial practice. Frank Gilbreth set up the Taylor Society in New York in the fall of the same year. The official beginnings of scientific management are attributed to a meeting in October at the Manhattan apartment of one Louis Brandeis. Brandeis, known as "the people's attorney," was a U.S. Supreme Court judge. As a Taylor acolyte he was motivated to improve the methods of scientific management to help workers and advance the benefits of productivity to society. He saw efficiency as "the hope of democracy."[33]

Each member of the Efficiency Society brought a specialization. The Gilbreths' method assessed labor according to type, creating improvements in task rate by grouping similar movements together. This is the origin of their neologism, the "therblig"—a reversal of the pair's surname. This term referred to the smallest gesture in any overall workflow. Breaking a job into isolated micro-movements for optimal arrangement became the process of establishing the "one best way" of performing it. Today, whenever I hear engineering colleagues asking for a "BKM," they invoke the lineage of the Gilbreths in seeking the best-known method for a task.

Frank and Lillian Gilbreth's iconic workplace reform was reducing the bricklayer's stoop through the provision of on-site scaffolding. As a former bricklayer himself, Frank surmised the energy and effort that could be saved by placing bricks within arm's reach of the worker.[34] This principle was the bedrock for many subsequent reforms the pair would make in a range of locations. The archive of Gilbreth films provides before-and-after insight into the unnecessary motions involved in a variety of tasks, including card punching, pear washing, soap packing, and produce labeling.[35] In many of the reels, a portly, officious, waistcoated Frank supervises proceedings and accompanying information slides and statistics. Productivity comes alive as both a quantitative and a qualitative measurement in these initial forays into industrial public relations, some of the first examples of promotional film.[36] The camera's ability to track the worker's body, hands, and eye movements creates an enriched level of accuracy in recording the labor motions under observation. Unlike the "stopwatch men," as the Taylorites were often known, the Gilbreths used film and other light-based imaging devices to capture activities taking place at speeds beyond human perception. Providing an empirical basis for the physiology of labor, time-and-motion films summoned the spirit of more artistic chrono-photographers, such as Etienne Jules Marey's mesmerizing renderings of human and animal form in motion.[37] The still images produced by the slow-motion camera enabled a new kind of awareness of the manifold movements involved in a task, a visual record of achievement. Applied to work sites, these technical systems had the benefit of removing managerial bias in capturing field data. For the first time, workers could see the activity on which their performance would be judged. Trained to recognize and covet optimization—the point of scientific management being to "eliminate waste"—workers could begin to contemplate managing task loads for themselves. The worker could start to see the beauty and elegance in efficiency.

One notable demo in the Gilbreth archive shows the method involved to "train a lady to become a champion typist." Sitting at her desk and typewriter, the worker in this film calmly processes line after line of text against the backdrop of a ticking clock.[38] Her fingers move, her left hand rises as she moves the carriage to return. The only break in output is to adjust the page and place a tick on the completed document. Departing from this set framing, a subsequent shot shows the typist's face in portrait style with particular attention focused on her eyes. The written slide explains the purpose of the film, to demonstrate "Early Studies of eye movements in conjunction with the motion of hands." Gilbreth's new keyboard layout minimizes both hand stretching and head turning. The wide eyes and demure smile playing across the typist's pale face convey delight at her industry as much as the modesty of an earlier era.

Next, the typist's hands become the focus for further close-up inspection. A grid of squares is transposed over footage of the busy fingers, assisting the measure of activity relative to the space occupied or touched in each square. The grid's addition is a development from the blank backgrounds of Malvey's films, producing a layer of scientific certainty to the visions on screen. Scott Curtis explains the performativity of these Gilbrethian methods, which, through inventions such as the stereocyclegraph, made the most of photography's affordances. The stereocyclegraph involved applying tiny light bulbs to workers' fingertips to photograph the smallest motion. Capturing micro-movement for subsequent assessment generates a trace of labor that otherwise would be lost. However accurate these representations may have been, their effect was to turn film into a landscape of data ripe for survey and inspection. The Gilbreths enabled "one kind of image (detailed, moving)" to be transported and reified "into another (simplified, still)" so that the elements of a task could be identified. Their cinematic depictions of small-scale gestures created "a graphic image of what efficiency and inefficiency look like"—a means of encouraging, by way of capturing, speed.[39]

The portrait of the individual worker on camera is a new kind of labor performance, an act choreographed and directed for a witnessing audience. In *The Psychology of Management* (1904), the book that arose from her doctorate, Lillian Gilbreth makes an explicit link between the worker's desire to have his performance recorded for history and the ambitions of actors hoping to have their artistry captured for posterity on film. From this perspective, scientific management could be pitched as an obvious solution to workers' frustration at not having a record of ac-

FIGURES 1.3–1.6 "Gilbreth trained this lady to become a champion typist"—selected stills from the Gilbreth collection. Work performance is recorded and optimized through technologies of measurement. These compositions establish the conventions of a cinematic gaze in industry.

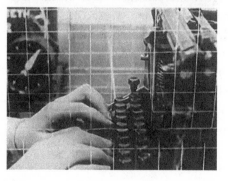

complishment for the day's toil. The measurement of motion efficiency relative to output generates an archive of achievement, much like the actors and singers who were also "grasping the opportunity to make their best efforts permanent through the instrumentality of the motion picture films and the talking machine records." In Gilbreth's account, knowledge that the record will be compiled creates interest in the work, for with it "comes the possibility of a real, scientific, 'athletic contest.'"[40] For the worker, attention "is concentrated on the fact that he as an individual is expected to do his very best." The psychological dimension to this is most notable: "He has the moral stimulus of responsibility. He has the emotional stimulus of competition. He has the mental stimulus of definiteness. He has, most valuable of all, a chance to be an entity rather than one of an undiscriminated gang."[41]

Gilbreth was writing these words at a time that Taylorism faced vocal criticism from workers concerned about its heartless quantification methods. She aims to assuage fears by arguing that, "under Scientific Management, the spirit of individuality, far from being crowded out, is a basic principle, and *everything possible is done to encourage the desire to be a personality.*"[42] In the case of the typist, working against her own previous record and embracing productivity becomes a way to match and better a previous version of herself, and, in turn, a way to be recognized. Gilbreth anticipates that individual performance will ultimately draw out new kinds of pleasures for workers that will rival the security and comfort of the group: "This chance to be an individual, or personality, is in great contradistinction to the popular opinion of Scientific Management which thinks it turns men into machines."[43]

The Gilbreths' introduction of motion to time-and-motion study is pivotal in the history of productivity. Applied to manual work, the cinematic apparatus transforms the worker's conception of her job away from a team or gang to a personal achievement. This visual account, and the performance of productivity for a witnessing eye, coincides with the first mainstream experiences of cinematic vision. The intimacy of the close-up, focused particularly on the face and eyes, provides coordinates for appraising the worker as a particular kind of actor. The typist's gaze is offered for scrutiny, her movements open to mastery and replication given the assumed benefits of reform. Time-and-motion studies in this way educate viewers in the dynamics of empathy and recognition through filmic projection. Like the male gaze that would come to be associated with the pleasure of Hollywood narrative,[44] industrial film normalizes the manager's view of a world waiting to be optimized. Identifying with the recorded image turns work into a science, labor into information, and the worker into an individual: "Photography helped make scientific management an event, a moment beyond the usual practice, in the workplace."[45] Improving on one's own prior record became a seductive prospect and a mark of distinction. For the typist, accomplishing ever greater productivity—becoming "a champion," in the words of the film—is a victory she alone can possess.[46]

MAYO'S MISSING WOMEN

The Gilbrethian method of finessing the contribution of gifted individuals continues in the Hawthorne experiments held at Western Electric's factory in Cicero, Illinois, in the 1920s and 1930s. This investigation of workers' morale and output, conducted in partnership with Harvard Business School academics, remains the iconic study of productivity in the factory. Following a series of experiments in modulating the temperature, light, and layout of work in the Relay Room, switching start and break times, and documenting the effects of providing lunch, researchers found that participants increased their productivity over the duration of the study. The Hawthorne studies accrue layers of scholarly analysis appraising the work's unparalleled scale and ambition, the dexterity and resilience of the researchers' effort to adjust methods in the field, and the flaws in both method and execution of study findings.[47] The Hawthorne effect, a concept that is liberally if inconsistently applied in management scholarship,[48] has become a textbook case of inductive logic, the social science equivalent of the placebo effect.

A field team headed by Harvard's Fritz Roethlisberger interviewed roughly forty thousand workers at the Hawthorne site, with specific subteams focused on small groups of workers in the Relay Room and the cabling department. In the best known of these smaller studies, five female assemblers and a parts assistant were chosen to work in an area shut off from the main factory floor. Recording outputs by way of an automated ticker, workers' productivity was monitored and plotted on graphs reflecting their individual performance in comparison with one another and according to specific variables, such as hours of sleep.[49] Rest times, changes to starting and stopping hours, and free meal provision were just some of the measures used to test the relationship between motivation and output volume. For the project's duration, the group's pay rate was calculated relative to the smaller team of contributors rather than the customary number of up to one hundred teammates on the regular shop floor. This financial detail clearly matters to any assessment of the productivity gains among workers in the study, as is now recognized.[50] In official records, however, these wage adjustments were downplayed in favor of the psychological and even physiological concerns of interest to the research consultants.

The women themselves varied in age from eighteen to twenty-eight and had Polish, Norwegian, and Bohemian heritage. Richard Gillespie notes that one operator was actually fifteen and had lied about her age to gain employment. Like the broader Hawthorne population, many were breadwinners for first-generation migrant families. The pressure to maintain employment at a time of growing economic instability (the study ran during the unfolding Depression in 1927–32) is a further consideration affecting the research, since the work itself was not obviously fulfilling. Telephone relay assembly "required manual dexterity, along with a willingness to repeat the same task every minute or so for almost nine hours per day, five and a half days per week."[51] Both hands were needed "to place pins, bushings, springs, terminals, and insulators between plates, insert a coil and armature, then screw the assembly together," equating to "thirty-two separate operations for each hand."[52]

At the time of the Hawthorne study, Harvard's Fatigue Laboratory was a test bed for the latest theories of employee conditioning and well-being, consolidating the emerging field of workplace ergonomics. Elton Mayo, the Harvard professor Western Electric held on a retainer, drew liberally on existing fatigue research in developing his own approach to employee productivity. His book, *Human Problems of Industrial Civilization*, maintained that some workers were better suited to withstand the physical and mental effects of repetitive job tasks, a Darwinian principle accordant with the book's ambitious title. For Mayo, the "capacity to be unfavorably influenced by repetitive work differs between individuals in respect of, for example, what can be tentatively called intelligent endowment and temperament."[53] Not a trained doctor (he dropped out of medicine before fleeing his homeland Australia), Mayo was appointed to his first U.S. academic post on dubious credentials thanks to some influential references.[54] His success at Harvard is typically attributed to a combination of charisma and suggestive if abstract ideas. As part of a wealthy Adelaide family, he had mixed in high-class company throughout his life, networking successfully to attain his first teaching job at the University of Queensland. Mayo counted the anthropologist Bronisław Malinowski among his close friends. Intellectually, he drew from the child psychologist Jean Piaget and Alfred North Whitehead alongside Freud, Jung, and other advocates of therapeutic technique.

Mayo discontinued a medical degree three times during his youth, and his Master of Arts was awarded under dubious circumstances later in life.[55] Still, as a member of the wealthy elite growing up in South Australia, Mayo had access to opportunity, and his engaging personality wooed patrons in business and physiology to support his pursuits. Mayo's attractive style—his reliance on transference, as Abraham Zaleznik puts it[56]—seems to have played a role in perceptions of his competence, whether from financiers, protégés, or study participants. Mayo's idiosyncratic interview technique mixed therapy and work—indeed, blurred this boundary purposefully, if we are to believe his assistants. His preference for interviewing women alone is a feature of his life story. According to Trahair, at various stages Mayo treated his wife, Dorothea, and her sisters for "irrational fears," to the point of having one sister-in-law, Barbara, sent to "a quiet room in a new hospital" so he might interview her twice daily.[57] There are many silences in Trahair's biography when it comes to these diagnoses and their causes, although the following passage is suggestive:

> Mayo talked with Barbara for two days. His first task was to master an emotional problem aroused by the remarkable likeness between Barbara and his longing for Dorothea, who was in Sydney with their newborn daughter Ruth. He had seen Dorothea beset by irrational fears, and he had been able to help her overcome them. Now he saw the same fears in Barbara, and his heart ached for the presence of Dorothea to help him separate his erotic interest in Barbara from the equally powerful need to be a detached and expert clinician.[58]

Most troubling is the detail that in late 1921 Barbara "decided to undergo an operation from which she knew she would probably not recover." Readers are not informed of the nature of the operation. Trahair instead reports that Barbara "asked Mayo to await a communication from her after death. He agreed, and waited in vain; but then he did not really imagine that contact with the after life was as easy as Barbara had expected."[59]

Mayo's biographer provides little context for us to piece together what precisely is happening in these vague recollections, and I have found no other commentary curious enough to delve deeper. Management historians appear to have overlooked these aspects of Mayo's private life, emphasizing instead the benefits his counseling provided for returning war veterans.[60] Of course, these circumstances may say less about Mayo than the power of men over women at this moment in history. The fact that he was not a trained doctor suggests, at the very least, that Mayo enjoyed a peculiar amount of intimate power over his female relatives. We might wonder, though, at the legacy of the one-on-one interview in mentoring and performance management in the workplace today. Such processes rest on an isolated and often unaccountable relationship of power and dependence between manager and worker, and it is important to acknowledge that it stems from a moment in history that unambiguously infantilized and incarcerated women. Mayo's silent female relatives are always in my mind as I encounter his diagnoses of productivity at Hawthorne.

Mayo's prominent position in management theory is further weakened by an account of the gender bias that inflects his application of Piaget, a developmental psychologist. Piaget's theory of equilibration explains how certain qualities of reason and affect emerge in the course of maturation. Piaget's approach to early childhood and adolescent development explains the acquisition of social behavior in sequential detail, a method described as genetic epistemology. The idea of equilibration— "that mental growth is governed by a continual activity aimed at balancing the intrusions of the social and physical environment with the organism's need to conserve its structural systems"—is an enduring principle throughout Mayo's published works.[61] Piaget's theory of child development provided the foundation for appropriate behavior to be expected of workers, women, and other subordinates. This heritage forms the conceptual frame for the vast schedule of interviews conducted by the social science team at Hawthorne. One-to-one dialogues carried out by specially trained managers were seen as essential to uncovering the basis of workers' sentiment. Attention to the holistic social and personal life of the individual was thought to get to the heart of any grievances—or, in Mayo's psychoanalytic parlance, "neuroses"—affecting performance on the job. The conviction that these details would provide suitable material for management also justified the unprecedented investigations taking place in the Relay Room.

Records at Harvard's Baker Library show that the data collected over several years of the Relay Room study extended to organ health and blood count, in line with dominant ideas of fatigue studies and its relation to athletic capacity and fitness. Judgments conveyed in the records mix medical opinion, morality, and anthropological classification in assertions such as "body and ears normal" to "underwear is clean and sufficient." The information gathered about the five assemblers expanded beyond physical attributes to extensive investigations of home, neighborhood, and family life. To the Hawthorne researchers, any insight that could be gleaned from the outside work environment was fair game in the quest to uncover the secrets of enhanced productivity. Observations covered the content of workers' lunches, dental health, footwear choices, and number of hours slept at night, in addition to more vague assessments ("She is subject to worries"). Moving the workers from the test room to a nearby clinic for regular medical examination added a further layer of scientific scrutiny and data gathering to the research program. This deliberate confusion of research, work, and medical interrogation sidestepped the power dynamics of employee-management roles and a host of consent issues. "The doctors exploited the doctor-patient relationship to ask the workers questions that the women might otherwise have been unwilling to answer," Gillespie notes, "including the timing of their menstrual periods. A heavy paternalism suffused the relationship of the researchers to the workers and colored their perceptions."[62]

This unique mix of physiological and psychological appraisal had distinct consequences for the women who failed to meet preconceived expectations. Adeline Bogatowicz and Irene Rybacki were two workers initially chosen for the relay assembly study whose conduct challenged the researchers' aims. Repeatedly scolded for disobedience—talking too much during the workday—the girls were ultimately dismissed from the experiment for "uncooperative behavior."[63] Hospital visits were the source of particular consternation for Bogatowicz, who was regarded as especially "antagonistic" on these occasions.[64] Following her expulsion from the test room, she eventually left the company. Rybacki, whose output had noticeably decreased in the lead-up to Bogatowicz's marriage, remained at the company but not in the study.

The women's friendship clearly affected the speed and efficiency of the test room, even if the field notes of proceedings offer little sympathy or material to expand on such observations. In his account of the troublesome pair, Mayo attributed Rybacki's deteriorating effort to a poor blood count. This retrospective diagnosis remained a favored piece of evidence in promotion for the Harvard team's methods. "Under medical treatment she rapidly recovered in respect of both cell count and haemoglobin percentage and in subsequent discussion disavowed her former criticisms of the Company," Mayo wrote. "She added that at the time of making these criticisms she was suffering a 'feeling of fatigue'—which was considered possibly to have been indicative of her organic disability."[65] As Gillespie surmises, such observations reveal "a persistent tendency in Mayo's work to transform any challenge by workers of managerial control into evidence of psychiatric disturbance": "Rybacki's assertions that she would work as she liked became evidence to Mayo of fatigue and Bolshevism, and her objections to having her conversations secretly recorded were indications of paranoia."[66] Note that conditions that seem reasonable expectations of any workplace today are considered grounds for "disability" in Mayo's time.

So many years later, it is necessary to reiterate that the cornerstone study of productivity in the manufacturing era, a research program that influenced the theory and practice of management for decades, simply removed two workers that conflicted with its goals. The study's success came "only after the two girls who had the lowest output were dismissed and replaced by selected output leaders who account for the major part of the groups' increase, both in output rate and in total output, over the next seventeen months of the study."[67] The removal of talkative women from professional settings is not just a familiar story, or even a mere tale of silencing dissent; it reinforces how often women are expected to embody dexterity and docility in the exercise of labor.[68] Rybacki and Bogatowicz resisted the most invasive aspects of the Hawthorne investigation, a stance that ultimately prompted compensatory measures from management.[69] The decision to provide small parties for the girls on the day of their clinic visits—previously unthinkable privileges such as cake, ice cream, tea, and radio—was an effort to assuage the women's negative reactions to the indignity of scientific measurement. While such gestures were close to a form of bribery, they were also indication of the workers' successful determination "to influence the test room environment in exchange for their participation in the experiment."[70] Through their constant chatter, Rybacki and Bogatowicz flouted the new norms of scientific management, pursuing friendship and camaraderie instead of productivity.

FROM SERVILE TO QUANTIFIED BODIES

Researchers concede that we will never know the truth of what happened at Hawthorne. The politics involved in keeping influential stakeholders happy, and the pressure on Harvard academics to prove their worth as experts in a nascent discipline, serve as factors shaping the reported findings. What the record clearly shows, however, is that the productivity imperative failed to address all workers from the very beginning. The need for speed—the drive to enhance athleticism to lift output and improve efficiency—relied on a neat combination of economic precarity, social subjection, and corporeal incursion targeting women. The paternalistic and coercive authority enacted by Mayo and his colleagues provided a pernicious basis for the emerging field of management. In the longer history of organizational thought, the specificities of particular informants' experiences have been rendered irrelevant. The sanitized promotional material on Harvard Business School's website heralds Mayo as a man who improved workplace well-being by providing employees with an opportunity to express themselves to an interested listener.[71] Complaints of fatigue and hunger that recur throughout the Relay Room's extensive field data seem strange and cruel to a contemporary reader. Before the study, workers performed their repetitive assembly job forty-eight hours per week, including on Saturdays, with no rest periods except one lunch break. The human relations movement that is today accredited to Mayo takes its name from the "humane" conditions—such as the ten-minute rest periods—introduced in the test room. It is important to note that even these conditions, of adequate time for rest and sustenance, still constitute the source of struggle in the harshest manufacturing and assembly jobs across the world today.[72]

Complicating this history further, recent interviews with the former Relay Room participants suggest that involvement in the study was a highlight of their time at Western Electric.[73] The attention enjoyed by the women selected for scrutiny rendered them celebrities in a way that their lives might not have allowed otherwise. This is another lasting effect of this vast experiment in industrial research. Still, migrant women's confinement to routine jobs in the interwar years contributed to their objectification as workers whose primary purpose became the improvement of business efficiencies. Placed under extensive medical surveillance, subject to physiological and psychological judgment, they performed labor that contributed to the securing of management as a science, even if their activities regularly confounded the expectations of experts.

As its critical purchase increased over time, human relations theory successfully married incentive and control. The theory of the workplace-as-family traded on the notion of base instincts derived from Mayo's unique reading of Darwin and Freud. In this vision, fueled by Piaget's development ideals, workers were necessarily infantilized in an Oedipal relation to an authority (daddy) figure. Responsibility had to be proved through competitive and comparative merit against other colleague-siblings. The longevity of Mayo's influence is obvious in the performance management protocols of large companies today, which elicit morale and motivation through techniques of the one-on-one interview and mentoring. The management relation operates on norms of confession and self-appraisal that produce a regulatory effect.[74] In the isolated context of the interview, management is a relation of dependence, a process that mirrors the inferior status of women and other "minority" workers at the moment in history that such practices took hold. This raises new questions for the discipline of management studies, especially given Mayo's own unusual treatment of women. The Hawthorne Studies taught scholars many things. Among them, we might venture that productivity has always been a science premised on the exclusion of disruptive bodies and the silence of those with little recourse to power.

Productivity pioneers at the turn of the twentieth century and interwar period established many of the methods for measuring, assessing and comparing workplace performance that continue in labor administration today. Catherine Beecher, Lillian Gilbreth, and Christine Frederick's home economics research taught generations of women to be time-and-motion experts within the family home. Through these contributions, and the constant interplay between public and private skills acquisition, the logic of productivity gained widespread mainstream acceptance. This hidden history challenges the narratives we typically tell about the incursion of work into home life, especially in relation to new technologies. In the case of Frank and Lillian Gilbreth's motion studies, the significance of the visual record in identifying an individual's contribution secured a new kind of desire for improving oneself and swiftly achieving tasks by amassing evidence. Meanwhile, in the productivity studies taking place at Hawthorne, Harvard professors applied the principles of fatigue studies to test the athletic capacity of workers. These methods assumed that the right combination of inputs and training would ensure optimal physical condition. When we hear the language of life coaching today, with its promise to guide individuals to achieve career goals, we might not pause to consider how athletic terminology became a suitable metaphor for the workplace. Productivity consultants intentionally encouraged workers to change their sense of accomplishment from the group to the individual. Through self-imposed discipline, workers could transform their labor into a championship contest with colleagues. This powerful combination of management and engineering innovation helped to remove collective thinking from our understanding of work and its organization.

Overall, the idea of productivity that emerged in business and management circles over the twentieth century consecrated a selective understanding of both the time and location for labor. Privileging the experience of workers outside the home during industrialization, in factory and office settings, neglected the central role of time and self-management in the command of home enterprises. As we will see in later chapters, it is these strategies of organization outside the Organization that bear more direct relevance to today's conditions of immaterial labor. The experience of women and racially subjugated minorities who secured the reproduction of domestic life offer an important complement to the official account of scientific management, even while the practices of middle-class women reinforced the logic of delegation and supervision that companies also enshrined. But this chapter has also revealed moments when these power structures came under direct challenge. The preoccupations and personal friendships of factory workers clearly competed with incentive schemes developed by managers seeking to optimize employee performance. The tenets of productivity have long been contested, including within the very moments that are typically used to generate legitimacy for its claims.

The progressive principles informing the beginnings of productivity theory relied on the idea of moral perfectionism, a worker who could rid "the evil" of inefficiency and make the most out of time.[75] The secularization of productivity in subsequent decades laid these virtuous principles aside. The rise of the executive class called for a new kind of athleticism, a separation and retreat from the considerations of others, to match the winner-takes-all logic of global capital. How this happened is the focus of part II.

II Practice

2 Executive Athleticism

Time Management and the Quest for Organization

The history of productivity is not owned by the Organization. As the previous chapter shows, the ideas of time and self-management embedded in today's entrepreneurial techniques have as much foundation in the home enterprise as in the corporate firm. Popular genres of time management have always complemented the formally recognized methods promoted by cultural institutions, a point this chapter extends by focusing on a specific case: the self-help instruction book. Beyond the elite environs of prestigious university campuses and the closed loop of big business, mass-market time-management manuals have been crucial in the dissemination of productivity ideals and their commonsense principles to a wider public. They are a key component of the "cultural circuit" Nigel Thrift ascribes to the operations of "knowing capitalism."[1] Through time management self-help, the personal relationship to efficiency takes hold. Starting in the late 1950s, with James McKay's *The Management of Time*, and gaining momentum with Alan Lakein's *How to Get Control of Your Time and Your Life* (1973), productivity literature remains a fixture of departure gate bookstores and middle-brow publishers catering to the psychological vicissitudes of white-collar work. These instruction books—which are often accompanied by associated lecture series, classes, and audiotapes—are the predecessors for today's TED talks, influencer blogs, and webinars. Enlightened teachers impart lessons to audiences seeking secrets to a more efficient work life. These guru-style leaders assume the role of guide or donor in the quest to find greater productivity. Their bootstrapping narratives are a further step from the selfless frugality and moral duty governing earlier forms of efficiency outlined in chapter 1. Productivity for the executive class celebrates separation from the concerns of others in the interests of self-enhancement. It is another front in the broader neoliberal project to erase the vocabulary of collectivity from work.[2]

Productivity genres address the urgency of now, offering remedies for the turbulence of day-to-day administrivia. Their tactical tips contrast the deliberative and abstract management skills imparted to business students aspiring to professional vocations, although the distinction between "management gurus" in formal and informal teaching genres can be difficult to discern.[3] For every overflowing inbox suffered by middle managers without a secretary, time management self-help provides colloquial armory for workers deep in the corporate trenches. It is a tactical and temporary defense mechanism in the longer battle known as office "firefighting."

The following analysis illustrates how time-management maestros occupy the role of coach for a competitive office worker whose individual feats increasingly come at the expense of colleagues. By learning the art of productivity, the aspiring executive is guided to acquire skills that ensure professional ascent and glory while others are left behind. Drawing on Peter Sloterdijk's notion of athleticism, I read time management self-help as codified practice, a form of training through which workers become capable of the ever more daring acts of solitude and ruthlessness necessary to produce career competence. Productivity's self-enhancing rigor is an evolution of Foucault's idea of *asceticism* for the postmodern domain of corporate institutions.[4] It is the means by which productivity genres ensure the myopia necessary for professional commitment while simultaneously diminishing awareness of the work of others. Time-management training has the effect, if not the function, of obliterating recognition of collegial interdependence in contemporary workplaces. Fitting its neoliberal moment, productivity's inward focus further entrenches the erasure of collective thinking that the first efficiency engineers sought to accomplish. Analyzing popular productivity practices in textual form shows the significance of these genres in extending the logic of efficiency to the individual, and the consequences of this development.[5]

One of the great ironies of time management as a genre is its dependence on amnesia: it is written to suit an attention span that fits the chaotic world of business. Forgetfulness and distraction is assumed of readers in the structural makeup of book chapters that stick with simple, brute-force layout and few exercises in poetics. The actual content of texts references a fairly unchanging cluster of tried-and-true methods (ranked and refined To Do lists; daily affirmations; time logs; single handling; delegation; embracing seclusion) as well as highly reciprocal recommended reading lists. Successful writers adopt a fearless approach to self-citation and relish recounting the advice of more famous forebears, often without conventional acknowledgment.[6] In this sense, time-management training operates at the level of myth as well as ideology. Catchy concepts are repurposed with slightly different nuances, each minimally inflecting and reshaping a palimpsest of an original. The writing is punctuated and enhanced with pithy quotations, a mixture of religious, spiritual, and conventional wisdom alongside "quasi-scientific appeals to neurology and psychology."[7] Analyzing a number of manuals in succession quickly reveals the false premise of any professed novelty on behalf of authors. To use the vocabulary of Judith Butler,[8] productivity pedagogy is quintessentially *performative*: its assertions gain traction through repeated circulation and citation, even when the basis for such truth claims have little empirical trace. My analogy to gender acquisition is deliberate. The acquisition of professional subjectivity as taught and demonstrated in these texts appears intended to inspire subsequent acts of mimicry. With this in mind, my intention in what follows is to suggest an opening in the hegemonic status of time management in professional life on recognition that one is not born but, rather, becomes productive.[9]

I.

The initial wave of mass-market productivity titles bears close relation to the first flush of corporate downsizing in North America in the 1970s. In preceding decades, the postwar settlement and the rise of the firm had created a climate that facilitated the prospect of a job for life, even if such positions "tended to eventuate rather than be mandated."[10] The occupational stability implied in this period was captured in the IBM slogan "No layoffs, ever." The promise was one of a host of post-Mayo efforts to "humanize" the workplace in the hope of generating loyalty from workers and discrediting the need for unions. In this context, worker productivity attracted a new kind of scrutiny due to external threats made visible by war. The competitive edge of Japanese management techniques was a notable source of concern; indeed, Lillian Gilbreth was one management consultant who visited the country to acquire new expertise to trade back home. Another contributing factor affecting the career prospects of white salaried men was the emerging civil rights agenda in the United States. The Organization Man famously described by William H. Whyte became subject to unprecedented internal job competition as women and other under-represented minorities succeeded in gaining greater access to office work and management responsibilities.[11] The 1970s thus saw a change in the amount of auxiliary, career-enhancing effort required of employees to prove their value in a more challenging marketplace for talent. Like the assembly workers studied at Hawthorne, and the factory hands and secretaries optimized by the Gilbreths, members of the professional class were invited to contemplate the rewards on offer if they actively identified with management thinking.[12]

The self-actualizing practices of time management in the office extended the initial principles of scientific management by developing skills that marked the worker as responsibly exercising a new kind of freedom. This latitude to conduct one's activities away from direct management surveillance is nowhere better crystallized than in David Allen's time management hit *Getting Things Done*: "If you had the freedom to decide what to do, you also had the responsibility to make good choices, given your 'priorities.'"[13] The ability to create order by distinguishing among various tasks is the difference between productivity for the professional and the enforced, repetitive output required of the manual worker. For the salaried class, exercising discretion is productivity's chief skill. In the words of the management icon Peter Drucker, a recurring authority in time-management texts, "Working on the *right* things is what makes knowledge work effective."[14] Productivity improvements manifest as the ability to detect inefficiencies and eliminate waste from one's schedule. As we will see, this process involves delegating to others all tasks that are deemed too trivial to be worth the attention of the successful.

One of the earliest examples of time management instruction is the System Company's *How to Systematize the Day's Work: 87 Plans and Shortcuts Used and Proved at the Desks of 43 Executives*.[15] This early twentieth-century manual defines the basis of personal system as "the ability to get the thing done; to get it done thoroughly, and to get it done on time."[16] The book's notable feature, as its title and publisher suggest, is the insistence on applying a system to achieve success. Man "invents his own system . . . because he finds it necessary. He has to discover a way to keep ahead of the other fellow and in devising such a way, he cultivates not only system, but his initiative and originality."[17] At this point in history, discretionary skill and prioritizing tasks are not the main measure of productivity. Rather, executive wisdom is shown by relinquishing control of one's affairs to an automated system that can be trusted to carry out the right process and order for work. Systems thinking provides the model for appropriate business conduct at an organizational and individual level. Once the basic structure and schedule has been established, any human interference in the smooth running of the system is to be minimized.

Chapters on "System in the Man" and "System in the Desk" include diagrams of orderly bureaus, files, and folders, as well as other useful equipment for the office worker seeking superior professional tools. Basic tenets of productivity are evident in illustrations that demonstrate the most efficient way to access previously filed information. The desk layout is organized, Gilbreth-style, to promote the smallest number of movements. Retrieving files from a desk drawer, for instance, should require no more than three motions.[18] When it comes to the files, a "compartment should be devoted to 'Letters Ready to Dictate,' another one to 'Matters to Do To-day,' another to 'Things to Take up With A,' etc."[19] The category "Ready to Dictate" reflects the expectation that support staff are available for the turn-of-the-twentieth-century executive. Once again, effective time management is made possible by delegating work to others.

The "Hold Over" file—a tool "for holding papers pending information or follow-up"—is to be kept on the right hand side of the desk, the

FIGURE 2.1 The appropriate number of movements to file. From System Company, *How to Systematize the Day's Work*, 1911.

FIGURE 2.2 System applied to the desk provides order and reassurance that work can be organized.

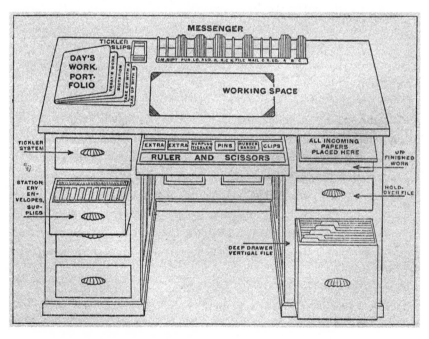

location for unfinished work yet to be disposed. "These are the papers we wish to hold over for some purpose or other. The time is not yet ripe to give them attention." The "Tickler" file, which complements the "Hold Over" file, is to be kept to the left side of the desk. The tickler is "an auxiliary brain," a "second memory for the desk man."[20] Organizing memos according to the day and month of their relevance allows the user to pace and prepare work to transpire at a time designated in advance. By systematizing responses and applying appropriate categorization, the amount of information addressing the worker becomes regulated. In this instance, systems thinking rests on the belief that the human brain is an imperfect instrument that can be enhanced with external equipment:

> Your brain has a capacity limit. Don't overload it. Don't fill it with details. Don't burden it with worry.
>
> Get a system.
>
> Make your system your storehouse. File therein the little cares that wear and tear — the important details that annoy.
>
> Make your system the guardian of the necessary, the grave of the needless. Leave your work at night, free and unshackled. Your system will bring your duties before you the next morning — the next week — the next month.
>
> Train your system to remember all that it should not forget — to forget all that it should not remember.[21]

In this passage, the limits of human capacity are overcome by placing faith in a higher power. The system delivers protection and consolation against all manner of anxieties, and the accumulating expectations of paperwork processing for the desk clerk. In today's talk of office automation and virtual assistance, the recourse to system holds a familiar ring. Delegating decision making to systems is increasingly portrayed as a rational response to the paralyzing experience of digitally mediated information overload. But this latest instance of adopting an "auxiliary brain" did not develop immediately. In the context of the 1970s, when time management manuals really accelerated, the reassuring voice of productivity came from a different source: the self-made guru.

II.

Time management self-help in the 1960s and '70s hinges on the insights of a writer who guides individuals toward increased efficiency and effectiveness. This style of instruction resembles mass-market management thinking, in which leadership, charisma, and calling are blurred.[22] Bringing together the anecdotal appeal of older self-help pioneers with the branding strategies of corporate public relations, time-management maestros answer the need for an actionable program to confront mid-career myopia. Typically, the guru-author offers a trademark formula for readers to adopt as part of a reformed daily routine, such as "the 7 minute difference," "leave the office earlier," or my personal favorite, "eat the frog."[23] The function of each adage is to insert ritual awareness into one's day, much like a religious refrain. The maxims act as a filter to keep the mind attuned to long-term aspirations. In Lakein's example, the motto "drift, drown or decide" summarizes three simple options. A worker can *drift* through the job, oscillating aimlessly among various tasks; he can *drown* in the deluge of tasks being requested of him, never to triumph over the sheer quantity of work; or, he can *decide* to take control of his time, pursuing only those tasks that fit the priorities identified in the course of self-reflection. The process of determining priorities is coordinated early in the books. As an opening exercise, readers are usually invited to list their life goals through a series of questions designed to establish guiding principles. These primary objectives—sometimes referred to as a personal "mission statement"—serve to place the apparent urgencies of daily tasks in a more comprehensive hierarchical order. Extreme methods are not out of the question when it comes to identifying one's life purpose. In *Winning at Work without Losing at Love*, Stephen Arterburn suggests writing the sentences that will appear on your gravestone in an effort to elicit proper perspective.[24] The result of this internal analysis is a set of anchoring statements that can be applied at regular intervals during the day, a force to resist the short-term drama of office urgencies.

Another memorable Lakein imperative asks, "What is the best use of my time right now?"[25] The question provides a further prompt to remember previously identified goals, especially as the demands of others begin to accumulate throughout the day. Constantly assessing the surrounding environment and conditions, the phrase provides a point of reflection to recalibrate intentions and maintain focus on broad-scale purpose. Like many gurus, Lakein suggests categorizing tasks according to importance—A, B, and C—with A-1 being the most significant accomplishment currently required. The act of prioritizing is precipitated in the book by a series of inquiries, prompts ("What are your lifetime goals?" "How would you *like* to spend the next three years?"), and brainstorming activities that can advance these hopes. Lakein is one of many popular writers who invoke "the 80/20 rule" as a way of explaining the appropriate amount of time to spend on different tasks. The so-called rule is actually a liberal extension of the Pareto principle in economics, in which 80 percent of outputs are generated by 20 percent of inputs. In enterprise productivity, this lesson is variously used to explain how 20 percent of a company's clients—or, indeed, employees—will deliver 80 percent of the results. Applied to the individual, the premise means that workers should strive to focus on tasks that are both highly demanding and highly rewarding.[26] The bulk of demands on one's time have minimal payoff and should be avoided where possible. According to this principle, time management is a way to justify a lack of attention to certain tasks when the rewards are negligible.

PRIORITIZATION

Prioritization is the primary lesson of time-management pedagogy in this early phase of the genre. Establishing priorities involves applying the right category for a task through the practice of "time diagnosis," in Drucker's terms.[27] The books urge heightened attention to the content of one's activity to generate confidence that a system of categorization will deliver better results. In *Getting Things Done: The ABCs of Time Management*, Edwin C. Bliss explains: "Action can be broken down into five categories: Important and Urgent, Important but not Urgent, Urgent but not Important, Busy Work, and Wasted Time."[28] An approximation of Bliss's formula appears in the Time Management Matrix outlined by Stephen Covey in the wildly successful *The 7 Habits of Highly Effective People*.[29] In this much repeated rubric, time-management problems are shown to arise from a kind of entropy that occurs in organizations that specialize in generating tasks that are "important but not urgent." Learning to tell the difference between competing temporal demands becomes the responsibility of the worker, a skill that "divides effective individuals from ineffective ones," according to Bliss: "Most of the really important things in our lives are not urgent. They can be done now or later. In many cases they can be postponed forever, and in too many cases they are. These are the things we 'never get around to.'"[30] Indeed, the bulk of office work falls into the category "urgent but not important." These are tasks "that clamor for immediate action" but rarely amount to much significance in the grand scheme of things.[31] Time-management gurus focus on these tasks in such detail because they are a regular source of diversion from headline goals. These jobs "are marginally worth doing" and "provide a feeling of activity and accomplishment" even while they regularly derail attention from the items that would deliver "far greater benefit," Bliss explains.[32] As the next chapter elaborates, checking e-mail messages has become the exemplary instance of this category type in recent years. The feeling of accomplishment that comes with clearing an inbox or organizing a calendar is a momentary pleasure that often reflects an inability to influence the broader agenda governing one's work. However, as we will see shortly, this narrow focus on the short term also has the unintended consequence of placing in the "important but not urgent" category a number of long-term health, family, and leisure goals that are difficult to keep buoyant faced with the barrage of day-to-day pressure.

Drucker's classic work *The Effective Executive* (1967) describes time management as the process of adjudicating between matters that are critical, "Things that need not be done at all," and "Things that can be done by somebody else just as well, if not better."[33] Here again, prioritization initiates a self-reflexive assessment of the worthiness of tasks relative to one's sense of status. Time-management manuals build awareness of efficiency and the need for prioritization not simply by instruction, then, but by conjuring processes of self-examination that amount to a measure of one's worth. In many guides this involves an explicit audit. John Adair's *Effective Time Management: How to Save Time and Spend It Wisely* (1982) advocates "keeping a time log" as part of the chapter "Developing a Personal Sense of Time."[34] Adair draws on Drucker's advice to "make sure you know where your time goes" if you are to have any chance of bringing it under control. Creating an inventory of time is intended to force readers to confront whatever schedule features are creating the perception of undue busyness. Note the anecdotal authority in Adair's caution:

"I warn you in advance, from personal experience, that you could be in for a considerable shock. Yet that very shock could jolt you into action. It is like an electric charge to start up the motor of your will."[35]

Ideally, the time log is filled out progressively, each day, for several weeks. Every hour is accounted for and coded according to a rubric the reader devises. The time period for the audit has to provide a representative sample of routine activities of various kinds. The outcome of this exercise (also mentioned by Alec Mackenzie, who is among a number of authors to include a sample spreadsheet for readers to use[36]) is "to notice opportunities for improvement. . . . For example, you may discover that you are spending much more time than you thought possible on reading newspapers and trade journals or compiling routine reports. Could the latter be delegated?"[37]

At the conclusion of the audit, readers should ask themselves whether the time spent in each category appropriately reflects their top-level priorities. "What are the items which take up significant portions of your time and contribute nothing?" Adair asks. "What would happen if they weren't done at all?" When it comes to discretionary time—time that is free from obvious obligations—the audit works rhetorically to persuade the reader to consolidate such moments into larger blocks, thus enhancing the likelihood of uninterrupted attention. Once the amount of unproductive activity has been identified, large portions of work can be passed to a subordinate or secretary, including "constantly recurring problems, routine matters or work to do with details."[38] The time log instigates a process whereby mere "activity" is refined and recast as an obstacle to meaningful work that delivers results. The art of time management is enacted by avoiding any task that fails to advance the individual's goals. The purpose of pedagogy is therefore twofold: to justify inattention to unworthy tasks and to provide motivation on important items when an immediate payoff or incentive may be lacking.

PROCRASTINATION

When difficult work cannot be avoided or delegated, productivity advocates espouse mythical techniques such as the Swiss Cheese approach, a dictum that appears regularly in personal efficiency manuals. The principle reminds readers that spare moments can be used to advance some tiny portion of the larger whole. In Lakein's use, the Swiss Cheese approach is a tonic for procrastination. It is a way to get started on a tough but important goal "by poking some holes in it." Applying Swiss Cheese turns large projects into smaller, "instant tasks," knowing the difference a few minutes can make. The full list of "holes" available to the worker includes these "simple tips to get started":

- get more information
- try a leading task (e.g., sharpen your pencil)
- take advantage of your current mood
- give yourself a pep talk
- make a commitment to someone[39]

Lakein's formula is a method for overcoming procrastination and associated feelings of helplessness, even if you do not have time to fully accomplish a pressing objective on a busy day. Swiss Cheese turns pessimistic attitudes upside down. "Admit to yourself: 'I just cannot plan,'" Lakein urges. "Then say to yourself, 'But if I could plan, what would the plan be?' Now, set about to answer the if question."[40] Cheese-puncturing methods generate action and provide a basis for beginning work. Their intent is to create mindfulness, an awareness of surroundings, and a sense of perspective on what appears to be paralyzing.

Another anti-procrastination method is the "eat the frog" technique, which means always starting the day with the most difficult task on your To Do list. The idea is that even if the reader may not like the job, the feeling of accomplishment that comes with getting something so dreaded out of the way can provide enough fulfilment to keep the worker buoyant for the remainder of the day. Brian Tracy's book *Eat That Frog!* pools "the 21 most effective methods for conquering procrastination and accomplishing more"; according to Amazon.com, more than 1.5 million copies have been sold in forty-two languages.[41] Frog-eating creates a simple means to ensure positive and substantial progress toward a long-term goal before the bustle of the day interferes. Identifying what constitutes the day's frog is the crucial step to ensuring high returns and satisfaction.

A related dimension to overcoming stasis is dealing with desk clutter. In the following example, Bliss applies a simple schematic to reestablish order:

Whenever you find your desk becoming chaotic, take time out to reorganize. Make a single pile of all your papers, then go through them (making generous use of your wastebasket) and divide them into categories:

1. Immediate action

2. Low priority

3. Pending

4. Reading material[42]

According to Bliss, these four categories exhaust the options for what should be done with written files and correspondence. The art of "wastebasketry" is avoiding "the temptation . . . to leave other high-priority items on your desk so you won't overlook them." Decluttering the desk, as we saw in the System Company instructions, panders to the belief that organization can be achieved with scientific precision. Productivity lore asserts that "you can think of only one thing at a time, so select the most important one and focus all your attention on it."[43]

LISTS AND RULES

Lists constantly populate time management self-help, with detailed instructions and lengthy questionnaires forming the substance of entire chapters. A typical example is this brief lesson from Bliss on "how to handle correspondence quickly and efficiently":

1. Have incoming mail screened and sorted, if possible. If you open your own mail, sort as you open (with wastebasket close at hand).

2. Handle each letter only once. Avoid papershuffling. Do whatever has to be done (checking, forwarding, phoning, replying) immediately, instead of postponing action.

3. If a brief reply is possible, write it on the incoming letter or memo, use a photocopy for the file, and return the original to the sender.

4. If possible, put your dictation on a tape, belt, or disk (see "Dictating Machines").

5. Use form letters and form paragraphs for routine correspondence.

6. Don't make frequent revisions. Perfectionism is time-consuming.

7. Get to the point.

8. If you have a long memo, make an outline before dictating.

9. Avoid unnecessary copies. They waste somebody's time to make, distribute, file, or read.

10. For internal correspondence, try "speed-letter" forms with carbons already inserted and with space for a reply.

11. Don't write when a phone call will do. Especially if there is something to be negotiated, or ideas to be exchanged, do it by phone or face to face, instead of on paper. Use memos primarily to announce, to remind, to confirm or to clarify.

12. Use short, terse words. Don't perpetrate polysyllabic obfuscation.[44]

Bliss's guide is a precursor to the professional self-help proliferating today in so many life-hacking websites. Point 12 is reminiscent of *Fast Company* magazine's guide to composing compelling e-mail,[45] reflecting its staple interest in productivity secrets of successful executives. Across the decades, both instances of advice serve to reassure workers that it is appropriate to dispense with letter writing's previous formalities in the interests of efficiency.

Productivity thinking means adopting an uncompromising attitude toward time. Authors regularly begin their books with the simple analogy that time is a resource, just like money. "It can be borrowed, saved or squandered," writes Adair.[46] Once time is exhausted, though, it cannot be replaced. As Mackenzie observes, "Few people have enough; yet everyone has all there is."[47] The purpose of time management manuals is to retrain the reader's ontological bearing in the workplace, from the short-termism of daily tasks to a larger, more grandiose view. Readers engage in goal setting for the short, medium, and long term. Adair uses research conducted by Shell in the 1960s to explain the benefits of "helicopter vision," a term that captures the need to

· Look at problems from a higher vantage point with simultaneous attention to relevant details.

· Place facts and problems within a broader context by immediately detecting relationship with systems of wider scope.

· Shape one's work accordingly on the basis of a personal vision.[48]

Allen similarly outlines the benefits of elevated thinking—of setting priorities that are discernible only at "30,000 feet." This approach literally invokes the experience of the frequent flyer, whose superficial engagement with the routine world excuses participation in the labor of the social.[49] In these ways, productivity thinking explicitly demands an active distance from the reality of life on the ground.

Even at a more modest scale, the significant legacy from this first wave of time management self-help is to deliver a set of techniques that legitimately isolate the worker from the needs of others. To make sure that established priorities can be advanced without interruption, Lakein recommends "dialing your own number and leaving the phone off the hook so anyone calling you will get a busy signal."[50] Mackenzie has an entire list devoted to "avoiding telephone interruptions," which includes a cutoff switch, silencing the ring to a blinking light, unplugging the phone, and even moving to another room.[51] In the language of time management, these practices are par for the course in "regulating traffic"—that is, placing limits on the amount of social interaction you will allow during business hours. Productivity entails heeding cautionary warnings about the time-sapping neediness of colleagues. As Lakein explains, in describing a common request from peers, "'Do you have a minute?' usually means "May I have your attention now to talk about something that will take an unspecified length of time?'" Successful time management means learning to recognize the dangers of "oncoming traffic," lest these distractions push workers off the desired course.

III.

For Alan Lakein, gaining control of time "is in many ways analogous to good muscle tone."[52] From the 1970s onward, this athletic sentiment recurs in the language of time management self-help. Lakein is the first productivity author I have found to suggest a natural equation between freedom and the exercise of discipline. "It might sound like a contradiction in terms," he writes, "but . . . the biggest payoff of all in achieving greater *control* of your time and your life is greater *freedom*."[53] In *Getting Things Done*, David Allen similarly claims, "You can train yourself, almost like an athlete, to be faster, more responsive, more proactive, and more focused in knowledge work."[54] The "art of stress-free productivity" centers on the adoption of a simple workflow diagram. Allen's system guides readers through the stages of assessing the urgency or priority of a task. In this version, there are only ever three reasons that something is on your mind:

· You haven't clarified exactly what the intended outcome is;

· You haven't decided what the very next physical action step is;

· You haven't put reminders of the outcome and the action required in a system you trust.[55]

Allen urges readers to write down To Do tasks—collecting "all of things that are 'ringing your bell' in some way"—to inspire a foolproof completion plan. This logistical work is affective as much as it is practical in effect: "You must be assured that you're doing what you need to be doing, and that it's OK to be *not* doing what you're not doing. Reviewing your system on a regular basis and keeping it current and functional are prerequisites for that kind of control."[56] Allen's book is a direct descendent of the time-management advice in the System Company manual, which overcomes all of the "little cares that wear and tear—the important details that annoy." Allen's system provides an organizational apparatus that reliably accounts for any permutation of task. This practical utility echoes the spirit of productivity predecessors by outlining a digestible refrain for adherents. Once you see the need for action, he writes, there are only three options: *do* it, *delegate* it, or *defer* it:

1. Do it. If an action will take less than two minutes, it should be *done* at the moment it is defined.

2. Delegate it. If the action will take longer than two minutes, ask yourself, Am I the right person to do this? If the answer is no, *delegate* it to the appropriate entity.

3. Defer it. If the action will take longer than two minutes, and you are the right person to do it, you will have to *defer* acting on it until later and track it on one or more "Next Actions" lists.[57]

It is easy to see how Allen's system, when plotted this way, has emerged as a popular strategy to navigate an inbox of e-mail messages, for instance. It is not incidental that the hashtag acronym for the book's title, *Get-*

ting Things Done (#GTD) came to prominence in the late 2000s, alongside the spectacular growth of e-mail and social media use in knowledge work.[58] While Allen's advice shares features of earlier techniques of time management before the digitization of office work, what has changed in the past decade in particular is the quality and quantity of information being processed by the worker. New computing technologies and platforms propel more data at and about individuals, rendering the desk- and document-bound regimes of time mastery increasingly outmoded.

Allen's response to this changing experience of knowledge work—the sheer weight of information overload wrought by digitally connected offices and colleagues—is to appeal to the worker's frustrated creativity. Allen engineers an important shift in assumed value from the system itself to the intelligence of the individual who adopts the system. In GTD, as the next chapter shows in more detail, there is beauty in the smooth operation of a system that allows individuals to transcend the worries of the world. To reach this level of superiority, workers are invited to embark on a schedule of disciplined training that culminates in a state of relaxed confidence. Allen uses specific physical analogies—the rower's swing, the karate punch—to explain this productivity ideal, which is synonymous with the psychological state of flow.[59] Allen is not the first business coach to draw on sporting metaphors to convey the exceptional needs of talented professionals; nor is he alone in borrowing from non-Western cultural traditions to illustrate an alternative to corporate workplace success. Allen is attracted to "the high levels of training in the martial arts" because they "teach and demand balance and relaxation as much as anything else. Clearing the mind and being flexible are key."[60] In productivity pedagogy, training both mind and body is an essential part of professional development.

Part III explores the growth of mindfulness practice as an extension of this principle beyond the written manuals analyzed in this chapter. For now, focusing on this literary form of self-production, we see that "disciplining and aestheticizing moments are intrinsically interwoven."[61] As Ulrich Bröckling notes, "Practice—doing the exercises—here means both regular and regulated repetition for the purpose of achieving perfection, as well as a playful *exercitium* intended to give one's own life a self-chosen and thoroughly formed structure."[62] Literary self-production takes an observable form in time-management manuals, beginning with the opening set of instructions that explain "how to get the most from this book." This phrase is a chapter heading in what is probably the best known of self-help classics, Dale Carnegie's *How to Win Friends and Influence People*. It echoes in Alan Lakein's advice, in 1973: "Don't be afraid to mark up the book, reading with pen or pencil to make the book yours," he writes. "Underline the key ideas, and make notes in the margins. List the numbers of the pages that are most important to you in the inside front cover for easy reference."[63] Compare this with Carnegie's original tips: "Read with a crayon, pencil, pen, magic marker or highlighter in your hand. When you come across a suggestion that you feel you can use, draw a line beside it. If it is a four-star suggestion, then underscore every sentence or highlight it, or mark it with '****'."[64]

The explicit endorsement to repeat, reflect, and remember prepares readers for a new way of thinking, the lifestyle change that the author seeks to arouse. Time-management manuals rely on popular cognitive science principles of habit formation, acknowledging that repetition is necessary for new thought patterns to take hold.[65] In discussing habit, Mackenzie is one of several productivity figures to cite William James, the psychologist who also influenced the early writing of Lillian Gilbreth.[66] Allen epitomizes these generic traits of time management self-help when he advises readers to "make a cassette tape that contains the determinations you've made about how to implement change." He continues, "If you make such a tape based on this book, it will change your life. That's a promise. Trust me."[67] Further formal conventions—such as repeating each chapter's point in conclusion and facilitating synthesis through end-of-section bullet points—accommodate the demand that readers revisit the book regularly to rekindle its energizing lessons. The predictable structure and content is the literary performance reinforcing the message that life can be simplified, tasks can be managed, and control can be gained when faced with the messiness of daily life. The personal address characteristic of self-help literature creates a layer of identification with the author's experience, increasing the likelihood of conversion to productivity reform. We will see more examples of this in coming chapters, as the self-help and wellness industry converge.

It should be clear that the problems time-management literature emerges to solve arise from a historically specific intersection of gender, age, and occupational concerns. In manuals published in the 1960s and '70s, the reader is presumed to be male, with a secretary and stay-at-home wife supporting his duties.[68] Moving in to the 1990s, the experience of women ascending company ranks expands the reach and register of time-management anxieties. Laura Stack, author of *The Productivity Pro*, and Kris Cole, "one of Australia's bestselling business authors," capitalize on the specific difficulty faced by women seeking to combine work and home obligations.[69] To readers today, these texts serve as useful archives of a moment when the ideal of "work-life balance" seemed to be a peculiar problem for female professionals, as if balancing intimacy with labor were a gender-specific problem. Across the productivity genre as a whole, particular moments stand out as especially annoying time wasters, from traffic jams and commuting to waiting in line for a doctor's appointment. The condition of time sensitivity that recurs in these scenes appears especially acute for a middle-class demographic poorly conditioned to the socially deferential position of waiting.[70] Authors attempt to contextualize "schedule stress" by placing it in relation to life-or-death issues—that is, matters more deserving of legitimate concern. Questionnaires are also provided to gauge the true sources of readers' anxiety. Results of these self-assessments reveal intersecting influences (divorce, health scares, moving house, children and other dependent relationships) that coincide and converge with career progression, accentuating professionals' feelings of time pressure. In this sense, one of the most sobering outcomes of reading time management self-help is learning the range of activities that gurus define as "important but not urgent." The prioritization process advanced in the books regularly places vacation time, hobbies, and health checks in the category of tasks that can be deferred until some later time. Note the examples Bliss uses to illustrate such procrastination:

> that special course you want to take to upgrade your professional skills; that new project you would like to suggest to your boss after you find time to do the preliminary fact-finding; that article you've been meaning to write;

that diet you've intended to begin; that annual medical checkup you've planned to get for the past three years; that visit to a lawyer to have your will drawn; that retirement program you've been planning to establish.[71]

Compare this with Allen's "Typical Partial 'Someday/Maybe'" project list of 2001:

- Get a bass-fishing boat
- Create promotional videos of staff
- Learn Spanish
- Find Stafford Lyons
- Take a watercolor class
- Get a digital video camera
- Get a sideboard for the kitchen
- Northern Italy trip
- Build a lap pool
- Apprentice with my carpenter
- Get Kathryn a scooter
- Spotlight our artwork
- Take a balloon ride
- Build a koi pond
- Build a wine cellar
- Digitize old photos and videos
- Take a trip through Montana
- Have a neighborhood party
- Set up a not-for-profit foundation
- Set up remote-server access at home
- Learn Photoshop software capabilities[72]

Allen further suggests a list of subcategories to add to the master "Someday/Maybe" list, including:

- CDs I might want
- Videos to rent
- Books to read
- Wine to taste
- Weekend trips to take
- Things to do with the kids
- Seminars to take[73]

These deferral lists are a neat time capsule of middle-class life at the turn of the twenty-first century. The mixture of paid and unpaid activities, voluntary and family work, professional and domestic pursuits anticipate the blurring of labor and leisure tasks that will be explored further in the next chapter. References to already obsolete technology only add to the poignancy of these collected aspirations, which read as so many dreams that will never be fulfilled unless one adopts a rigorous program of productivity—and even then, it is potentially too late. Allen's dot-point style brings clarity to the process of introspection, an unimpeded view that helps to assess whether projects align with life goals. Used appropriately, the GTD system reforms habitual short-termism to ensure that readers have no cause to regret the life not lived.

FROM SORTING THINGS OUT TO CARE OF THE SELF

In this chapter, the art of time management evolves from a system of classification befitting discrete units of time and information to a mode of self-care aspiring to meet the transformed conditions of immaterial labor. As a form of subjective training, time-management texts express a commitment to finding the right attitude toward familiar scenarios that can be better handled through the application of proverbial wisdom. As Kenneth Burke explains, the function of proverbs is to provide "*strategies* for dealing with *situations*." He writes, "In so far as situations are typical and recurrent in a given social structure, people develop names for them and strategies for handling them. Another name for strategies might be *attitudes*."[74]

As we have seen, time-management techniques encourage an *attitude* toward knowledge work that accepts personal responsibility for productivity.[75] The lessons imparted by efficiency gurus teach readers "what to expect, what to look out for" in the customary settings of the workday.[76] Heeding these signs, the reader is able to enact a more appropriate attitude to propel action and ensure that the most important tasks get done. Written in 1938, Burke's "Literature as Equipment for Living" already diagnoses the pleasure in accomplishment that productivity literature makes popular: "The reading of a book on the attaining of success is in itself the symbolic attaining of that success. It is while they read that readers are 'succeeding.'" At a time that the industry for self-help was barely in existence, Burke argued that "readers make no serious attempt to apply the book's recipes" in the majority of cases: "The lure of the book resides in the fact that the reader, while reading it, is then living in the aura of success. What he wants is easy success; and he gets it in symbolic form by the mere reading itself. To attempt applying such stuff in real life would be very difficult, full of many disillusioning problems."[77]

From today's vantage point, we might posit that the further function and pleasure in reading productivity pedagogy is that it grants readers time to think about time. For many salaried employees, working to satisfy multiple obligations across a range of social roles, this opportunity can be rare. Reading for advice is not just a useful exercise in grasping content; it is also a way to take "time out" from the pace and priorities set by office norms. This is why so many manuals explicitly incorporate an exercise of temporal awareness in their early pages. A recurring example is the simple directive that the reader sit quietly for two minutes—without using a clock to count the seconds—to calibrate sensitivity to time passing.[78] In this exercise, the pace of daily life and the coercive power of the calendar schedule is acknowledged to pervert natural awareness. This is one reason that time-management manuals emphasize adherence. Reminders to revisit key points and reread chapters at regular intervals are all evidence that productivity is a regime that aspires to cognitive programming. Even if we are mobilized to develop effective habits, productivity practices require sustained attention and discipline to withstand the ordinary momentum of daily life. Our fallibility as humans makes us vulnerable to losing control over our time. In the next chapter, we will see how technology trades on this sense of vulnerability, offering the promise of transcendence from human flaws.

The formulas offered by productivity authors—a repetitive combination of inspirational adages, performative citation of alleged authorities, and lack of interest in scientific accuracy—offer a type of instruction that wanes in popularity amid the subsidized training schedules of official corporate life. As the ranks of middle management swelled in the organization era of the 1950s and 1960s, popular business paperbacks provided a reservoir of accessible expertise for a generally male executive class seeking to secure reputational capital and the benefits of lifelong employment. By the 1970s, this literature targeted middle managers charged with the task of recurring layoffs and the growing reality of corporate downsizing. Employees experienced a change in power dynamics as team-based workplaces came to vogue and productivity ideals became peer-facing. It was no longer the manager standing watch to observe an individual's outputs that characterized the assessment of productivity. The colleague and the client took over as the overarching influences pressuring workers to stay busy on and off the job.

In this context, personal productivity literature exemplifies what Mark Banks calls "instrumental leisure."[79] These activities take place outside the formal hours of a job and generate further layers of capital to reinforce class privilege. Instrumental leisure incorporates the broader suite of lifestyle preferences that ensure middle-class hegemony in social and cultural space.[80] Time-management practices operate on this principle, teaching "methods of working that fill gaps between the worlds of enterprise, government, education and everyday life."[81] As corporate cutbacks throttled many of the benefits of white-collar work, as professionals lost the formal guidance and explicit instruction once typical of their vocation, and as office employees came to terms with the unlikely prospect of a secure career in a single organization, productivity literature occupied a psychological void. In Western business culture, it continues to address a salaried class in need of recognition and reassurance. Efficiency training encourages workers to see themselves as capable of separating from the pack and, with the right motivation, destined for a prosperous future, even in times of economic distress.

Time-management manuals' combination of solace and pragmatism is a specific kind of recreational sermonizing. Heralding myths of origin and calling for acts of disciplined repetition, their methods address users as potential followers requiring indoctrination. While these systems bear the hallmarks of a faith, what they generally lack is any conception of a higher power holding one's enlightened actions to account. Instead, productivity's prophets turn the erratic potential of task management into a smooth and controllable workflow. Irrespective of one's actual job description or task load, the books serve the purpose of performing satisfying solutions to the day's inevitable conflicts, making sense and order out of chaos. The guru's voice assumes a spiritual dimension for a world that lacks reliable signs and guides. Unlike previous periods of efficiency thinking, however, where aspiring to attain thrift and economy brought one closer to God, this next stage of productivity practice strips the need for a religious rationale. Time management self-help is inwardly focused; its project is personal enhancement rather than care for others.[82]

These new efforts in professional strategizing are part of productivity's project of subjective reform that commenced in the cinematic visions of scientific management and extended to plotting individual outputs in comparison with co-workers in factory settings. In popular productivity techniques, time management moved even further into the intimate realm of individual psychological self-surveillance. The monitoring behavior invoked in personal time management conforms to Sloterdijk's notion of "practice."[83] The practicing subject seeks to realize the better version of oneself that is somehow stymied by everyday encounters. Throughout Western history, Sloterdijk argues, individuals have lived with a constant sense that there is a heightened or elevated position attainable through diligent work. This process of internal self-reckoning is a revolution conducted "in the second person singular": "I am already living, but something is telling me with unchallengeable authority: you are not living properly. . . . It is the authority of a different life in this life. This authority touches on a subtle insufficiency within me that is older and freer than sin; it is my innermost not-yet."[84] Applied to productivity, the "subtle insufficiency within me" is made visible through technologies of capture—the film record, the relay ticker, the time audit spreadsheet. The worker's newfound sense of efficiency and purpose prompts a need for reform and improved technique. "In my most conscious moment, I am affected by the absolute objection to my status quo," Sloterdijk writes. "My change is the one thing that is necessary."[85] Business self-help books are a key technology through which "readers can improve their relationships with themselves," as Bröckling convincingly explains. "This particularly involves writing methods that serve self-exploration, self-affirmation and self-obligation. The enterprising self . . . is a literary program consisting of, among other things, autobiographical admissions, diary notes, stories of wishes and encouragement, aphorisms, a cathartic writing-out, and finally of contract texts, in which the individual makes a binding agreement with herself to reach certain goals."[86] Scheduling and assessing oneself become practices of care, beneficial asceticism in the pursuit of productivity. Time-management prowess becomes a means of satisfying, navigating, and successfully mobilizing the "vertical tension" of career ambition. Normalizing the self-interested qualities of workers, encouraging individuals to seize control of their fate and advance their goals, productivity reproduces the hierarchy of the organization as common sense. It is not incidental that both Sloterdijk and Allen use the language of sports to describe the exertions of the practicing. It is this great secular belief system that emerged alongside the labors of the industrial era to provide a language for celebrating the competitive principles of training and self-enhancement.

For Drucker, the ultimate management guru, the effective executive's motto is "Know Thy Time."[87] For the raft of time-management disciples he inspired, it is only a small step to see the appraisal of personal productivity as the equivalent to Socrates's statement "Know thyself."[88] Drucker warned the aspiring professional that "only constant efforts at managing time can prevent drifting."[89] This unrelenting drive (and its reliance on water imagery) is also central to Sloterdijk's notion of "shore subjectivity."[90] Superior individuals are those who have the will to separate themselves from the river of life and enjoy the unimpeded view from the shore. Using Sloterdijk to understand the insatiable appetite for business advice books, this chapter has demonstrated that trustees of time-management truisms are the donors initiating a post-secular conversion to the practice of productivity. The role of technology in consecrating this induction is the topic of the next chapter.

3   The Aesthetics of Activity

Productivity and the Order of Things

To feel productive is to recognize as a personal accomplishment the qualities of efficiency endorsed by modern computing technologies and management mantras alike. This chapter connects productivity applications—software programs designed to facilitate "getting things done"—with the textual tradition of time management that the previous chapter describes in detail. I begin with some initial efforts to apply insights on the behavior of knowledge professionals to the business environment of the tech industry, where the benefits of "productivity" are often taken as common sense. In an IT context, productivity is usually understood in one of two ways: to explain enhancements in "user experience" that certain design features enable—most notably, around improvements in speed and comfort—or generically, to market business-oriented products to suit the changing needs of enterprise customers. To take some obvious examples in my time at Intel, when a business user is working outside the office, "on the go," a device with a longer battery life delivers greater productivity. Likewise, a wireless external display may save time that is otherwise wasted looking for the right connector cable in a conference room. Both of these "use cases" are instances of enhanced productivity, even if they reflect quite different social scenarios.

This chapter focuses on *personal* productivity tools as a deliberate contrast to dominant ideas of productivity in corporate settings, which usually serve the interests of the enterprise. My interest is in software that is either designed or adopted by workers to orchestrate a new kind of logistical labor that arises when technology assumes the role of subordinate for life's trivia. Productivity apps are software solutions that help individuals arrange schedules, workloads, and activities—the *how* as opposed to the *where* or *what* work gets done. Software provides an accommodating infrastructure for activity. In this sense, as we will see, productivity apps do share one similarity with other enterprise user scenarios: they typically avoid any mention of the quantity of work being done in the course of deploying specific tools. Productivity apps are a way to order work that avoids discussing work limits, job content, or questions of power that ultimately determine ownership of tasks that require action. In this way, time-management tools obscure the politics of labor and its delegation in the quest to maximize efficiency.

In 2014, Luke Stark and I conducted an audit of personal productivity services, prompted by media commentary suggesting a boom in productivity software.[1] The study consisted of (1) an overview of productivity software to isolate popular apps in this category; (2) a breakdown of capabilities for sixty-five productivity apps, determining what they do; and (3) details for a sample of twenty-five app developers—their leadership profiles, business size, and other products affiliated with the same company. Apple's App store was the primary focus of this study.[2] In the Apple and Google Play stores, "Productivity" is its own category, distinct from other alternatives, such as "Wellness," "Business," and "Utilities." Since developers themselves designate the category in which their apps reside, understanding the subdivisions within and against productivity tools sheds light on the markets assumed for these services. Examining the functionality, aesthetics, and use cases contained in specific apps illustrates the many ideals productivity is intended to capture.

At the time of the survey, the productivity category had six subcategories: task managers, note takers, utilities, brainstorm, stay on task, and manage your time. A substantial proportion of apps offered pared-down versions of popular desktop or web-based software programs, such as Adobe Acrobat, Yahoo Mail, Google Drive, Microsoft Office, or Apple Pages products.[3] Further high-demand services were those we might term productivity *platforms*—browsers and mail clients in particular. Emoji apps held the number-one spot among paid productivity apps and the number-two spot among free productivity apps. This interesting finding suggests that pictorial symbols are regarded by many as an efficient way to communicate emotion between users—and the explosion of emoji and GIF apps since the time of our study only confirms this point.

Two different collections of apps, "Productivity 101 Essentials" (presenting eighteen apps subdivided into the categories "Task Managers," "Note Takers," and "Utilities") and "Getting Stuff Done" (a larger grouping of fifty-eight apps subdivided into the imperative categories "Stay on Task," "Take Note," "Manage Your Time," and "Brainstorm") offered a suite of options for users to consider. Similar curated collections also appeared on the landing page for productivity apps in Google Play, where a range of new tools are regularly featured in a packaged display. At the time of our survey, only about half (34 of 63) of the apps featured in the App Store's showcase collections were among the top downloads in the productivity category.[4]

The apps proclaim a repetitive set of affordances, much like the gurus in the previous chapter who recycled tried and tested insights of predecessors. The key tension between the various tools is the option of doing a lot or doing a little: some app developers advertise "all-in-one" products that combine task management, note taking, and calendar and messaging capabilities, along with contacts and social media access. Others make a commitment to fulfilling one function well, answering the need for focus and efficiency in productivity. Within this broad spectrum, products distinguish themselves further at the level of aesthetics and functionality. These factors manifest as claims to excellence in user experience (UX): a growing basis for distinction in the crowded marketplace for technology tools, and one not limited to the productivity segment.

David Allen's "Getting Things Done" (GTD) brand was prominent across the productivity apps surveyed, especially those listed as time-management aids. As we saw in the previous chapter, for GTD adherents efficiency springs from relaxed control of everyday tasks, a form of mastery that permits a shift in focus to higher levels of planning. Apps that cater to this aspiration store tasks and subtasks, restricting users' focus to the most pressing items. Some apps, such as Do It (Tomorrow) take this technique to an extreme, allowing only a day or two of future planning time.[5] Others permit both immediate and short-term planning. Timers are a consistent feature in this genre, promising enhanced qualities of attention. 30/30, for instance, is clearly grounded in the Pomodoro technique developed by Francesco Cirillo in the 1980s. In this formula the secret to greater focus involves breaking work intervals into twenty-five-minute blocks, each separated by a three- to five-minute break. This meets the recommendations of other time-management gurus to "regulate traffic" and ensure blocks of uninterrupted time to accomplish prioritized To Do items. The 30/30 program leverages this system as part of an embedded regime; other apps, such as Task Player, combine Pomodoro with metaphors taken from other bounded media artifacts, such as the music playlist.[6] The design feature encourages users to toggle through various items of the To Do list thoughtfully and creatively. These decisions flatter the user to exercise discretion and artistry in the quest for efficiency.

One of the foremost challenges for app designers is to determine how to translate productivity methods into an embodied, daily practice. As the previous chapter showed, text-based manuals include explicit inducements to read and annotate productivity mantras in the interests of securing adherence. For technology designers, habit formation is increasingly seen as a benefit of wearable devices that have the capacity to nudge users' behavior toward desired outcomes. Productivity downloads dependent on a screen interface deploy "intuitive" design in an effort to make use of the software habitual. By making UX features "free-flowing," designers claim minimum attention in fostering the practice of time management, encouraging users to focus on the content of their projects. Specific technical features, such as natural language parsing, allow users to write "natively" without conforming to a particular format. Voice recognition in phone systems is similarly pitched as a simple and easy method of transferring information from user to app. A strong focus on the iPhone and iPad's gestural capabilities is prominent in many tools, with the "swipe" a favored interaction. Todoist even incorporates an element of ersatz resistance near the end of a swipe, modeled on the movements of material objects such as sliding drawers and cabinets when they are slowed near the end of their track.[7] This intentional resistance acts as feedback to the user, reinforcing the proffered movement and generating a fleeting sense of accomplishment. In these ways, app developers demonstrate Donald Norman's concept of "visceral design," where "juiciness" and immediate recursive cues affirms the bond between user and action.[8] In our observation, gestural interfaces sometimes belied their claim to intuitiveness: videos dedicated to explaining basic instructions for an app were often posted on developers' websites, proof that not all interactive design is equally accessible.

THE AESTHETICS OF ACTIVITY

Most smartphones come with basic note-taking, reminders, and scheduling assistance loaded into the operating system. The appeal of downloading an additional productivity tool, and one over another, therefore depends on the style or ethos conveyed by the brand. The apps surveyed employed minimalist design—sans serif fonts; strong vertical and horizontal lines (if any); and color palettes made up of neutrals, pastels, and jewel tones—to communicate a "clutter-free" feeling. For Clear and Taasky, color schemes act as important points of differentiation for very similar services that list and order To Do items. The claim of Taasky's headline—to be "Beautiful, simple and easy to use"—exudes the confidence necessary to overcome the more dubious marketing claims that follow. ("It's a scientific fact that a human can only focus on one thing at a time. That's why we added the main priority feature, which stands out only one priority task.") For Taasky, "Every category has its own colour to avoid chaos."[9] By contrast, Clear's "playful and clutter-free interface" uses warmer hues to make productivity "fun." The app's website demonstrates design interactions that "make it quick and satisfying to mark tasks as completed" through a heavy reliance on various swiping gestures.[10] Simplicity is intentional, encouraging users to "stop worrying and start doing." In the accompanying video, a male user makes good use of a coffee shop break to add items to his grocery list and mark tasks completed in rhythm with jingly upbeat pop music. The tagline: "Life is messy. Simplify with Clear."

More established and comprehensive software packages, such as Evernote, extend their artistry to the physical realm. The website boasts a catalogue of auxiliary items for sale, including office stationery and luggage, to integrate on- and offline productivity. In these ways, productivity software generates an *aesthetics of activity*. Getting things done smoothly and efficiently should look and feel beautiful; marketing for productivity services routinely invokes the value and pleasure in leading

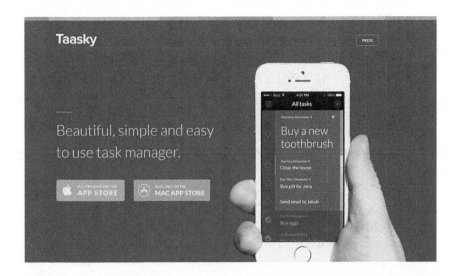

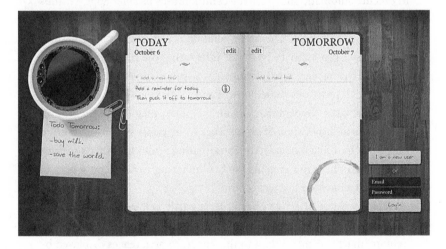

FIGURE 3.1 The digital desktop. The aesthetic style of productivity apps enables the choreography of a To Do list that is always repopulating. Source: http://www.taasky.com.

FIGURE 3.2 Invoking past technologies of time management, such as the paper diary, adds comfort, texture, and a touch of nostalgia to the virtual workday. Source: http://www.tomorrow.do.

an efficient life. Through their feature sets, user-experience design, and promotional copy, productivity apps regard the quantity and content of work being done as incidental to the manner in which it is performed. Productivity becomes effortless with the adoption of simple platforms that perform the labor of connection and coordination. As we will see, this labor is taken for granted as necessary for smoothing the way for the ongoing expectation of more work and data to come.

Almost universally, productivity apps emphasize their connectivity— their ability to synchronize a user's account across multiple devices and platforms (desktop, tablet, phone, and so on). This capability is frequently promoted as invisible and automatic. The speed of synchronicity is attributed either to the software itself or to the individual user whose previously limited abilities are enhanced by the product design. An app such as IFTTT (If This Then That) uses the grammar of coding to execute automatic shortcuts for common uses of *other* apps.[11] It thus makes a feature of automating multiple layers of communicative labor in one unique package. The IFTTT solution is just one of a suite of tools that promise productivity by better integrating the functions of disparate social media platforms. Exemplary use cases (applets) stitch together regular work processes so that users can avoid so many versions of what Ian Bogost calls "hyperemployment."[12] Applets magically synchronize the tedious multiplication of online work by instantly sharing Instagram photos on multiple media feeds, coordinating reminders across various devices and operating systems, or bookmarking websites on a host of context-specific note-taking accounts.

The aesthetics of activity are at least partly achieved by way of the "smartness" of the program itself. Services such as Mynd, Smart Day, and Tempo Smart Calendar adapt to the signature preferences displayed by the user.[13] A few apps also offer the option (sometimes as a paid upgrade) of additional analytics and cumulative data displays, even exporting such feedback in spreadsheet form. Swiftkey Note (now Swiftkey Keyboard) is a plug-in that allows a phone's keyboard to "adapt or customize to the natural working style" of its user.[14] The keyboard "learns" your vocabulary with an adaptive API (application program interface) that the company describes as "magical prediction technology."[15] An added benefit is the ability to access typing statistics to better measure the user's efficiency. Making sense of oneself through these visualizations facilitates awareness of one's actions with a view to optimizing activities, continuing the enlightened insights first delivered by the cinematic gaze of the time-and-motion camera. The primary difference between the typewriting secretary of the Gilbreths and the smartphone user today is the lack of distinction between the device that provides both labor and leisure.

Promotional materials for productivity aids stoke the desire for self-improvement. To Do lists capture the lifestyle preferences of people who are not only wealthy (their multiple devices prompt the need for synchronicity) but health-conscious: exercise routines and meditation practices sit alongside grocery lists with raw and organic staples. Leisure and lifestyle pursuits involve regular travel by plane, often to foreign countries, and particular kinds of consumption ("order stemless glassware"; "pick up dry cleaning"). The productive lifestyle depicted is a regimen that is always being performed all the time. The focus on accomplishment without effort—the fast, smooth, intuitive flow of uninhibited work—suggests a certain circularity to success: productive people are capable of being ever more organized, and since their creativity is expressed in the efficient management of tasks, this work of collection, scheduling, and organizing can potentially continue ad infinitum. Productivity tools cut through competing demands for attention to help workers focus, freeing up time and energy for the most demanding and rewarding work. Paradoxically, the capabilities of productivity software create expectations of always more activity. This state of anticipatory achievement must be regulated by the very same software systems that create awareness of productivity in the first place. As the next chapter discusses, when productivity apps enable *too much* activity, another category of product can step in as a helpful corrective. Health and wellness apps, especially those designed for mindfulness or meditation, offer a form of repair for the otherwise insatiable appetite for action. Here we see overlaps with the corporate benefits programs popular in contemporary organizations and a set of implicit assumptions about work limits. In the contemporary workplace, productivity is encouraged as long as the worker's body is capable. When the same body is disabled, wellness services provide the healing necessary to resuscitate living labor.

Productivity platforms serve the function of creating sense and structure out of chaos: identifying, facilitating, and coordinating tasks and assembling the infrastructure for juggling jobs and appearances. Many emphasize the specific visual pleasure to be gained by arranging tasks in the right order, making a feature of the original mandate for prioritization in time-management manuals of decades past. In productivity apps, process trumps content. Advertising for services consistently celebrates capabilities—"synchronicity," "smart," "seamless"—rather than the material realities of work. This focus on the artistry of doing softens the callousness of a digitally mediated environment with seemingly endless quantities of things To Do. An aesthetically appealing app serves to displace questions about the volume or character of work that requires action. Instead, developers celebrate technology's sublime abilities to remember, predict, anticipate, and deliver.

The aesthetics of activity evident in productivity tools is a tangible manifestation of the engineer's desire to provide better living through software. In proliferating apps, productivity is a creative practice enacted at the level of individual commitments and schedules. Achieving productivity is not about the outcomes of paid labor or the results of a day's work. It is a sensibility, a "user experience" of smooth and seamless integration, designed to compensate for a (work)life that, without diligent monitoring, risks falling in to disrepair. Productivity apps fuel a lifestyle that does not differentiate among work, home, and leisure space while striving for greater efficiencies. Apps provide both the technological and psychological infrastructure to navigate a world that is simultaneously felt to be unstable, improvised, challenging, and seductive—characteristics at the core of the labor experience for today's knowledge professionals.

THE ASCETICS OF ACTIVITY

At a deeper level, the religious dimensions observable in productivity apps also suggest an *ascetics* to time management.[16] With names such as "Self Control," "Omnifocus," "Rescue Time," and even "Freedom," these platforms offer liberation as much as consolation from everyday social entanglements. Asceticism is the practice of enforced restriction; disciplined habits that generate constraints on certain behavioral indulgences in the service of transcendence. In the next section, I consider these religious dimensions as a point of entry into more public concerns that computing devices have become vessels for temptation and the source of new moral failings.[17] A number of productivity tools reflect anxiety about the amount of digital dependence taking hold in modern culture—a concern that I also explore in part III. For now, I consider how online activity appears implicated in the suspension of appropriate time perception, which causes some very old ideas—of confession, abstinence, and salvation— to emerge as rehabilitative features in the words of productivity's tech prophets.

THE INDIVIDUAL AS FAILURE

In his address to Google employees in 2007, Merlin Mann, creator of the 43 Folders website and icon of the online GTD movement, begins with an anecdote: appealing to workers on a personal level, Mann tells the story of his e-mail history. The tale begins with infatuation, as he shares the wonder and excitement of discovering e-mail's "astonishing" new horizon for contact. As the volume of his online communication increases, however, Mann admits to growing feelings of inadequacy. His relationship to e-mail deteriorates from an initial love plot to the point of being overwhelmed and paralyzed by messages. Introducing the audience to GTD techniques, Mann offers a solution to a familiar kind of inertia, even among employees at one of the world's most admired companies.[18] The anecdotal mode is purposeful here, as it is in so many pedagogical contexts.[19] Mann draws on self-help's formulaic structure, which charts a recognizable course: "You think I'm not like you, but listen. I had your problem. I overcame it. Here's how. Copy me and see that you can be successful, too." Mann's "Inbox Zero" technique follows the same tenets of paperwork efficiency touted in the System Company's manual for using a tickler file (see chapter 2). The only novelty in the present era is the technological development that sees e-mail inherit the mantle as the primary platform delivering reams of information to workers.

Mann's career as a motivational speaker and creative talent builds from the example of bootstrapping pioneers such as Dale Carnegie, whose lectures to Depression-era Manhattanites punctuated shrewd business advice with multiple anecdotes.[20] In Mann's case, the cathartic function of his introduction also draws on the Augustinian tradition of confession dating back to the fourth century. To confess is to speak the truth of oneself, to access and retrieve the essence of interiority and offer it to others for judgment.[21] A generic trait of other self-help programs (e.g., Twelve Step AA), confession's retro-introspection calls for an honest and attentive self-criticism to generate a new manner of living. The conversion process initiated by the confession has mobilizing power. The pattern or refrain "I too had your problem, but look at me now. If you only adopt my methods, you can be cured" encourages followers to identify with a leader, see the light, and find a path of better thinking that animates righteousness. In time management, as we have seen, reinvention is reinforced by repetitive practices that include positive affirmations and carefully selected catchphrases. The latter are further endorsed by a populist neuroscience that encompasses an evangelical optimism, evident in the oft-cited maxim to "visualize" change. We will see in the next chapter how this intersects with mindfulness.

In combination, productivity's confession-conversion as demonstrated by Mann works on a religious level to the extent that it avoids inherently political structural questions and instead demands a leap of faith. The link between inward focus and individualism is ensured through the aura of the celebrity task manager, whose elevated status facilitates the recruitment of others. At the time of the Google Talk, Mann's stardom (he is introduced as a "superhero" by his host) rides the wave of enthusiasm for other dot-com prophets whose unique qualities and innate genius inspire others. But his personal charisma rests on a disavowal of this status. His website is not an icon of the GTD trend so much as a modest exercise in "finding the time and attention to do your best creative work."[22] For the regular GTD believer, the discourse of confession articulates personal improvement with personal productivity.[23]

PRODUCTIVITY AND SELF-DISCIPLINE

Productivity techniques that encourage periods of abstinence and withdrawal from the network are another key instance of ascetic practice. Self Control and Cold Turkey are downloadable applications that block a computer's access to desirable online sites (those that might occasion regretful indulgence) and the established peril of e-mail. The tagline for Cold Turkey—"I'm watching you"—winks knowingly at dystopian visions of surveillance with its claim to "temporarily block you off of social media sites, addicting websites, games and even programs!"[24] Also noteworthy in this genre, Self Control offers a "spirit of escape" for users faced with the challenge of too many online obligations.[25] Its creator, Steve Lambert, cites the influence of Mann's Google speech in dreaming up his application's design. Self Control is Lambert's effort "to deliberately create time for me to create that even I couldn't sabotage." The app offers assistance for individuals looking to focus "on the work that, hopefully, they care the most about, for their livelihood and for their well-being. It's about making the best of a bad situation."[26]

Like the confessional process outlined here, productivity programs require users first to acknowledge a problem. In this case, it is the ceaseless temptation of stimuli available in a smorgasbord of Internet sites and all-consuming media platforms. The pleasures of online life are reframed as threats to a healthy balance of productive activities. Forced deprivation provides the path back to focused, peak performance. This somewhat militant approach repositions the sociability of networked communication as coercion, a challenge of will for an individual unfairly targeted by threatening influences, neuro-marketing, and attention-seeking design. Reclusive behavior becomes a means of reasserting control, taking back ownership of one's time and attention.

The block-and-avoid tactics underpinning these productivity apps repurpose the same pointers from time-management literature of decades past in recommending a "golden hour" of uninterrupted time each day, a "prime time" for performance. But in the online context, the prevention model invokes a health-oriented moralism reminiscent of Catholicism, with its prevailing metaphors of denial and restraint. Too much socializing with friends is a temptation to be trained out of workers if they are to remain appropriately productive. Productivity can be attained through reprogramming existing cognitive reflexes—the spoof tool Pavlok makes this point by invoking Pavlovian psychology in its "5 Day" treatment plan.[27] A techno-fix not only retrains habits to more socially sanctioned rewards; it also offers a no-nonsense solution to common etiquette dilemmas—the friend who sends constant messages, the instant messaging buddy who ignores a "busy" status. Removing the user's availability for distinct periods allows a new form of algorithmically determined scheduling that avoids the awkward adjudication of manners. Delivering an increasingly elusive sense of solitude on demand, productivity apps of this type unleash the individuating tendency of the self-help tradition by prompting consideration of the ultimate question: could your biggest productivity problem be you?

A further religious strain observable in productivity software is the desire to access an elevated perspective—a clear separation from the drama of quotidian interaction and a master plan for life itself. Quantification apps such as Rescue Time and Vitamin-R join project management suites such as Omnifocus in the aim to deliver fully integrated maps of the territory of waking life.[28] These examples allow users to track work/life cycles by day, hour, or minute so that energy levels and communication patterns can be identified for improvement or greater discipline. The ultimate goal is to siphon off periods of greater concentration from the mass of undifferentiated data and demands. The pivotal religious experience delivered by these services is the sense that you can *be* like a God, in charge of your destiny, for at least twenty-five minutes a day. The apps exist to provide users with uninterrupted time to be creative—to get on with the "real" work of producing the pitch, idea, or insight that others in the office will likely miss. This process manipulates the unwieldy "order of things" presented by incessant online contact and notifications to make space for guilt-free concentration.[29] Such mindful attention may allow room for extraneous matters, but only after the most noteworthy targets have been met.

With three recurring qualities—confession, abstinence, and omniscience—digital productivity tools offer the foundational elements of a religion. Apps provide solutions to the inadequacies of an individual who, upon successful inculcation into its systemized set of practices, is destined for a higher calling. As the first step in the process, *confession* initiates conversion to a reform program. Recruitment is premised on admitting the deep truth of one's fallibility and the need for help. This acknowledgment of personal failure becomes material to be rehabilitated through techniques of mastery, whether it is transcending the day-to-day concerns of this life through the adoption of right habits or the elimination of obligation entirely through regimes such as a "four-hour work week."[30] In the second step, *abstinence*, the seeker similarly admits to character flaws, acknowledging the sin of relationships outside work. This resembles early tenets of efficiency thinking that sought to rid "the evil" of inefficiency.[31] In the logic of productivity, relenting to the demands of the social amounts to quasi-incompetence that is close to a lack of will. The "sinner" calls on a higher power to reward accomplishment and punish unproductive activities through the policing tactics of blocking and surveillance. This resigned ethics effectively gives control over access to seductive communication to a stronger force. Technology becomes akin to a judging deity, a suprahuman fix for problems that, ironically, are generated by technology itself. In the third feature in the triad of productivity ascetics, *omniscience*, software provides a route to the ultimate good: pure creativity. Quantification and metrics allow the user a divine perspective on how human actions can be optimized. This knowledge informs the all-seeing, all-knowing technology user to perform at a higher level than the previous, unaudited self and to surpass the performances of others. Escaping the fate of peers through data insights and behavior tracking, the successfully productive subject focuses attention on being brilliant and imagining a world of greater things.

PRODUCTIVITY AND FREEDOM

Each of these versions of productivity orthodoxy involves a vision of mastery and control that entails freedom from obligation but not from work. The inconvenience of other people,[32] the mutual dependence that collective liberation requires, pales in significance compared with the accomplishments of the individual. Prioritization regimes outlined in time-management manuals for the place-based organization taught readers to classify tasks and disruptions from the urgent to the not so urgent, the important to the trivial. As chapter 2 showed, anything that can be delegated is done so, according to ruthless regimes of calculation. The "How To" section of R. Alec Mackenzie's original edition of *The Time Trap* shows the politics of order involved in these productivity precedents. Among the "things" that count as trivia are updates on overdue reports alongside telephone calls from one's wife. In describing tactics to avoid "the avalanche of paperwork," Mackenzie maintains, everything comes down to assessing "which materials ought to come into your desk and which ought to be screened out mercilessly by your secretary."[33]

The secretary was both subordinate to and a public face for the ex-

FIGURE 3.3 Freedom's software promises liberation from the social at the push
of a button. Source: http://www.freedom.to.

ecutive. In the network era, productivity apps are the *interface* for a new
kind of delegated labor. For today's resource-depleted, on-demand workplace, the subordinate takes the form of the smartphone with a range
of embedded features providing assistance. The notion of freedom that
these tools animate, however—whether freedom from silencing a ringing telephone or from locking oneself out of social media—remains the
same. Productivity operates on the premise that "taking time for oneself
is a form of liberation."[34]

Productivity software thus extends time management's long-standing
mission to produce a hierarchy of attention for workers seeking the rewards of elite performance. This is the freedom to act and make history
through the consequential decisions confined to the privilege of high
office once all other administrative burdens have been passed down the
workplace hierarchy. Placing productivity apps alongside earlier genres
of time management produces a useful historical contrast. It allows us to
note that the rise of techno-mediated efficiency infrastructure occurs in

tandem with post-Fordism's reconfiguration of the sexual contract and the gradual emancipation of women from subservient workplace roles. Productivity apps are the digital assistants that are increasingly required when the gendered labor of the secretary and the wife are not so easily available. In post-feminist work cultures mediated by personal mobile devices, business and home-based administration are less likely to be delegated to others, even if, as we are realizing, a key component of productivity thinking is to absolve responsibility for certain kinds of labor. In the wake of the significant rupture brought about by feminism, the affective labor of the secretary is a luxury few workers will know. The very need for productivity tools to carry the burden of organization today allows us to appreciate the extent of the administrative and logistical labor once provided by women and other "delegates."

The notion of freedom the productive lifestyle celebrates is, perversely, the freedom to work. In practice, and at best, this activity means liberation from a raft of unrewarding labor that others must still perform. This understanding of freedom as the power to delegate fits with broader attitudes that have shaped the development of the Internet and its technologies through history. As Tom Streeter notes, it is a vision that naturalizes the power of men over women to the degree that the freedom it promotes is understood "in terms of the power to command, to walk out the door, to deny the work of nurturing and the material fact of interdependence."[35] It is also a vision that is specifically North American: a "habit of understanding freedom negatively, blindly, as freedom from government, freedom from dependency, freedom from others."[36] The idea of freedom through creative labor relates to the broader glamorization of work in successive dot-com booms and the origin stories attached to pivotal leaders. The quasi-religious appeal of these narratives resonates strongly with long-standing aspirations of particularly U.S. workers to pursue a spiritual calling in work.

While motivational literature of the 1970s and '80s helped managers to maintain their distance from those under their watch, productivity apps are a sign that, in the present, the qualitative distance between manager and employee has largely collapsed. This is one way to understand the revolution that constant connectivity has wrought on organizations. With their emphasis on streamlined workflow, productivity apps evolved in tandem with management protocols inviting employees to display autonomy and responsibility in the exercise of new kinds of freedom. Software design provides an aesthetics that makes the superior arrangement of work a source of pleasure. By allowing the possibility of minute and constant decision making, the recursive satisfaction of creating order plays to users' desire to take charge of their activities. "Motivation is triggered by making choices that demonstrate to ourselves that we are in control," writes Charles Duhigg. "The specific choice we make matters less than the assertion of control. It's this feeling of self-determination that gets us going."[37]

In their start-up attitude toward self-help, productivity apps also absorb a more generic, do-it-yourself hacker ethic that regards personal and professional tasks as challenges to be overcome through efficient programming. As in "cognitive capitalism" more broadly, the obligations of life and labor become interchangeable versions of administrivia; productivity's gift is to deliver results in the private and public zones that are now equally crucial to displaying competent professional subjectivity. This is the link between the historical analysis in the first two sections of this book and the empirical findings of *Work's Intimacy*: through the adoption of productivity practices, responsible individuals create regimes of anticipation, protection, and recovery to meet the temporality of computationally inflicted schedules. This labor is preparatory and reparative as much as it is obligatory. In the move from personal productivity to personal logistics, entrepreneurial workers smooth the way for the ongoing expectation of task and project management that is the condition of workplace flexibility. Table 3.1 foregrounds the schematic and material difference this makes to the aspiration of time management when the Organization no longer determines the experience of time shared by all workers. Plotted this way, we can see how work practices enabled by mobile devices calls for a new language of labor and limits—else we are rendered permanently captive to the unrelenting challenge and oppression of finding "flow."

TABLE 3.1. The changing experience of time outside the organization, from personal productivity to personal logistics.

	PRODUCTIVITY	LOGISTICS
Objective	Complete	Coordinate
Resource	Tool	Provision
Time	Measured	Anticipated
Hours	Clocked	Billed
Location	Fixed	Distributed
Asset	Sold	Circulated
Data	Stored	Synched
Loyalty	Firm	Network
Power	Enterprise	Worker

TRANSITION: FROM THE BOUNDED ORGANIZATION
TO PERSONAL LOGISTICS

Time management's chronic labor performance epitomizes the regime necessary to ensure ongoing employability in a "new spirit of capitalism," even though the corporate form no longer serves as the epitome of the chronopolitics needed to assert labor rights and work limits.[38] Productivity manifests as a ritualized practice. It is a lifestyle enacted at the level of activity, as pure form. While it encompasses qualities of a religion, it lacks any narrative of redemption that would relate adherents to a larger whole. Productivity isolates and sanctifies the actions of individuals. It elevates an elite class of worker beyond the concerns of mundane others.

These two factors mark its difference from previous visions of labor and its possible politics. In the organization era, workers gained power and privileges through association with a firm. Career ambition was couched within the terms and the "social ethic" of a company and its standing within a community.[39] By contrast, today's white-collar workers learn to manage themselves in proximity to a workplace that is felt to be omnipresent, ambient, and intimate. In this pervasively "virtual" space and time for work, employees are less tethered to a particular office or workplace but must cultivate their own personal regimes of psychological resilience for day-to-day affect management. Productivity is the refrain heralding the activity of mobile professionals entrusted to internalize company mandates, accomplish results, and maintain a pleasant composure. If productivity practices show overlaps with other examples of work on the self through Western history, noting these precedents helps to illustrate the limitations of its secular ethics, its unceasing athleticism, in Sloterdijk's terms. Productivity turns the workplace into a contest among individuals who vie for the ultimate neoliberal victory: the opportunity to remove themselves from the demands of the social. The language of Thatcherism is useful to press a possible analogy: if there is no such thing as society, then there is no such thing as a workplace. Neither statement is true if one believes that citizens and co-workers are vital for mutual flourishing. Yet the partial truth each statement conceals is that, left unchecked, a bias toward individual success will be harnessed toward the imposition of inequality.

The labor of time management is a recursive distraction that has postponed the need to identify a worthwhile basis for work as a source of spiritual fulfilment. The urgency of this conversation is only becoming more pressing as automation threatens workers of all kinds to prove their "value add." The boom in productivity software over the course of the past decade reflects the struggle workers face in trying to achieve goals and claim ownership of their time in the face of management's and network culture's equally immersive surveillance. Productivity tools categorize, with the aim of eventually integrating, different elements of a user's world. Tracking services, reminders, and behavioral nudges turn everyday activities into objects of measurement—and, hence, adjustment and improvement—by a "quantified self."[40] Just like the time management pedagogy of decades past, GTD's "affect of efficiency" emerges from adopting specific techniques "of thinking about doing and not-doing."[41] This transforms the volatility of contemporary living into actionable steps that provide a better pace and orientation for daily encounters.

The personalization of analytics that sees individuals choosing to measure their own productivity is an accomplishment that began at least a century ago, as the discipline of psychology joined forces with management consultants pioneering a new industry of subjective engineering (see chapter 1). Unlike earlier individuals engaged in forms of professional strategizing, however, the self-sufficient worker downloading GTD apps today takes on the imperative of productivity despite a generalized lack of employment and institutional security. The difference between time management in the organizational era, defined by To Do lists, clock time, and a highly gendered division of labor, and time management in the network era, when employees at all levels are equally responsible for their productivity, is the ontological condition of precarity. There is no guarantee that increased output will earmark star performers as worthy of ongoing investment by their employers. In this work context, prior versions of management oversight are less obvious or necessary, since the innate value of productivity is rarely questioned by workers. It is no coincidence, I have been suggesting, that this is also the moment in which the commonsense tenets of individualism and freedom became embedded in technology design. This is how a cooperative politics targeting the *amount* of work being performed proves elusive. Isolated activities are directed away from any collective measure or reward, although there are signs that cooperative efforts to redistribute the profits of personal productivity may be coming.[42]

Linking the tradition of professional self-management first introduced in self-help literature with techniques reprised in the productivity industry today, we see a recurring trend: asociality espoused in the name of superiority. Productivity apps materialize a mode of thinking that takes seriously the possibility of transcending the social, at least for programmable periods. While spiritual transcendence is not the main objective—this will be the focus of chapter 4—attempts to triumph over trivia produce a hierarchical workplace in which unrewarding tasks can be delegated down to other, less powerful employees or, if that fails, to a device. In celebrating this structure as freedom, productivity tools normalize exceptionalism, endorsing this as the epitome of professionalism.

The heroic individualism characteristic of Silicon Valley myth—from Bill Gates to Mark Zuckerberg, from Stewart Brand to Steve Jobs—further legitimizes notions of individual genius in the name of advancing civilization and success. The ascetic dimension of productivity tools blocks distractions but also the purportedly unimportant neediness of other people. This continues an influential legacy of thought in the technology sector that subscribes to the mission of promoting the acts of a few especially brilliant people above the struggles of others.[43]

Personal productivity is an epistemology without an ontology, a framework for knowing what to do in the absence of a guiding principle for doing it. The meaning produced by productivity is the aesthetic pleasure of pure order, a method in which to do things so that they appear superficially manageable. Such a practice erases any need to question the overall structure determining *which* things are important, because if we spend enough time choreographing *what* should get done, there is no need to deal frankly with *why*. The desire for time management underpinning productivity applications therefore takes a particular notion of time for granted. It assumes that time, like the worker, can be managed according to the imperatives of capitalist production, and it does this in an unreflective way. This context further illustrates productivity's appeal as a work-related ethics that, while it shares some of the spiritual functions previously accorded to capitalism, is today better understood as a *post-secular practice*. In the shift from the printed page to the network, time-management techniques accrue some of the mythology of Silicon Valley culture.[44] These romantic sensibilities, missionary callings, and proto-bohemian work styles add further mystique to the charismatic qualities of time-management prophets. Contemporary productivity tenets capture dominant ideas of industry and creativity that high-tech demigods are thought to embody, where commitment to work takes the form of a vocation or calling.[45] But the fact that productivity is self-oriented, not other-focused, marks its difference from most classical notions of religious devotion. Productivity pivots on the belief that right actions will liberate an extraordinary class of worker from the concerns of this world.

Productivity holds such profound power as a rationale for work because it manipulates an ethical dimension that lingers from the original spiritual foundations of capitalism. Animating a set of procedures and biases that encourage attention to oneself, the productive lifestyle is an "aesthetics of existence" accordant with the global economy's necessary secularism.[46] As corporate business practice surpassed borders and belief systems in the Greed Is Good 1980s and '90s, productivity took on the thrust of Puritan principles shorn of their U.S. parochialism. Productivity provided a model of social involvement that could be embraced either adjacent to or in spite of religious belief because it holds the same qualities of disciplined practice. Religion and productivity share similar traits: each summons a participant whose success is judged by the ability to cultivate effective habits. In the practice of today's effective executives, productivity self-help mixes spiritual consolation with cognitive science in a compelling ideological cocktail.

Subscribing to the lessons of productivity gurus in text or app form provides superficial bearings for workers in the absence of grander narratives for action. But whereas capitalist values were once better aligned with a desire to move closer *to* God through frugal efficiency, productivity's mandate of outsourcing and delegating labor suggests that we now seek to become Godlike ourselves. Exercising creativity, the ideal productive worker justifies his difference from colleagues whose lack of self-discipline condemns them to stagnation. This is a particularly pernicious vision of freedom since its condition of autonomy is the refusal to place any hope in improving circumstances for others. Productivity's spiritual valences seek a Pentecostal conversion of the Godlike power to control time and space; indeed, the point is to maintain a state of elevated flow that suspends accountability to any local coordinates. It is enough of an affront that this lifestyle actively endorses substituting action for thought. Taken to its logical extreme, the chapters in this section show that to be productive is to subscribe to a belief structure without an ethics, an epistemology without an ontology, and a repetitive set of gestures meant to console us when faced with the knowledge that there are always too many things to do, but there may never be a sense of meaning behind the disorder. To find a better vision of labor, one that can overturn the binaries of self-other, master-slave, executive-secretary, and programmer-user that propelled the Organization for so long, we need a different vocabulary for time and self-management. This is the task of part III.

III Anthropotechnics

4   Mindful Labor

In parts I and II, I show how time management in the workplace came to be seen as a quest for professional accomplishment through a series of formal and informal injunctions. Productivity's original engineers instituted a model of enterprise-oriented athleticism that demanded ceaseless devotion to activity and training. Capturing the heroics of individual performances became the foundational calling for a nascent management science to document, measure, and improve. Meanwhile, an array of self-help techniques promoted by popular gurus assisted the *personalization* of productivity. Time-management textbooks, celebrity consultants, seminars, and apps reinforced a gradual evacuation of labor politics understood in terms of work limits. Career competence and superiority came to rest on the ability to triumph over trivia, judiciously reserving one's efforts for the best kind of labor. Productivity thus became a status metric, a demonstration of success in post-secular capitalism.[1]

Turning this history of time-management techniques to the present, this chapter focuses on a discernible backlash that has emerged against constantly connected productivity tools and the general middle-class susceptibility to busyness. It is inspired by a range of phenomena—screen Sabbaths, disconnection experiments, and technology detox camps—that extend the abstinence regimes of some of the more ruthless productivity tools analyzed in chapter 3. The politics of "non-use," "technology refusal," and "calm technology" are debated across industry, scholarly, and activist settings, addressing the seductive effects of always-on devices in an age of user-centered design.[2] Building on these trends, my interest is in how mindfulness in its current technological manifestation relates to preceding time-management practices. New to California in 2013, and struck by examples of mindfulness apps reported in research by Ellie Harmon, I asked for her expertise in developing market intelligence on software and hardware developers gathering at industry conferences such as Wisdom 2.0. The findings in her comprehensive report for Intel, as well as the analysis in her excellent doctoral thesis, "Computing as Context: Experiences of Dis/Connection beyond the Moment of Non/ Use," deeply inform my analysis in what follows.[3]

Mindfulness manifested in any number of digital and analogue forms over the course of writing this book, from wearable appendages to corporate wellness programs and a booming market for stress-relieving coloring pages.[4] The hypothesis I want to explore is whether these ordinary examples of asceticism satisfy the desire for a form of punctuation from social labors that lack obvious temporal constraints. Mindfulness appears to offer an acceptable source of relief from the breadth of online preoccupations that are part of high performance corporate cultures as much as they are a way to manage the broader shift to contingent employment.[5] Software promotion makes this clear: in an infographic showing essential services for remote office workers, Lauren Moon, a staff member at Trello, lists the Headspace meditation app as a vital solution for "when you are feeling overwhelmed."[6]

Mindfulness is not new in American culture, as others have noted.[7] Chapter 1 revealed how nineteenth-century housewives were encouraged to spend their dawn hours in quiet spiritual contemplation, away from the needs of others. The turn to mindfulness in relation to today's work conditions in fact suggests that our current combination of mental and manual labor is not dissimilar to that of traditional women's work: immaterial labor involves generating affect, a sensibility, or a feeling. As Arlie Russell Hochschild established, "service with a smile" is the ultimate form of suppressing one's own well-being to please others.[8] Mindfulness may be a sign that there is a shift under way in the qualitative nature of time in contemporary capitalism, when emotion work is a feature of all employment types, to varying degrees.[9]

At the very least, the popularity of mindfulness techniques marks something of a limit point or moment of exhaustion for workers struggling to meet the imperative of time management in the transformed surroundings of the contemporary workplace. The evident need for mindfulness practices reveals the inadequacy of productivity as a way to think about work at a time that finite material labor outputs—from manufacturing goods to the paper-based office—no longer capture the quality or extent of labor being performed. In the post-industrial economies of the West, work has transformed from factory-based manufacturing trades to service and knowledge professions involving endless iteration and circulation of intangible goods. This is a character shift in the outputs gained from work hours (technically, the measurement for productivity) as the experience economy demands different skills and competencies.[10] For example, precariously employed gig workers and service and hospitality staff wrestle with productivity pressures that involve fashioning a lifestyle flexible enough to support "surge" work.[11] To be mindful in this environment is to create an infrastructure to withstand the intensities of labor supply and demand. By contrast, in traditional office jobs, where corporate wellness programs devoted to self-care are taking hold, mindfulness offers practical strategies of disassociation and retreat from the ceaseless drive for greater efficiency. Mindfulness is a temporary fix for the challenges of contemporary work life—a means of "making it through the day," as Lawrence Grossberg wrote in defense of rock music.[12] As we will see, mindfulness practices also provide repair for the heightened degree of reflexivity involved in emotion work.

Aside from the critiques of established iconoclasts—Evgeny Morozov, for example, describes mindfulness as a "racket"[13]—the rise of mindfulness has not been linked to labor conditions explicitly and remains largely removed from scholarly sympathy. Understanding mindfulness is therefore my contribution to the vocabulary for labor politics that is required to describe "cognitive capitalism."[14] Theories of "immaterial" and "affective labor" draw necessary attention to the psychological effects of jobs that involve specific or deliberate relation to feeling.[15] Hochschild's pioneering account of air hostesses and parking inspectors showed how manipulating feelings (one's own and those of others) created a unique kind of alienation from the self. What I call *mindful labor* is a further extension of these intellectual lineages. It identifies a process of subjective reform that applies to a broad range of jobs today. Mindful labor refers to the degree of work involved in producing and maintaining affective composure in the absence of collective labor politics. It describes the methods employed to relieve the burden of stress that productivity places on individuals. At a time when the responsibility for productivity has been successfully interiorized (through the century-long process described in previous chapters), mindful labor is the means by which workers train themselves to accommodate otherwise unsustainable work demands.

Mindful labor is admittedly limited as a form of organized resistance. Critics of commodified mindfulness note there is a clear contradiction in applying meditation methods for the purpose of enhanced personal gain.[16] Yet these increasingly mainstream techniques for producing professional propriety offer crucial insight into the obstacles now thwarting collective thought and action regarding labor limits. My own experience suggests that mindfulness offers a form of self-help for harried workers that may be useful in the short-term.[17] In addition, mindfulness encourages awareness of some basic elements for a new kind of politics that is needed when so many are involved in the exercise of mental as much as manual labor. Acknowledging the spiritual legacies at the heart of mindfulness can mobilize sentiment regarding productivity's vacuous post-secularism. As my concluding chapter argues more forcefully, mindful labor in the service of shared professional survival sets a new direction and temporality for workers to find common purpose outside the Organization.

THE POWER OF NOW

Mindfulness technologies discussed in this chapter bear a strong relationship to the varieties of self-help, New Age, and American Zen Buddhism that have influenced branches of Western science as part of the complementary and alternative medicine movement. Beyond the medical profession, the broader impact of Zen Buddhism on American culture over many decades is remarkably consistent, even if, as Eve Kosofsky Sedgwick explains, the "Buddhist encounter with 'Western culture' must also be understood as an encounter with a palimpsest of Asian currents and influences (and vice versa)."[18] R. John Williams lists hundreds of popular publishing titles dedicated to Zen and the Art of X that have followed the breakthrough novel *Zen and The Art of Motorcycle Maintenance*.[19] Fans will recall that the final episode of the television series *Mad Men* concludes as the protagonist, the advertising executive Don Draper, finds inspiration for Coca-Cola's most influential ad campaign in the course of meditation. In the technology sector, mindfulness practice strengthened following the example of the Silicon Valley icon Steve Jobs, who meditated before appearing onstage at career-defining product launches, and employed a guru during his tenure at Apple.[20]

A focus on being in "the moment" overlaps with the teachings of New Age figures such as Eckhart Tolle, author of *The Power of Now* (1997), who regularly appears in the reference lists espoused on the speaking circuit for mindfulness gatherings.[21] For these leaders, the serendipitous joy of *now* offers liberation from the pressure of constant striving. By narrowing our temporal horizon to the most elemental level, practitioners of mindfulness embrace their surrounding reality with all of its color and texture, leaving behind undue concern for specific problems. At this simple level, mindfulness presents a tactical response to the obligations of social participation, marking a break from the worries of the world. It provides a pause button for the expectation of empathetic reciprocity, a way to claim territory for the self by suspending awareness of time's passing.

Mindfulness advocates in the technology world draw mainly from the school of healing associated with Jon Kabat-Zinn, founder of the Stress Reduction Clinic at the University of Massachusetts Medical Center and a long-time student of the Buddhist luminary Thich Nhat Hanh. Kabat-Zinn brought legitimacy to the practice of mindfulness-based stress reduction (MBSR) for medical outcomes with the bestselling introduction, *Full Catastrophe Living* (1990).[22] The treatment program outlined in the book addresses patients who are suffering chronic pain or illness, living in palliative care, or recovering from trauma.[23] Several chapters in this early publication focus on workaholism and job-related stress. In subsequent books, such as the phenomenally popular *Wherever You Go, There You Are: Mindfulness Meditation in Everyday Life* (1994), Kabat-Zinn caters to these more everyday preoccupations, extending the relevance of mindfulness to an array of life circumstances.[24]

From the outset it is important to note that Kabat-Zinn explicitly rejects the religious underpinnings for mindfulness to enjoy its benefits.

"Mindfulness is basically just a particular way of paying attention," he writes:

> It is a way of looking deeply into oneself in the spirit of self-inquiry and self-understanding. For this reason it can be learned and practiced, as we do in the stress clinic, without appealing to Oriental culture or Buddhist authority to enrich it or authenticate it. Mindfulness stands on its own as a powerful vehicle for self-understanding and healing. In fact one of its major strengths is that is not dependent on any belief system or ideology, so that its benefits are therefore accessible for anyone to test for himself or herself.[25]

Reading this passage, it is tempting to see mindfulness as the latest example in a long history of incorporating Eastern spirituality into Western contexts. Explicit recourse to the phrase "Oriental culture" hardly disguises a form of Orientalism that is evident in the work of other time-management gurus discussed earlier in this book.[26] The selective adaptation of others' belief systems for personal utility is part of a complicated history of mutual influence that has always taken place between formal and informal business genres in the East and West. The rise of Toyotism, or "just-in-time" production, and the Taoist influence on theories of organization illustrate this in earlier moments of management theory.[27] In his account of the influence of Zen on American pop culture, Williams makes a compelling case that Buddhist concepts became a permanent feature of contemporary capitalism in direct relation to productivity panic that Japanese management techniques caused in corporate boardrooms of the 1970s.[28] For personal productivity, however, the state of mindful meditation creates distance from these anxieties about enterprise competition. Turning perception inward draws attention to the ways we as individuals are affected by the needy world outside. To be mindful means to respond rather than react. Acknowledging a default disposition toward activity encourages practitioners to withhold immediate impulses, to process stimuli in such a way that actions have deliberate intention. The objective of mindful practice is to access a state of non-judgment, as Kabat-Zinn explains: "Mindfulness is cultivated by assuming the stance of an impartial witness to your own experience."[29] Arresting the reflex of judgment goes against the disciplined regime of self-assessment that productivity thinking requires. It also subverts the predominant workplace norm, resuscitated in Silicon Valley tech culture, that celebrates a "bias towards action."[30] Mindfulness is instead dedicated to producing "moments of peace and stillness, even in the midst of activity": "When your whole life is driven by doing, formal meditation practice can provide a refuge of sanity and stability that can be used to restore some balance and perspective. It can be a way of stopping the headlong momentum of all the doing and giving yourself some time to dwell in a state of deep relaxation and well-being and to remember who you are."[31]

Kabat-Zinn's mindfulness practice involves a combination of corporeal surveillance, breath control, and yoga to find tranquility and self-healing. The MBSR program recommends an initial training period of eight weeks to appreciate full effects and successfully overcome established habits. Patients at the Massachusetts clinic use their residency to learn the technique, bond with a cohort of fellow students, and test their capacity to carry on independently at home, with the help of guidance tapes available for purchase. The combination of a daily "body scan," yoga, and meditation instigates a new kind of awareness and auditory procedure for the self. This curated attention is a way to discern messages that the body may be sending but that fail to find an audience due to competing messages and cognitive priorities. For pain sufferers, the technique aims to alleviate the dominance of signals that privilege negative interpretation of bodily discomfort, a form of neural rewiring that meditation facilitates. For trauma patients, mindfulness welcomes open recognition of painful memories to help the body find physical release. This is the essential benefit of breathing with intent. "It is as if the breath contains, folded into itself, a power that we can come to simply by following it as if were a path," Kabat-Zinn writes.[32]

Applied to other ills, mindfulness counteracts the weight of particular signals that overwhelm the mind—specifically, the connotations of urgency that attach to work and other social requests. Mindfulness enacts a sensitivity program that instigates a return to the body's natural mode of information transmission. It removes the cognitive barriers that arise from external interaction and get in the way of recognizing the significance of vital signs. In the specific setting of the workplace, this method helps identify how the pressure of professional performance sometimes shuts down attentiveness to self and body. Working through lunch, back-to-back meetings, or sitting hunched over a computer screen, office dwellers are sometimes forgetting to breathe.

On a broader level, mindful practices of attunement are said to elicit a more holistic sense of connection with humanity, the cosmos, or whatever overarching framework participants determine as the guide for broader life purpose. We will return to this grand ambition a little later, given its potentially universalist assumptions. For now, the key to mindfulness in the Kabat-Zinn tradition is that it offers a method of "non-doing":

> It is the only human endeavor I know of that does not involve trying to get somewhere else but, rather, emphasizes being where you already are. Much of the time we are so carried away by all the doing, the striving, the planning, the reacting, the busyness, that when we stop just to feel where we are, it can seem a little peculiar at first.... [W]e tend to have little awareness of the incessant and relentless activity of our own mind and how much we are driven by it.[33]

In describing the "incessant and relentless activity of our own mind," Kabat-Zinn not only captures the quality of brain activity that constitutes the matter of everyday experience; he also formalizes the unique properties of mental labor that knowledge workers contend with each day. This work of chronic self-analysis involves both formally documented outputs compliant with explicit management norms and accompanying regimes of self-interrogation. In contemporary workplaces, productivity's demand for prioritization and efficiency—the informal registers of professional competence we saw in earlier chapters—typically occur without training or support. In this environment, mindfulness offers a mode of repair and solace from the combined psychological and organizational requirements placed on workers. Through specific instructions that assist in recalibration and refocusing, mindfulness emphasizes being over doing, at least for short periods. It therefore flips the default rationale of productivity even while its techniques reaffirm many of the same lessons of time management gurus of decades past.[34]

In the period since MBSR first gained prominence, a new wave of practitioners has brought an accompanying growth of interest in mindfulness. Curiosity reached something of a crescendo in 2011, when Thich Nhat Hanh was invited to speak at Google's Silicon Valley headquarters. His two-and-a-half-hour talk "Mindfulness as a Foundation for Health" has more than a half-million views on YouTube.[35] The session epitomizes the company's commitment to mindfulness programs for employees, including the appointment of an official "Jolly Good Fellow," Chade-Meng Tan, to convene Google's "Search Inside Yourself" leadership program. Mindfulness meditation groups continue to operate in other Bay Area corporations, with varying levels of official sanction.[36] At software companies such as Medium and Twitter, meditation and mindfulness are encouraged, and employees are eligible to receive conference passes to events that feature philosophical conversations between like-minded company founders.[37]

An emerging ecosystem of technology hardware designers has flourished in proximity to these trends and the growing influence of conferences such as Wisdom 2.0, the lead gathering of mindfulness evangelists inspired by the organizer and author Soren Gordhamer. The book *Wisdom 2.0: Ancient Secrets for the Creative and Constantly Connected* was published in 2009, and the first conference bearing the name took place in 2010. With the involvement of major media players such as Arianna Huffington, whose app, "GPS for the Soul," received heavy promotion at the 2013 event, the conference has been a lucrative marketing vehicle for technology start-ups seeking exposure for mindfulness products. The meeting provides a platform for business leaders championing alternatives to traditional corporate management models, whether through adhering to "wisdom" principles, in the case of LinkedIn's Jeff Weiner, or more wholesale organizational reforms, such as the Holocracy method promoted by Zappos's chief executive Tony Hsieh.[38]

A standout in the list of mindfulness technology vendors gaining attention with the growth of the industry is Muse, an intelligent headband that enables users to "Listen. Focus. Relax. Track. Improve. Accomplish."[39] With a price tag of about $250, the slim device sits on the user's forehead, with four EEG sensors monitoring brain activity. The data gathered by sensors is sent to an accompanying smartphone or tablet app to generate readings for analysis. The headband's purpose is to generate feedback on the inner workings of the mind, awareness of which will prompt ongoing training and behavioral reform. In this way, it operates much like the time-and-motion capture technologies introduced by the Gilbreths, or like the Harvard Studies that measured workers' athletic capacity with heart monitors in the 1920s (see chapter 1).

Trevor Coleman, the founder of Muse and chief operating officer of InteraXon, explains the benefits of brain tracking in these terms: "A heart rate monitor will give you information about what's going on with your heart while you're exercising, that helps you exercise better. In the same way, you wear Muse doing mental exercises, and it gives you information about how your brain is functioning during these exercises. . . . More information helps you improve yourself over time."[40] Muse encourages users to build "healthy brain habits," because "we now have overwhelming proof that we can improve our health, happiness, and performance in all aspects of life by taking time to strengthen our minds." The exercises Coleman promotes are about "developing the skill of attention." Distraction is a natural reflex, in this view, a sign that your mind has been "pulled off course." The benefit of Muse is to advise when you are experiencing distraction, and train you to be "pulled off course less often." Coleman recommends thinking of Muse as an Olympic coach available in your phone: always "making sure that you are at every moment motivated, connected, and performing at your best."

Coleman's claims about athleticism are matched in the rhetoric of other mindfulness technology evangelists, such as Paul Campbell of the company bLife. Although Campbell is not an athlete himself, his love of sports led him to develop a brain-tracking product based on methods he observed being used at Athletes Performance Inc. (now EXOS).[41] Learning how athletes trained, Campbell adapted similar procedures "to elaborate the science of mind fitness, or personalized fitness for the mind."[42] The result is bLife, a smartphone app "rooted in science" that provides assessments, exercises, meditation guides, and other tools to populate an "informative personal dashboard." The benefits of this accumulated data and feedback are said to include "deeper sleep, reduced stress, healthier relationships, and more productivity in life and work."

The company slogan, "Be Better," conveys its commonsense objective of self enhancement.

In his introduction of the product at a TEDX talk in Venice Beach in 2013, Campbell describes a "scientific revolution taking place" in a movement "that requires all of our participation."[43] Like the productivity gurus featured in previous chapters, Campbell begins his pitch with an anecdote that precipitates his conversion to mindful technology. Despite his success as a technology entrepreneur, Campbell confides to the audience, his personal life was falling apart when he experienced a stroke at age thirty-one. He started investigating meditation soon after. The health crisis, closely tied to the developer's work habits, prompted a change to his lifestyle and the motivation to inspire similar transformations in others.

In these examples, technology evangelists make a virtue out of contradiction by invoking mindfulness, which emphasizes non-action, and training, which necessarily requires repeated activity toward a goal. Common in each of these visions is the idea that the work involved in accessing the meditative state is secondary to the accomplishment of the state itself. Press coverage for mindfulness technologies confuses the situation further. The link to physical training is explicit in this commentary on bLife: "Mental pushups: Can a new app train your mind like the gym trains your body?" Yet the article fails to identify how training the mind in such a way brings about any benefit. Muse likewise claims "Improved Focus, Positivity, Sleep & Social Skills" as the result of its "Customized Action Plan for Healthy Brain Functioning." But there is little scientific evidence behind these effusive statements. Instead, the apps merely celebrate reform in general. The imperative is not just doing but doing *more*. "Do more with your mind," urges Muse, while its head-worn competitor Thync declares it will "unlock more of our minds and bodies without drinks or pills."[44] Thync's white patch, placed on the side of the forehead, has the appearance of a pirate's missing eye patch, or a tiny white boomerang. The company's slogan, "This is what good feels like," reflects an intention to provide natural relief from stress and an alternative to more toxic ingestible substances. The electromagnetic pulsing that emanates from Thync's patch works in two modes, "energy" and "calm," to "shift your frame of mind," according to a promotional video.[45] The three examples chosen for the website demo—a football player, DJ, and restaurant chef—all work in industries involving abrupt changes in intensity. For these professionals, event-based performance depends on a combination of physical and psychological exertion. Technology is the assistant for mindful transitions in the workday. It is not incidental that the workers chosen as representative for the technology inhabit a world of work that is outside that of the traditional office worker.[46] Indeed, looking closely at the video, each character appears to juggle multiple roles in a never ending workday (of student, in the case of the football player and chef, and promoter and sound engineer in the case of the DJ). Given the character of gig work, where even existing jobs are complemented by a range of auxiliary labor in anticipation of holding on to the possibility of ongoing employment, the mindfulness app allows training and recovery techniques to ensure peak professional performance.

Over the period of writing this chapter between 2014 and 2017, prototypes for mindfulness technologies have come and gone, and companies such as Muse have refined their business models to target health-care providers and alternative healing practitioners directly. For this market, the headband offers a pedagogical role, especially for first-time users and those unfamiliar with meditation. Much like the original MBSR clinic, the app's step-by-step instructions help individuals prepare for the experience. When they put on the device, users become part of a disciplinary regime: the ritual signals commitment to the practice while claiming time for the specific purpose of self-care. One way to distinguish the properties of mindful labor is to note the role of these hardware appendages in getting users into the *right frame of mind* to attend to themselves. As the Muse headband calibrates with one's brainwaves, guided exercises create attunement with the technology: "During the exercise, a woman directs you (through headphones) to close your eyes, relax, and breathe. As your mind calms down, you'll hear light winds. The less focused you are, the louder the winds. If you reach an ultimate state of zen, you might even hear beautiful birds chirping."[47] The *Business Insider* correspondent who wrote this description later admitted, "I never heard birds. And in all honesty, it was pretty noisy for me the whole time." Ellie Harmon had a similar reaction when she visited the Muse demo booth at Wisdom 2.0.[48] Both investigations convey the sense that a user's inability to sync with the headband can have a counterproductive effect:

FIGURES 4.1 AND 4.2 The multitasking millennial. The Thync wearable patch provides affective adjustment and on-demand composure through the different phases of a fractured workday. Source: Thync, "Camille Chef" promotional video.

in failing to provide a calm state, mindfulness technology can actually generate anxiety.[49]

Meditation devices and their software infrastructures sit comfortably among a broader set of treatments endorsed by the booming wellness industry. As a component of corporate-sponsored lifestyle programs, these "scientific" tactics for affect modulation appeal to health-care providers and employers seeking convenient means to monitor employees' moods and activity. In other instances, wellness wearables serve the needs of an elite demographic seeking drug-free alternatives for pleasure and performance. As the next chapter explains, the subcultures surrounding these digitally enhanced rituals reflect the priorities of a new generation of entrepreneurs seeking to animate perceptual regimes that link individuals to the rhythms of the natural world, whether through sober weekday parties or the euphoria of SoulCycle workouts. The consensus shared by all of these efforts in time and energy manipulation is a belief that tension can be ameliorated through internalized consumer transactions. As others have noted, the commodification of mindfulness makes it a privilege of the wealthy.[50] Like the asocial tendencies of previous time-management techniques, mindfulness offers quasi-scientific justification for its particular version of spiritual transcendence that comes more easily to those who can pay to protect themselves from concern for others.

The mindfulness technologies outlined here signal an evolution from recommended meditation practice in that they relocate the intentionality of self-reflection from the person to a device. The most radical aspect of mindful meditation is the momentary suspension of a command and control view, the unraveling of the usual equation between temporal and self-sovereignty. Relying on a machine to optimize corporeal operation negates this possibility. In the visions of hardware and software designers, there is pleasure in escaping the social world and its productivity pressures. But in contrast to Kabat-Zinn's endorsement to "remember who you are" by following the path of your breathing, mindfulness technologies and prosthetics perform the body scan on a user's behalf. The monitoring capabilities of new sensor-based appendages not only relinquish the transcendental aspirations of mindfulness practice, they do so in the guise of improved scientific validity. The sensor is the authoritative observer and point of perception reporting findings back to the user.

In the shift to "smart" devices, the practice of mindfulness moves another step further away from any original spiritual tradition. Just as Kabat-Zinn's MBSR method secularized the Buddhist underpinning for mindfulness, wearable technologies remove unnecessary human filtering and reflection. Technologies become omniscient agents trusted to scan the body's functions, producing data that expose a self that is otherwise hidden and oblivious. But by virtue of its algorithmic detection, this automated empiricism registers effect without cause. What is reported is separated from the conditions that produce the story. Mindfulness technologies relieve the user of the fundamental experience that meditative practice seeks to generate: a link between body signals and the specialized literacy needed to interpret them. The gap between mind and body is reified, contradicting the goal of mindfulness evangelists, which is to insist on their ultimate connection.

FROM ME TO WE

Explaining the role of yoga in everyday mindfulness, Kabat-Zin turns to etymology, writing, "Yoga is a Sanskrit word that literally means 'yoke'. The practice of yoga is the practice of yoking together or unifying body and mind, which really means penetrating into the experience of them not being separate in the first place. You can also think of it as experiencing the unity or connectedness between the individual and the universe as a whole."[51] Universalism is a casual expectation of secular mindfulness. As this description implies, attunement between mind and body at a personal level magically leaps to a connection to the entire world. Such an unencumbered disposition of cosmic openness appears regularly in the ideals of mindfulness advocates in Silicon Valley, particularly younger practitioners involved in the success of major social media companies. Justin Rosenstein is a leading example of this new generation of leaders finding notoriety in espousing mindfulness principles. Known for creating Facebook's "Like" button, Rosenstein made headlines with "Do Great Things: Your Role in the Human Project," his speech at Wisdom 2.0 in 2013.[52] Like other self-help gurus already mentioned, Rosenstein shared a number of biographical details in his talk to preface his conversion to mindfulness. His awakening came after a significant period of time away from ordinary routine, living in the wilderness and traveling the world. His speech provides this background as a positioning exercise for his latest company, Asana, a project-management software service. The Wisdom 2.0 plenary goes on to share Rosenstein's particular version of universalism, which sees the entire world as one giant team, with new communication technologies providing pathways for sharing love. Seeing the world as a team—the conduit from "me" to "we"— conveniently removes status distinctions or questions of wealth and equality. It also incorporates all other forms of association that might affiliate individuals with a larger cause. For Rosenstein, accustomed to designing interfaces for team-based work cultures, there are few better

FIGURE 4.3 Justin Rosenstein's 2013 Wisdom 2.0 talk, "Do Great Things: Your Role in the Human Project," is a definitive example of mindful technologists' casual universalism. Source: http://www.wisdom2conference.com.

notions of association than the hackneyed sporting metaphor. Yet his use of the term as the solution to major geopolitical problems conveys a missionary zeal that is worth further analysis.

The significance of Rosenstein's universal vision is more apparent when it is placed in relation to that of other celebrities in the Wisdom 2.0 community, such as the media mogul Ariana Huffington. While discussing "The Rise of Mindfulness in Society" with Kabat-Zinn onstage at the 2014 conference, Huffington mentioned Rosenstein as an exciting new participant in the conversation.[53] Kabat-Zinn and Huffington, who was on the promotion circuit for her book, *Thrive*, explored ancient traditions, bantering effusively about Huffington's Greek heritage to advocate the idea of "eudaimonia," a concept that roughly translates as "human flourishing." Throughout the celebrity pair's appearance, mindfulness is explained as the ultimate fusion of various belief systems articulated at different moments throughout human history. It therefore offers a path for enlightenment that is not hindered by ethnocentrism but brings all cultures together. Huffington said, "I love the fact that we are coming to the realization that all spiritual traditions and religions are really ulti-mately in their esoteric mystical forms saying the same thing. The kingdom of god is within." In the same discussion, Kabat-Zinn explained mindfulness to the audience as "a nascent renaissance that has the potential to be global this time, not just European." He also noted that "in Asian languages" the word for mind and the word for heart are the same and that medicine and meditation "have the same Indo-European root."

Huffington's assumption that all faiths are essentially interchangeable and the quest to prove a universal connection across cultures continues a convention evident in other New Age prophets to downplay spirituality in the interests of maximizing the message appeal. As we have seen, this is also a feature of time management self-help that works in combination with the market to ensure that productivity pedagogy captures the widest audience possible. In each case, discipline is privileged over content. All spiritual motivations are equally worthy as long as they conform to the notion that the individual can connect her flourishing to the wider world. Coming to terms with one's location in a social structure of distributed power, privilege, and wealth can be forgotten by focusing attention on the moment.

In an appraisal of the mindfulness trend in *Wired* magazine in 2013, Noah Shachtman queries the "religion-lite" elements of its most recent Silicon Valley practitioners: "Siddhartha famously abandoned the trappings of royalty to sit under the Bodhi Tree and preach about the illusion of the ego. Seeing the megarich take the stage to trumpet his practices is a bit jarring."[54] Kabat-Zinn's cooptation of Buddhist practice for mainstream consumption fits the history of time management I have been outlining throughout this book. Like productivity, mindfulness becomes an accommodating system because it transcends religious belief and welcomes a range of cultural values as irrelevant supplements to its basic infrastructure. Mindfulness for professional benefit is a postsecular exercise: adopting its ascetic discipline does not require belief in something meaningful to inspire the activity. To be mindful in the Wisdom 2.0 sense is to see virtue in the commitment to practice itself as a source of strength.

Mindfulness is a form of self-appreciation without self-knowing, to adopt Patricia Clough's description of the circulatory economy of affect.[55] Embracing the principle of non-doing is a way to cope with an environment of digitally mediated experience that encourages acts of "updating to remain the same."[56] Mindful labor is the work of recalibration needed when brain and body so regularly fall out of attunement in the intensified conditions of cognitive capitalism. In the hands of technologists, mindful meditation becomes one more data trail that separates the self from activity that can be optimized and quantified. It is another means by which today's workers risk being alienated from the character and value of their labor.

FEAR OF MISSING OUT — ON YOUR NEXT JOB

In closing this chapter, I want to recall the medical origins of Kabat-Zinn's MBSR method as a healing program for the chronically ill. The regularity with which the mindfulness industry's most vocal advocates cite their own stories of breakdown prior to rehabilitation reveals the volatility and attendant health risks of hyperproductive and performative work cultures.[57] Leaders in the field of wellness technology at least acknowledge feelings of dis-ease, helplessness, and stress, even when they appear to be enjoying a career peak. What is troubling is how easily these admissions develop into so much marketing spin for their software solutions. Indeed, as I was writing this book, the founder of one of the most recognized mindfulness retreats in the United States, the technology detox collective Camp Grounded, died. In announcing his brain tumor to the community mailing list, Levi Felix asked supporters to book tickets to the camp as the best way to show care. The message even supplied a discount code: WeGotThis. "I want to express love for all of you," Felix wrote,

> for believing in what we do, following our story, being a part of the narrative, and celebrating what it means to be human. This is a unique moment in human history, let's play hard and shine. Thank You! Thank You! Don't forget.... [C]all your mom or dad. Squeeze your siblings. Tell everyone that you love them. Take time to meditate or breathe or just laugh. This is the moment. This is the experience. This is it and this is it. And this moment too. We're all in this together.[58]

Perhaps it is unsurprising that mindfulness has taken hold in the United States at a time that feelings of hopelessness and suffering appear to be part of the broader cultural zeitgeist.[59] As other scholars have argued,

meditation is a convenient means of offsetting the negative affects arising from systemic inequalities in the workplace and beyond.[60] Of the
many influences that may be at play, my reading contends, there is a
powerful correlation between this recent form of self-healing and spiritual repair and the experience of contemporary labor. Management techniques aimed at minimizing resources, combined with technology design aimed at colonizing attention, manifests as *a state of mind* that feels
overwhelmingly *full*. There are just too many things vying for "mind-
share" in workplaces that fail to acknowledge that the quality of information reception, processing, and dissemination has fundamentally
changed with digital media. In the appraisal of some social commentators, overdependence on technology inspires a need for detox programs
to overcome the newly diagnosed syndrome of "FOMO," or "fear of missing out."[61] These arguments acknowledge the growth in social networking platforms and software services that prolong the already considerable degree of communicative labor in both work and leisure time. This
context explains why companies such as Muse position their products
as a way to reclaim the "skill of attention." But helping users "recover
faster" from distraction not only downplays the amount of effort that
goes into designing software that trades on psychological vulnerabilities;
it also makes individual feats of athleticism the commonsense response.
Today's workers are deciding to stay connected to a device at least partly
because of a lingering dimension that is affecting all workers making a
living in precarious times: the fear of missing out on your next job. As
non-standard work becomes a new norm, and professional credibility
equates to availability, being "on call" is a feature of the labor market at
both the low and the high end.[62]

When activity is celebrated at the expense of meaning, as the previous
chapters argue, mindfulness is a salve for individuals who are expected
to display constant forward momentum in careers that do not tolerate
gaps or absence. Kabat-Zinn makes this explicit when he talks about
the difference between mindfulness and other health pursuits: "Exercise classes emphasize *progress*. They like to push, push, push. Not much
attention is paid to the art of non-doing and non-striving in exercise
classes, nor to the present moment for that matter, nor to the mind."[63]
This passage underscores the incongruity of using athleticism as a measure of accomplishment for mental and physical health. As the character

of both mental and manual labor has become more screen-based, exploiting the properties of the brain, the techniques of self-care required by employees call for renovation. In today's job market, when activity is a sign of viability, mindfulness is a way to square the balance between doing and being. This is what makes the commodification of mindfulness so distressing for those who value the spirit as much as the letter of the practice. The central idea of mindful meditation is to curate a state of non-striving, a deflation of the heroic ego that Western competitive capitalism typically celebrates. The adoption of mindfulness principles in technology design can reflect a disturbing utilitarianism—a partial adoption of asceticism that is actually the antithesis of productivity's insatiable appetite for self-enhancement.

In *Full Catastrophe Living*, Kabat-Zinn acknowledges that "it is no accident that mindfulness comes out of Buddhism, which has as its overriding concerns the relief of suffering and the dispelling of illusions."[64] Mindfulness encourages practitioners to come to terms with the false illusion that their time and obligations can be perfectly managed; to recognize that lack of control over one's fate is not only necessary, but liberating. This altered perspective on being decenters, albeit slightly, the egocentric command-control dynamic that the pact between temporal sovereignty and professional competence has long upheld. Applied to the workplace, this attitude can be a way to come to terms with the inadequacies of organizational life, including the circumstances that conspire to generate urgency and priorities according to one's location in a broader hierarchy. In this sense, mindfulness technology may be the inevitable result of a partnership between two kinds of professional: the information worker who craves a semblance of sanity in the office and the engineer whose impulse is to solve problems. As a strategy of time management, however, mindfulness is flawed in execution. Even if the process of introspection and self-healing provides a temporary method of coping with the affective overload of cognitive labor, in its current form mindfulness does not escape the broader logic of productivity governing the workplace, which personalizes responsibility for efficiency in the name of perfecting performance. This is what we see in the Trello marketing mentioned earlier in the chapter: for remote knowledge workers, mindfulness is just another app in the toolbox. The casual universalism of mindfulness technique also absolves one from having to consider the social infrastructure and the human dimensions that apportion work to some already stretched bodies more than others. Despite its origins in a belief system that seeks to erase earthly considerations of the ego, meditative practice has little chance to defeat the orthodoxy of careerism that attaches the incentive and reward structures of the workplace to the unique talents of exceptional individuals.

In its most evangelical form, mindfulness creates a sense of connection to an entire planet of like-minded practitioners. In doing so, it ignores staggering differences in financial and cultural privilege, equating the suffering of the wealthy with that of the oppressed. We can see in the statements of mindfulness enthusiasts how the desire for universal connection serves the worldview of the individual by transcending the realities actually encountered by colleagues, neighbors, friends, and other geographically located peers. The appeal to a cosmological framework, spurred on by the New Age underpinnings of mindfulness in the Big Sur tradition, naturalizes thought processes that are at once attuned with the world and acting in the best interests of its inhabitants. The non-action of a global elite to intervene in the structural inequalities of this, or any, particular moment, thus becomes justified.

MINDFUL WORKPLACES

A generous appraisal would hold that organizations such as Wisdom 2.0 have clearly fostered an ecosystem of wellness entrepreneurs with the capacity to transform workplace culture for the better. In companies that embrace mindfulness principles—Google, Facebook, and Medium, for example[65]—the conditions enjoyed by employees may yet prove influential enough to raise the standard of benefits for workers in less socially or financially rewarded roles. Corporate programs for employee well-being often face cynicism from workers well aware of the rewards for employers in minimizing health risks and enhancing productivity through preventative care. As my co-researcher Ellie Harmon concluded in her report on the industry, mindfulness is convenient for hardware and software developers in that the solution to excessive workloads is not to stop making technology, but to create products that support mindfulness maxims. This in turn is convenient for business because, as long as the facilities for healing and recovery are provided, there is no need to change the incentive structure that exhausts workers. Today, mindful labor is the self-regulation burden that falls on ordinary workers, as much as on their higher-level executives, who have a new obligation to make wellness achievable for their employees.

One of the most popular sayings in Kabat-Zinn's keynote repertoire is "Check your watch: it's now again. The only moment that matters." This chapter has shown how practitioners of mindfulness find empowerment in a newfound ability to manipulate time: to pause, reflect, and be in the moment, suspending awareness of past and future. The fact that this accomplishment appears revolutionary is a sign of just how ingrained productivity thinking has become. Mindful labor alleviates the psychological impact of efficiency norms by claiming periods of withdrawal and respite through determined rituals of non-doing. This rejection of activity for its own sake—captured in Thich Nhat Hanh's pithy quote, "Don't just do something, sit there"[66]—is the flipside of the productivity aesthetics we saw in previous chapters, where the appearance of getting things done provided its own kind of pleasure and rationale. In forfeiting participation in the constant drive to perform, mindfulness thus has the potential to occupy a place alongside other kinds of work refusal that acknowledge the biopolitical constitution of labor.[67]

In the many months of worrying how to write and finish this chapter, a time that investment in my actual job fluctuated wildly, I found solace in the very activities and practices of mindfulness I was studying. My progress on this book was affected significantly by a period of prolonged turbulence at work, completely befitting the picture of corporate life depicted in the self-help guides of chapter 2. Leaving aside the momentousness of my career change from academia to industry and a move to the United States from Australia, after I joined Intel, multiple shifts in managers and divisions, combined with the biggest company layoff in more than a decade, created a volatile transition. The level of stress I felt in this unstable environment, particularly in contrast to the pace of change in the university, is perhaps obvious only in retrospect. Researching mindfulness turned out to be a useful way for me to recover from a range of health symptoms arising from this period, from mysterious food allergies to vitamin D deficiency and a very scary bout of pneumonia.

As much as I dislike the macho "tech-bro" front of new-generation

Stoicists such as Tim Ferris, I have started keeping a diary again to keep my "monkey brain" at bay.[68] I meditate whenever I feel harried from too much inflated urgency and political melodrama at the office. Thanks to the nudging of my partner, we now have an adorable puppy who shows me how to chill and channel emotion through long walks and hilarious sighs. Sometimes he joins me when I roll out my yoga mat in the morning, raise my arms to the sky, and salute the not always reliably present Portland sun. While finishing revisions to this book, I even bought a portable mat to take with me on the road. This simple routine brings me a sense of joy from continuing even the tiniest ritual. These are not major political victories. Admittedly, they are solitary. But in relation to previous efforts to keep work concerns off my mind, they feel like progress.

An anthropotechnics of mindful labor may yet mobilize workers to issue new demands of employers, including the right to communal ritual and retreat. Yet the lack of philosophical substance behind key examples of mindfulness technology currently offsets the search for an appropriate ethics that would confront the accumulative bias of capitalist thinking. This is what Peter Sloterdijk conveys in his appraisal of Zen in the context of Western athleticism: "The movement as a whole, due to its basic therapeutic and atheoretical attitude, proves sufficiently impatient to be attractive for the spiritual aspirations of Western people, who only know life as a finale."[69] Sloterdijk implies that Buddhism's religious underpinnings are necessary for the practice to provide any real coherence. True mindfulness includes the accompanying acknowledgment that life is suffering and that death may bring not salvation but, rather, a rebirth, a return, and a repetition. Other critics, such as Slavoj Žižek, condemn Western Buddhism as "the most efficient way for us to participate fully in the capitalist dynamic" through its reliance on "the selfless 'now' of instant Enlightenment.'"[70] Siphoning the most utilitarian elements of centuries-old traditions, mindful meditation draws together a patchwork of platitudes to soften a capitalist system that continues in spite of its spiritual deficiencies.

If mindfulness is something of a Band-Aid for the productivity imperative, one source of optimism is the frankness of its prominent practitioners who actively admit the damage of high-octane workplaces and the health consequences of constant striving. This admission is an important starting point for contemplating alternative work futures. "Why we disconnect matters," argues Morozov in his appraisal of mindfulness evangelists:

> We can continue in today's mode of treating disconnection as a way to recharge and regain productivity, or we can view it as a way to sabotage the addiction tactics of the acceleration-distraction complex that is Silicon Valley. The former approach is reactionary but the latter can lead to emancipation, especially if such acts of refusal give rise to genuine social movements that will make problems of time and attention part of their political agendas—and not just the subject of hand-wringing by the Davos-based spirituality brigades. Hopefully, these movements will then articulate alternative practices, institutions, and designs. If it takes an act of unplugging to figure out how to do it, let's disconnect indeed. But let us not do it for the sake of reconnecting on the very same terms as before.[71]

Despite its solipsistic potential, mindful labor—work on the self, work that acknowledges the impact of one's personal choices on others—offers the prospect of a path back to the social, to a collective conversation about the cumulative impact of productivity's relentless call to action. While efficiency thinking and competitive careerism often isolates individuals from shared acts of imagining change, mindfulness is a glimmer of hope that the desire for other worldviews remains and that there are sublime experiences to be savored beyond the temporality of the office. Elaborating on all of these ideas will be necessary to regain a sense of solidarity in labor beyond the capitalist enterprise. This is the task of my conclusion.

Conclusion

From Careers to Atmospheres

In this book, I have shown how technologies of efficiency worked in tandem with an ascendant science of management to establish the language and practice of productivity. Over the course of a century, time management in the workplace enacted a progressively personalized relationship to efficiency. Subjective reengineering through career-enhancing training programs defined professionalism in terms that benefited the Organization and its machines. Sanctioned methods for time- and self-management, assisted by computational interfaces designed for atomized users, amplified workplace initiatives aimed at erasing the practical and ideological means of experiencing labor as collective. Casting workers as high-potential performers focused attention on improvement and forward momentum, removing the incentive for individuals to acknowledge their output in relation to group effort. The athleticism of time management in the workplace required a turn away from the social.

Under the growing influence of neoliberal economics, these developments helpfully facilitated the austerity measures that would become commonplace in corporate and other enterprise environments following successive financial downturns. Efficiency mantras prompted status anxieties and ambition in equal measure. Popular texts and technological tools supplemented professional curricula that were consolidating in universities as a new discipline of management took shape in both formal and informal pedagogies. For workers, the consequences of this history are profound. When everyone is personally challenged to be productive, discussion of adequate resources or additional colleagues to share the load becomes close to irrelevant. The entrepreneurial individual is trusted to perform a "permanent reform or revolution" of the self to avoid redundancy in a competitive job market.[1] Productivity's recursive rationale suits a generalized condition of austerity in which "anyone not prepared to 'fling himself into the fray . . . has already lost.'"[2]

This book maintains that the theories of time and performance that underwrote initial management techniques map poorly onto the present. The notion that work is carried out through a series of individual choices regarding time, based on unique interpretations of classification and order, ignores the structural conditions that govern today's organizations, not to mention the cumulative impact of so many apparently personal decisions on a social and global economic field. The latest productivity tools enacted through software platforms and wearable devices are the end of a long line of delegated logistical work that has been the burden of *some* bodies in *some* places to bear more than others. As Sara Ahmed notes, "When being freed from labor requires others to labor, others are paying the price of your freedom."[3] Recalling Sarah Sharma's words, a politics of temporal awareness "means recognizing how one's management of time has the potential to further diminish the time of others."[4]

The engineer and the manager emerged at a similar period in history.[5] Their shared heritage in turn-of-the-twentieth-century Progressivism explains a common aspiration to optimize operations through the production of time sovereignty. Time management is the exercise of this computational worldview that celebrates command and control.[6] As feminists have long argued, the idea of time sovereignty holds faith in the idea that time is territory that can be conquered—a belief structure that reinforces other patriarchal and colonial regimes of thought.[7] Of course, conquering terrain necessarily involves surveillance, navigation, and documentation. Each example chosen for analysis in this book—the scientific management of Taylorism; the human relations tradition of Elton Mayo; the self-auditing company executive; and the app-monitoring, mobile professional today—all embark on record-keeping pursuits. All illustrate the conviction that personalized modes of attention will identify and encourage peak performance from the individual. The productivity mandate in time-management tools posits the idea that it is possible to focus on consequential matters for predetermined periods. That we hold the power to control life's unpredictability through the deployment of protective infrastructures is the fantasy necessary for productivity's appeal.

The resilience of time management as an ostensibly achievable goal must be understood before turning to alternatives that may prove more accommodating and empowering for workers in the present and future. Acknowledging feminist, race- and class-sensitive histories means that the equation between temporal sovereignty and freedom in work must be constantly questioned. The pleasure of being productive—to work on the most visible, valued, and rewarded labor—should not come at others' expense. Productivity is not a virtue if it requires temporal subordination in the attainment of elite gratification.

I began this book by asserting that a delegation dynamic animates some of the most prominent companies operating on a productivity premise today. If there was any doubt that time mastery depends on inferior others, the names of these brands are enough confirmation: "TaskRabbit" is as dehumanizing as Amazon's "Mechanical Turk" in the landscape of virtual online assistance.[8] Advocates see these software platforms as evidence of the resources now available to workers to earn a living outside the inconvenience of corporate mandated schedules. There are important opportunities to seize amid these circumstances, which I discuss in more detail shortly. Set against the longer history of labor struggle, however, the rise of on-demand labor apps is a mixed blessing, revealing what is at stake when servitude is required to advance the benefits of productivity. Digital platforms are the distribution point for an unregulated job market that separates employment from employers and thus the expectation of baseline income and benefits. The configuration of work as it is carried out in these transactions means that employment location, management, scheduling, and pay no longer align in one place.[9] Another way to say this is that "platform capitalism" ruptures the relationship between employment and time.[10] What is traded for the convenience of a contract, contingent, or "gig"-based lifestyle is any hope that workers *can* control time. The service economy facilitated by third-party apps celebrates an attitude to work and to income that is improvised and ad hoc, forever arriving "just in time."

As we saw in chapter 3, the labor of synchronizing schedules and commitments in this decentralized, hyper-flexible environment culminates as a new kind of personal logistics. Instead of the organization bearing the burden of coordinating time, the injunction to use time resource-fully now falls on everyone. This creates a hierarchy of privilege between those who choose their schedule (the consultant as much as the Uber driver) and those who are scheduled (the day laborer or the Starbucks staff member suffering yet another "clopen").[11] In the latter category, re-sponsibility for embodying the future moves from the employer to the worker. Thus, only some kinds of employees or vendors will experience this change as empowering. In passing the responsibility for time man-agement to the individual, so-called sharing economy platforms create value for those who have already established the coordinates to plan time in advance and the financial capacity to outsource work that is trivial. The most successful companies apparently "disrupting" employment in the new economy therefore continue the longer history of productivity outlined in this book. By promoting an unequal hierarchy as freedom— for the worker *and* the person hiring—digital platforms enthusiastically endorse delegation as the commonsense mode of achieving efficiency.

ESCAPING THE ENTERPRISE

The forms of measurement and reward celebrated in the practice of pro-ductivity are terms originally set by the enterprise. Mundane metaphors— the career path, the organizational ladder, the management coach urg-ing you to focus and win—reinforce notions of linear progression. These concepts of success celebrate individual efforts in ways that profit compa-nies and their owners. As we saw in previous chapters, despite the vocal emphasis on teamwork in contemporary work settings, careerism's insu-lar focus on advancement is necessarily egocentric. It requires an invest-ment in one's self and a degree of comfort and ease with ushering one's own interests in contrast to others'. This is a legacy of self-witnessing, recognition, and will to improvement that began in the earliest studies of employee output. In the lean organization, personal triumph means dis-pensing with the ties of collegial solidarity and care, even while work is simultaneously conferred an ethical, at times spiritual, status. Now that the idea of the stable career path appears to be under threat—or rather, as the notion of the long-term job with company perks becomes ever more exclusive—we can appreciate how much the prospect of a salary and a course for ascent created a mutually beneficial relationship to time for workers and employers alike. These expectations involved understanding one's life in terms of scheduling: static and predictable bundles of time that would ensure order in the office and work plans that adhered to particular weeks, quarters, and years. So while there are clearly negative effects of sharing economy platforms when compared with this neat framework, other examples reflect more positive changes to traditional organizational norms of workload distribution. These alternatives to the servitude model harness the power of online and offline communities to provide a more communal way to talk about time, income, and assets.

The emergence of coworking spaces is one instance where we can see growing numbers of independent, remote, and contract workers gathering together in a shared location to pool resources and networks. By paying membership fees to the community on a month-to-month basis, coworkers invest in an infrastructure for the development of new identities, affiliations, and rituals that compete with the corporate-career reward structure—to the point where enterprise customers are turning to successful shared office operators such as WeWork to solve their problems with talent retention.[12] In addition, consumer-driven platform innovations—Airbnb, Kickstarter, Etsy, and others—provide tools to generate work and income so that livelihoods need not depend on traditional 9–5 employment. Many of these start-ups share with mindfulness technologists a desire for more meaningful work beyond the ideals of productivity that defined employment in the organization era.

In a plenary talk at the O'Reilly Media Next Economy conference in 2015, Yancey Strickler, chief executive of Kickstarter, used an image of the punk band Fugazi to convey his belief that do-it-yourself (DIY) ethics are the future of small business. At the same event, Stewart Butterfield, co-founder of Flickr, explained the basis of his new company, Slack, a collaboration platform for distributed work teams. Using design methods that put the emphasis on groups and collaboration, Slack prioritizes projects and collective threads to facilitate conversations that stretch beyond the perimeters and objectives of any one company. Recognizing that individuals may be split among multiple jobs and tasks, with numerous ongoing interests and income streams, Slack's user-friendly screen interface helps workers manage multiple commitments by granting them different "channels" that can be turned on and off according to need and availability. Slack offers workers more control over the tools of communication than more cumbersome enterprise software. It provides easy ways to change settings in the interests of rest and respite, modulating work-related notifications and noise without sacrificing connection to groups that provide ongoing solace and support.

Slack is one way that I maintain contact with colleagues and friends through the various iterations of job, location, and institutional affiliation that are now customary for my peers. This mode of contact renovates drab corporate-issued interfaces that typically address isolated monadic individuals encountering a campus-bound world in pre-programmed calendar bundles.[13] By the time this book is in press, there will be many more tools for knowledge workers seeking a new way to choreograph time and labor as part of a larger life's work, beyond the specifics of the employment relation. Like the crowdfunded product launches that Kickstarter enables, software platforms and code are important armory in the quest to release our ideas and productivity from the enclosure of the firm.

To close this account of time management, I offer two further case studies that express the positive qualities to be found in productivity when it involves building atmospheres for social connection outside the temporal dictates of the organization.[14] While neither example is without flaws, I see both as useful stimuli for advancing further efforts in worker-led futures, anticipating the final provocations that conclude the book.

ATMOSPHERES I: COWORKING SPACES

Returning to the example of coworking, in 2016, struck by the growing number of shared office locations appearing in my local neighborhood around Portland, I began talking with Thomas Lodato about his research on coworking spaces. For my job at Intel I was interested in the burgeoning ecosystem of start-ups and small businesses arising from these venues; Lodato and I wanted to find out what the "co" in coworking really captured. Did it mean community—as so much of the advertising for coworking spaces maintained? Or did it mean something specific to the kinds of collaboration enabled by the physical layout of the buildings inside? Over the course of a year, he and I shared notes from fieldwork conducted across the United States, Europe, and Asia, drawing together overlapping observations.[15] In coworking, we observed, community refers to a combination of "camaraderie, collegiality and knowledge transfer fostered through spatial proximity."[16] In promotional copy for coworking spaces, community is often shorthand for what Seb Olma calls the "serendipity" of coworking, which can appear artificially manufactured in some contexts.[17] Current projections from the firm Emergent Research point to twenty-six thousand coworking spaces and something like 3.8 million individual members by 2020.[18] Whether or not these figures hold, the phenomenal growth of coworking can be understood in terms of the emphasis knowledge workers place on the right *atmosphere* for personal productivity: "Coworking's key benefit has been to offer *comfort* amenities—free coffee, beer, and snacks; inspirational quotes painted on walls and displayed through neon signage; on-site therapy dogs, massage, and yoga—in addition to aesthetically pleasing lounge areas that allow individuals to feel close to something; something that *might be happening.*"[19] The popularity of coworking as part of the post-2008 economic recovery also suggests that shared work location is one important factor in offsetting the instability of a precarious career path. While coworking providers do not directly generate employment security or job leads, they provide the social and material infrastructure on which such valuable connections and opportunities can be realized. While freelancers have always lived at the whim of the market, bearing the burden of securing their own contracts, tools, and resources,[20] it is the lack of social interaction in independent work that can negatively affect workers' well-being.

As more professionals face the prospect of a contingent lifestyle of informal, on-demand work, the loss of temporal stability can be offset in coworking by the social connection that temporary colleagues and communities offer in a harsh employment market. In the process, a heavy irony is sometimes attached to the physical and aesthetic layout of coworking venues to demarcate the move away from company life to something more playful and free. At Grind coworking in Manhattan, coffee tables designed by artists are filled with IT junk signifying the dated technologies of the out-of-touch office;[21] meanwhile WeWork drapes banners outside its buildings that say, "Thank God it's Monday," a tongue-in-cheek reference to the banal affects of corporate culture. Deliberately blurring office space with hospitality, critique with celebration, coworking providers fuel the spirit of independence and creative passion that marks a growing category of "solopreneurs" whose desire to evade the compromises of the corporation feeds a new industry servicing their productivity preferences.[22]

Coworking is the physical manifestation of a larger international community making use of Instagram accounts, Twitter hashtags, and Facebook pages to promote workstyles outside company walls. Search for #coworking or #digitalnomad on social media and witness the array of users promoting travel and adventures beyond the conventional career itinerary. In the course of writing this book, the gap year between college and full time employment was permanently commodified by brands such as Unsettled, whose coworking retreats provide "everything you need to be connected, comfortable, and collaborative: private accommodation, shared workspace, local guide, events, and an immersive community experience."[23] Nomad Cruise is another service that fuses travel with work ambition to deliver the ultimate "networkation."[24] These communities operate on the premise that the world can be navigated easily and efficiently through shared know-how—namely, through brokerage services that will facilitate safe passage through cities and countries that gain an economic benefit from wealthy workers' presence. Coworking spaces are a vital channel for this global class of mobile workers, securing the social and practical resources to enjoy a world *through* work. This plenitude of online and offline connectivity in the service of new livelihoods contrasts the extremes of productivity seen elsewhere in this book, where accomplishment in the organizational hierarchy depends on a turn away from the social. Yet it is hard not to recognize that the privilege of digital nomads often depends on a superficial engagement with local communities, just as the commodified form of community offered by coworking behemoths derives speculative value from the collision of real estate and business interests.

Daybreaker is an occasional morning dance party that began in 2013 and has since spread to numerous U.S. cities, as well as to Toronto, Paris, and London. Appropriately, it was conceived in a Brooklyn falafel shop by its founders, Radha Agrawal and Matthew Brimer, after a long night out. The idea was to "take the energy and inclusiveness of the night-club scene and infuse it into the weekday morning routine," inverting the conventional dance experience that requires darkness and drugs.[25] The predawn parties are designed to disrupt the monotony of the working week, allowing access to great music and inspiring locations for patrons to bliss out and relieve stress: "The idea is this: Arrive before dawn, dance like crazy to hot beats from popular DJs, and then go to work feeling amazing."[26]

Daybreaker's mix of live DJs, entertainers, and boutique fitness instructors come together to lead a party of typically four hundred to five hundred paying guests and begin the day on a natural high.[27] Before the dancing commences, pre-ticketed yoga sessions allow gathering attendees to wake gradually, while local vendors offer gourmet juice, coffee, and breakfast items as part of the price of entry. The further benefit of the dance dimension, as the sober clubbing trend also documents, is the chemical hit of the endorphin rush. The pleasure of this physical exertion accentuates what time-management gurus in previous chapters identified as the "Prime Time" of early mornings. "Morning is a time when you have the most amount of energy potential inside of you," Brimer notes in explaining Daybreaker's origins.[28] Promotion for the events celebrates both the mental clarity and the adrenaline hit that dancing at dawn delivers.

Daybreaker parties are another example of popular mindfulness practices seeking attunement with the body's rhythms and patterns. Like the mind-fitness trackers and meditators in the previous chapter, Daybreaker creates an opportunity to witness the body's natural sensations and experiences without the noise of stimulants or other signal-scrambling distractions. Daybreaker makes a spectacle of this vital knowledge, taking it to an extreme, at a time of day and week when this behavior is socially unexpected. Rather than turning inward, reflecting on the story of the individual's body, the gatherings purposefully explore the body's pleasures in combination with a large group. Daybreaker events are designed to unleash affective contagion: assembling a multitude of bodies to witness what they will do. In this way, Daybreaker extends the premise of other quasi-spiritual fitness companies who serve a niche market by offering sensuous aesthetic environments for members. These various start-ups (such as the SoulCycle chain made famous by Michelle Obama) exemplify a kind of physical exertion that fuses mindful techniques with athleticism.[29] They suit the requirements of an urban milieu in which contaminated environments provoke the desire for what Sloterdijk would call "immunological bubbles."[30] Unlike the healing ambitions of mindfulness, however, Daybreaker is explicitly hedonistic in its aim to unsettle the norms of the working week. Gatherings provide an oasis away from the grind of city life in assembling various nutrients that will replenish the mind and the soul in the midst of habitual routine. The events are typically located several steps removed from the heart of the city's financial district or the grittier parts of the urban scene. In a particularly popular Daybreaker form, parties are held on a boat on the Hudson (New York City), the Sound (Seattle), or the Bay (San Francisco), marking a temporary separation from the city grind.

Daybreaker is not the first morning dance phenomenon, but its international appeal suggests that there is something similar in the experience of living and working in large, affluent cities, whether New York, Los Angeles, or London. The audience imagined for the events shares the language and privilege of the white, wealthy elite also drawn to mindfulness technologies. Social media promotions for Daybreaker feature attractive, style-conscious, and youthful participants who have the time and means to participate in a rich sensory wonderland. The further point of interest is that the price of entry to the event clearly provides access to a well-heeled and well-connected clientele. Argine Ovsepyan, Daybreaker's organizer in Los Angeles, told CBS that the guests are generally "young professionals that are rocking life. . . . You could be next to an entrepreneur that runs three companies, which is pretty epic."[31] Burning Man is cited as a useful point of comparison, "without the dust, drugs or bikes."[32]

Daybreaker hints at the new coordinates for social networking that are appropriate for today's professionals who are tired of generic collegial formats such as Friday night drinks.[33] The growth in wellness and health-conscious lifestyles in proximity to the work cultures of the successful tells a story of affective reengineering among a new urban gentry whose boutique tastes have grown in tandem with the widening gap between rich and poor in the United States. News coverage for Daybreaker parties lists them with tags dedicated to the topic of "green living," an indication of Daybreaker's grander aspiration to encourage intelligent engagement with nature, paying heed to internal and external rhythms. The Daybreaker atmosphere encourages workers to experience the pleasures of time spent differently—to break with the commuter treadmill of corporate athleticism. The drug-free status of these events makes a feature of their health orientation, all the while opening the experience of elevation to a range of potential participants from different cultural and religious traditions. Like the productivity regimes explored throughout this book, Daybreaker transcends any one belief system to reawaken spiritual awareness through a simple and powerful premise: organizing joy at witnessing the dawn.

PRODUCTIVE ATMOSPHERES

In sharing these examples of productive atmospheres, my aim is not to hold them as exemplary or ideal case studies for a post-work future. As *Fortune* noted, describing the Daybreaker event at Macy's Manhattan department store in 2016, "It'll all be over in time to go to work."[34] I hold no illusion that these two subcultures are untouched by varieties of class and racial exclusivity or substantial networks of financial capital that bankroll their efforts. It is not incidental that both arise from a Manhattan milieu that harbors a degree of wealth that is unimaginable to the majority of ordinary workers. Where I do find hope, given the concerns of this book, is in the way that both coworking and day dancing play with the constraints of the workweek paradigm. Each example calls out the damage caused to workers' well-being by the 9–5 routine instituted by the organization. And each provides simple gestures of self-care, even luxury, that today's generic workplaces find it increasingly difficult to provide. Whether it is the cacao bar at breakfast or the refresher pack in the WeWork bathroom, these atmospheres for productivity offer amenities for a worker who is destined to endure a long and unpredictable workday.

In sum, what I like about both micro-movements is that they operate in the interests of the worker rather than the manager. In different ways, both offer spaces of support and repair for individuals who seek to practice the principles of mindfulness and find purpose in the work that they inevitably have to do. Coworking and Daybreaker reintroduce the pleasurable social relation that the efficiency metrics of the organization stripped from view. These communities use technology and local geography to introduce new rituals centered on shared time and presence. Attending Daybreaker or subscribing to a coworking space will not revolutionize corporate business practice; indeed, each clearly supplements its obvious failings. This raises the question with which I want to end my analysis: what models of productivity do we need—what forms of affiliation and ritual—for a future outside the corporation?

My conclusion, based on the material in this book, is that we need to move our aspirations for productivity from the corporate to the collective interest. Productive atmospheres are truly revolutionary when they undo the century of managerial strategy described in this book and initiate a form of collective solidarity that is not dependent on labor. We urgently need political visions that celebrate practices of selflessness and care to challenge the embedded egotism of enterprise-serving job norms and pervasive industry myopia. At a time of global environmental threat, the athleticism of accomplishment has to be rejected for its utter dependence on the growth mentality that exploits our finite resources.[35] In Sloterdijk's words, "Individual immunity is only possible as co-immunity."[36] Our decisions about work and our ability to classify which tasks are worthwhile are part of a larger societal discussion necessary to establish shared infrastructures that will sustain a range of meaningful work practices in the long term.

The provocations that follow synthesize the major lessons from this book, outlined in a set of principles for post-work productivity. They are intended to generate prototype workstyles, job experiments, and supportive environments that allow a multitude of valuable social contributions to thrive and succeed.[37] Despite the stress that attended my own recent attempt to reconfigure life and work, I am glad to have escaped the horizon of one professional location so as to better appreciate the importance of cross-industry alliances in developing alternatives to productivity. Working collaboratively in writing this book, I have found new colleagues and friends in a range of locations and fields. Our conversations have only just begun. Together, we are navigating the opportunities and limitations of existing work worlds, moving the measure of productivity from the angst of individual careers to the cultivation of atmospheres. I hope that these ideas spur for you an inkling of the lives that may be waiting for us in the wake of industrial schedules.

PRINCIPLES FOR POST-WORK PRODUCTIVITY

- Our sense of capacity and power escapes organizational determinism. We generate value and meaning through work that enterprise metrics do not capture.

- How long we work is not a measurement of heroism or commitment. Liberation from record keeping allows us to focus on meaningful activity.

- We once drew strength from co-location: shared employers and time and length of service. When these are withheld, or when they are no longer possible, we make our own networks of support to build livelihoods.

- We are self-managing and self-realizing in securing a collective immunology from overwork. Knowing our strengths and our limits is how we generate benefits for others as much as for ourselves.

- Mindful labor recognizes the connection between personal preference and external conditions for labor. To be mindful is to acknowledge the impact of our work on a social and material world.

- Careers are a model of comportment that suited industrial growth. The consequences of this way of working — the accumulation of already concentrated wealth; the polarization of labor and rewards — are too damaging to maintain.

- Productive atmospheres reward collaboration, coherence, and duration. Their workstyles resist opportunism and the formula of mobility as success.
- The technical, financial, and temporal privileges embedded in the organization can be collectively raided to build productive atmospheres of our own.

Postscript

A Belated Processing

POSTED ON | SEPTEMBER 11, 2016 | NO COMMENTS

Last week I finally wrote the email I have been dreaming of writing for years. It was sent to my publisher, along with the draft of my new book, *Counter-productive: A Brief History of Time Management*. It made a certain sense when I realized that the day I submitted the manuscript was also the anniversary of my mother's passing. She died fifteen years ago, of cancer. I have never really written about this event, and the many ways it has affected my life. I still don't want to share much about it, except to say that there are aspects of the book that are closely tied to my memories of her. These include what are imagined connections to different parts of her working life.

When I was young, mum taught home economics at the local school on Bruny Island, Tasmania, where I grew up. She went on to teach and direct religion and English literature at the Catholic school I attended in Hobart. It must have been some time during this later period that she acquired a book on stress that I found years afterward. It was this discovery, along with some other books related to health and illness, that inspired my interest in self-help. I saw them as symptoms of how she and other first-generation office workers developed strategies of consolation and recovery to face professionalism and its strangeness.

When my mother was very ill, she needed to leave work for certain periods, not all of which I can date well now. Eventually she took early retirement to savor life with my dad. They spent a lot of time apart while we were growing up, as she took on the breadwinner role and supported us through the perils of Australian farming. Their sacrifice in putting us through private education is something I always hold prominently in mind.

While she was a converted Catholic, mum adopted a range of new practices in response to cancer's disequilibrium. She did Tai Chi and meditation. She also started reflexology. One of many regrets I have from our time together is refusing the multiple offers she made to give me a foot massage with her new skills. As a punk rock wanna-be, these gestures seemed entirely weird and unnecessary to me. I think anger was my dominant response to mum's sickness. Often it still is.

I wish that I'd had more foresight to enjoy the gifts she was trying to offer.

In my book, I dedicate a chapter to mindfulness—one of several examples of time manipulation and self-suspension that workers employ in the quest for affect management. Reading the ideas of alternative medicine gurus as part of this research brought me to the point of experimenting with some of their recommendations. Now, when I meditate — or try — I have started to understand this as a belated appreciation of the spiritual pleasures my mother was finding towards the end of her life. It also makes me conscious that my response to her death, which has generally involved working and writing through it, may not have been an ideal strategy.

This personal history may explain why *Counterproductive* starts with an account of home economics and ends with an argument about post-secularism and co-immunity. In talking about the myopia of knowledge work, the book addresses many of the same issues of my previous writing projects, but somehow the structure has also become a mirror of certain stages in my own life narrative, filtered through mum. The relief I feel in having completed the manuscript makes me wonder if at least part of my sense of accomplishment has been to find a way to become closer to her, and the messages she was trying to share. While I can't yet figure out if I've succeeded, writing this postscript is a prompt to remember these ideas as part of the record of what the book became and what I have been processing.

Acknowledgments

My primary thanks go to Genevieve Bell for the life-changing opportunity she presented to me over a flat white in the Queen Victoria Building in early 2012. Genevieve's determination and skill forging a path for social science and humanity in the world of engineering inspire so many; her infectious energy helped me contemplate and eventually access the reality of working in a large technology organization. For this book specifically, her extensive library of time and home economics literature has been a constant delight and stimulation. Without her generosity in sharing connections, wisdom, and ideas, this project would have taken a very different and diminished form.

I likewise could not have produced this book without the substantial research contributions made by Ellie Harmon, Thomas Lodato, and Luke Stark. In addition to your own brilliant PhDs, I am happy to know that this publication will stand as an outcome of the thinking, writing, and friendship we have shared since the Intel Science and Technology Center for Social Computing brought us together in 2013. Similarly, I thank Tamara Kneese for her research on smart offices that helped me organize my workload and finish this book.

Every day at Intel I enjoy the privilege of learning from colleagues in engineering, marketing, management, user experience research, design, strategic planning and more. I am grateful to everyone who supported my perverse insistence that this book be finished and the many colleagues who urged me on. I particularly thank Maria Bezaitis and Michael Nordquist for protection while I continued to write despite strong headwinds. I also thank Gregory Bryant and Miles Kingston for taking the time to listen in a world that is not always conducive to hearing.

Key ideas in this book came to fruition through a series of columns guided by the expertise of Rebecca Rosen, who invited me to write for *The Atlantic*. I thank Ian Bogost for this invaluable gift. Specific arguments were explored and tested in various talks at the New School for Social Research (thanks to Shannon Mattern), the Digital Cultures Research Lab at Leuphana University (thanks to Wendy Chun, Paul Feigelfeld, and Armin Beverungen), Copenhagen Business School (thanks to Timon Beyes), the University of Pavia (thanks to Ursula Huws and the COST Network on the Dynamics of Virtual Work), the London School of Economics (thanks to Nigel Dodd and Judy Wajcman), Rochester Institute of Technology (thanks to Jonathan Schroeder and Janet Borgerson), the Chinese University of Hong Kong (thanks to Jack Qiu and Yujie Chen, for coworking research assistance), V2 Lab of Rotterdam (thanks to Seb Olma), the Free University Berlin (thanks to Jan Slaby), the Research Institute for Culture and Media Economies at the University of Leicester (thanks to Mark Banks), the University of Bristol (thanks to Rutvica Andrijasevic), the University of Toronto Techniques of the Corporation conference, the IT University of Copenhagen (thanks to Marisa Cohn), and the 2017 *ephemera* conference at Stockholm Business School (thanks to Sverre Spoelstra).

I acknowledge the vital support of the Pufendorf Institute of Advanced Studies at the University of Lund, where the final draft of the manuscript was completed. Thank you to my Swedish colleagues, especially Magnus Andersson and Stephan Schaefer, for making my dream of working in Scandinavia come true.

For feedback on the manuscript, as well as excellent reading suggestions, I thank Mark Banks, Michelle Dicinoski, Illana Gershon, Ellie Harmon, and two anonymous readers for their incredibly detailed help. Many others are thanked in the text. A further thank you to Michelle for considerable editorial work that saved my eyes, arms, and sanity at the end.

On a personal note, I thank Natasha Dow Schüll, Camille Morhardt, Margie Morris, Sarah Sharma and Judy Wajcman for their example and friendship at critical moments. I thank Craig Robertson for solidarity in filing cabinet nerdery and a place to stay in Cambridge. I thank

Rutvica Andrijasevic and Clare Unwin for UK care and tennis. I thank Carl DiSalvo for cross-country phone calls and Jock Given for regular reading exchanges. Tawny Schlieski and Jay Melican have been wonderful guides to Oregon. Ellie and Luke have been the best companions as well as loving godparents for Monty. Thanks to Susana and her team for cleaning our house so that Jason and I can write and sometimes even play together on weekends at home in Portland. And thanks to my family for ongoing comfort and reminders of other homes.

Finally, for keeping me together with warmth, intelligence, and hilarity every day, for his efforts in becoming the manager of our home enterprise, and for motivating me with his own exceptional writing that has flourished outside the Organization, I thank with all my heart Jason Wilson.

Notes

INTRODUCTION

1   Melissa Gregg, "Getting Things Done: Productivity, Self-Management and
    the Order of Things," in *Networked Affect*, ed. Ken Hillis, Susanna Paasonen,
    and Michael Petit (Cambridge, MA: MIT Press, 2015), 187–202; Melissa Gregg,
    "Presence Bleed: Performing Professionalism Online," in *Theorizing Cultural
    Work: Labour, Continuity and Change in the Creative Industries*, ed. Mark
    Banks, Rosalind Gill, and Stephanie Taylor (London: Routledge, 2013), 122–34;
    Melissa Gregg, *Work's Intimacy* (London: Polity, 2011).

2   I discuss the Fordist idyll that haunts notions of job security after the 2008
    crash in Melissa Gregg, "The Return of Organization Man: Commuter Nar-
    ratives and Suburban Critique," *Cultural Studies Review* 18, no. 2 (September
    2012): 242–61.

3   The first example of the phrase "work smarter, not harder" uncovered in
    the course of this research is in Alec Mackenzie, *The Time Trap* (New York:
    AMACOM, 1972). The longevity of the phrase as a productivity maxim reiter-
    ates the point I make repeatedly in what follows: that time-management man-
    tras offer vernacular speech acts as a substitute for structural workload reform.

4   McKinsey Institute, "Poorer than Their Parents? Flat or Falling Incomes in
    Advanced Economies," report, McKinsey and Company, July 2016, accessed
    March 19, 2017, http://www.mckinsey.com/global-themes/employment-and-growth
    /poorer-than-their-parents-a-new-perspective-on-income-inequality. See also
    Raj Chetty, David Grusky, Maximilian Hell, Nathaniel Hendren, Robert Man-
    duca, and Jimmy Narang, "Executive Summary: The Fading American Dream:
    Trends in Absolute Income Mobility since 1940," Equality of Opportunity proj-
    ect, accessed March 19, 2017, http://www.equality-of-opportunity.org/assets
    /documents/abs_mobility_summary.pdf.

5   Enrico Moretti, *The New Geography of Jobs* (New York: Mariner, 2013).

6   Andrew Ross, *Fast Boat to China: High-Tech Outsourcing and the Consequences of Free Trade—Lessons from Shanghai* (New York: Vintage, 2007); A. Aneesh, *Virtual Migration: The Programming of Globalization* (Durham, NC: Duke University Press, 2006).

7   Classic management textbooks pose this question on behalf of the factory worker, the typical model for productivity theory: see, e.g., Michael Burawoy, *Manufacturing Consent: Changes in the Labor Process under Monopoly Capitalism* (Chicago: University of Chicago Press, 1979).

8   "By now it's evident that the more hours workers put in under more exploitative conditions, the more management sees that it can extract from them, and the *less* it is willing to give them in return": Miya Tokumitsu, *Do What You Love: And Other Lies about Success and Happiness* (New York: Regan Arts, 2015), 153.

9   Stephen R. Barley and Gideon Kunda, "Design and Devotion: Surges of Rational and Normative Ideologies of Control in Managerial Discourse," *Administrative Science Quarterly* 37, no. 3 (1992): 363–99, accessed March 19, 2017, doi: 10.2307/2393449.

10   Carole Pateman, *The Sexual Contract* (Stanford, CA: Stanford University Press, 1988). Melinda Cooper and Catherine Waldby update this history to address new power geometries in *Clinical Labor: Tissue Donors and Research Subjects in the Global Bioeconomy* (Durham, NC: Duke University Press, 2014).

11   Angela McRobbie, *The Aftermath of Feminism: Gender, Culture and Social Change* (London: Sage, 2009). On the enduring quality of the subservient female voice, see Helen Hester, "Technically Female: Women, Machines, and Hyperemployment," paper presented at the Inhuman Symposium, Fridericianum, Kassel, Germany, 2015, accessed March 19, 2017, https://www.youtube.com/watch?v=ZSBefHq7C_0&feature=youtu.be.

12   "The Founder of Personal-Assistant Service Fancy Hands, Ted Roden, on How to Know When the Time Is Right to Start a Business," *Fast Company*, August 18, 2015, accessed March 19, 2017, https://www.fastcompany.com/3049278/ignite-positive-change/the-ceo-of-personal-assistant-service-fancy-hands-ted-roden-on-how-to.

13   Sarah Sharma, "Speed Traps and the Temporal: Of Taxis, Truck Stops, and TaskRabbits," in *The Sociology of Speed: Digital, Organizational, and Social Temporalities*, ed. Judy Wajcman and Nigel Dodd (Oxford: Oxford University Press, 2017), 131–51.

14   My use of the term "technics" is indebted to the work of Lewis Mumford, *Technics and Civilization* (New York: Harcourt, Brace, 1934). It also anticipates my use of Peter Sloterdijk to elaborate an anthropotechnics of mindful labor in later chapters.

15 This is one of several occasions in which I cite direct e-mail marketing campaigns that adopted different slogans over the course of writing. This version from 2014.

16 Guy Standing, *The Precariat: The New Dangerous Class* (London: Bloomsbury Academic, 2011); Rosalind Gill and Andy Pratt, "In the Social Factory? Immaterial Labour, Precariousness and Cultural Work," *Theory, Culture and Society* 25, nos. 7–8 (2008): 1–30; Brett Neilson and Ned Rossiter, "From Precarity to Precariousness and Back Again: Labour, Life and Unstable Networks," *Fibreculture Journal* 5 (2005), accessed March 19, 2017, http://five.fibreculturejournal .org/fcj-022-from-precarity-to-precariousness-and-back-again-labour-life -and-unstable-networks.

17 Lauren Berlant, *Cruel Optimism* (Durham, NC: Duke University Press, 2011).

18 In this way, my argument adds volume to Sarah Sharma's elegant account of chronopolitics and temporal asymmetry in *In the Meantime: Temporality and Cultural Politics* (Durham, NC: Duke University Press, 2014).

19 See Lisa Adkins and Maryanne Dever, eds., *The Post-Fordist Sexual Contract: Working and Living in Contingency* (Houndmills, UK: Palgrave Macmillan, 2016). As will become clear in later chapters, my writing on this topic is strongly indebted to scholars such as Rutvica Andrijasevic and Jack Qiu, who introduced me to the work of Pun Ngai and Jenny Chan. Lilly Irani, Winifred Poster, and Mary Gray all provide essential insights on the "hidden layer" of human labor behind productivity in dispersed digitally connected geographies. I reference these authors elsewhere in text.

20 As Erin Hatton shows, in the history of formal salaried employment, the possibility of alternative hours and flexible scheduling brought about by "temp" and part-time work has been particularly important for minorities to gain a foothold on middle-class incomes, even if this has not obliterated the 9–5 paradigm entirely: Erin Hatton, *The Temp Economy: From Kelly Girls to Permatemps in Postwar America* (Philadelphia: Temple University Press, 2011). Similar arguments are made in relation to today's "gig" economy, which I address in the conclusion.

21 This is one reason prominent knowledge economy companies such as Yahoo and IBM reinstated mandates for employees' presence on campus in recent years. In their efforts to retain leadership in technology innovation, each firm assumed that a degree of time, and therefore productivity, was lost in the effort to locate and connect remote colleagues.

22 Judy Wajcman, *Pressed for Time: The Acceleration of Life in Digital Capitalism* (Chicago: University of Chicago Press, 2015). See also Melissa Mazmanian, Wanda J. Orlikowski, and JoAnne Yates, "The Autonomy Paradox: The Implications of Mobile Email Devices for Knowledge Professionals," *Organization Science* 24 (2013): 1337–57, accessed March 19, 2017, doi: 10.1287/orsc.1120.0806. Ned Rossiter highlights the role of software in coercing management's inter-

ests in *Software, Infrastructure, Labor: A Media Theory of Logistical Night-mares* (London: Routledge, 2016).

23 Wajcman, *Pressed for Time*, 74.

24 Wajcman, *Pressed for Time*, 164.

25 Sharma, *In the Meantime*, 149.

26 The term is Sharma's, and her writing on temporal dissymmetry is a touch-stone for ethically situated writing about time in academia.

27 This is an evolution from my previous writing: see, e.g., Melissa Gregg, "On Friday Night Drinks: Workplace Affects in the Age of the Cubicle," in *The Affect Theory Reader*, ed. Melissa Gregg and Gregory J. Seigworth (Durham, NC: Duke University Press, 2010), 250–68.

28 Richard Sennett, *The Corrosion of Character: The Personal Consequences of Work in the New Capitalism* (New York: W. W. Norton, 1998), 97.

29 On the difficulty of attributing virtue in secular settings, see Alasdair Mac-Intyre, *After Virtue: A Study in Moral Theory*, 2d ed. (Notre Dame, IN: University of Notre Dame Press, 1984).

30 Fellow travelers that have inspired this project include William Davies, *The Happiness Industry: How the Government and Big Business Sold Us Well-Being* (London: Verso, 2015); Charles Duhigg, *Smarter, Faster, Better: The Secrets of Being Productive in Life and in Business* (New York: Random House, 2016); Geert Lovink, "Indifference of the Networked Presence: On Time Management of the Self," in *24/7: Time and Temporality in the Network Society*, ed. Robert Hassan and Ronald E. Purser (Stanford, CA: Stanford Business Books, 2007), 161–72; Tom Lutz, *Doing Nothing: A History of Loafers, Loungers, Slackers, and Bums in America* (New York: Farrar, Straus and Giroux, 2006); Adrian Mackenzie, "The Affect of Efficiency: Personal Productivity Equipment Encounters the Multiple," *Ephemera: Theory and Politics in Organization* 8, no. 2 (2008): 137–56, accessed March 19, 2017, http://www.ephemerajournal.org/sites/default/files/8-2mackenzie.pdf; Corinne Maier, *Hello Laziness: Why Hard Work Doesn't Pay*, trans. David Watson (London: Orion, 2005); Frank Partnoy, *Wait: The Useful Art of Procrastination* (London: Profile, 2012); Andrew Smart, *Auto-Pilot: The Art and Science of Doing Nothing* (New York: OR Books, 2013).

31 Max Weber, *The Protestant Ethic and the Spirit of Capitalism*, trans. Talcott Parsons (London: George Allen and Unwin, 1930). See the important additions to Weber's outlook in the context of U.S. self-help literature and its religious underpinnings in Micki McGee, *Self-Help, Inc.: Makeover Culture in American Life* (Oxford: Oxford University Press, 2005).

32 David Graeber, "On the Phenomenon of Bullshit Jobs," *Strike!* August 17, 2013, accessed March 19, 2017, http://strikemag.org/bullshit-jobs.

33 Barry Schwartz provides a thoughtful reading of labor incentives in *Why We Work* (London: Simon and Schuster, 2015). On meaningless work in aca-

demia, and how to overcome it, see Mats Alvesson, Yiannis Gabriel, and Roland Paulsen, *Return to Meaning: A Social Science with Something to Say* (Oxford: Oxford University Press, 2017).

34   Hence the rise of critical management studies as a fusion of sociology, political economy, and philosophy in European and Commonwealth nations. In this book, I focus on a specific lineage of charismatic business consultants who influence management theory as it has been conventionalized in the United States, since this corresponds with the popular texts and technologies that are also my objects. Management and organization studies has a comparatively progressive agenda in other settings, including Scandinavia, where I write this note. See Chris Steyaert, Timon Beyes, and Martin Parker, eds., *The Routledge Companion to the Humanities and Social Sciences in Management Education* (London: Routledge, 2016).

35   The acronym STEM stands for science, technology, engineering, and mathematics. These combined fields are currently subject to intense scrutiny and campaigning because of their role in shaping the professional ambitions of young women contemplating a career in traditionally male-dominated industries. However, my experience in technology so far suggests that gender bias is as much a problem in management theory and practice (i.e., the level of decision making in large companies), which only exacerbates the lack of diversity in engineering training. Of course, there are notable exceptions in the literature. The pioneering work on gender remains Rosabeth Moss Kanter, *Men and Women of the Corporation* (New York: Basic Books, 1977). Nicole Biggart provides detailed evidence of why women retreat from corporate workplaces to build livelihoods in keeping with their roles and values in her prescient *Charismatic Capitalism: Direct Selling Organizations in America* (Chicago: University of Chicago Press, 1989). Robin Ely, Pamela Stone, and Colleen Ammerman advance a more accountable history of graduate outcomes for women at Harvard Business School in "Rethink What You 'Know' about High-Achieving Women," *Harvard Business Review* (December 2014), accessed July 25, 2016, https://hbr.org/2014/12/rethink-what-you-kno w-about-high-achieving-women. Internationally, the Gender, Work, and Organization conference and the European Group for Organization Studies are important sites of activity. On the constraints arising from the professionalization of diversity work over the past several decades, see Sara Ahmed, *On Being Included: Racism and Diversity in Institutional Life* (Durham, NC: Duke University Press, 2012).

36   For another example, see Melissa Gregg, "The Deficiencies of Tech's 'Pipeline' Metaphor," *The Atlantic*, December 3, 2015, https://www.theatlantic.com /business/archive/2015/12/pipeline-stem/418647.

37   Megan J. Elias, *Stir It Up: Home Economics in American Culture* (Philadelphia: University of Pennsylvania Press, 2008); Laurel D. Graham, "Domesticating Efficiency: Lillian Gilbreth's Scientific Management of Homemakers,

1924–1930," *Signs* 24, no. 31 (1999): 633–74, accessed June 14, 2017, doi 10.1086 /495368; Jonathan Grudin and Gayna Williams, "Two Women Who Pioneered User-Centered Design," ACM *Interactions* 20, no. 6 (2013): 15–20, accessed June 4, 2017, doi: 10.1145/2530538; Jane Lancaster, *Making Time: Lillian Moller Gilbreth—A Life beyond "Cheaper by the Dozen"* (Boston: Northeastern University Press, 2004); Janice Williams Rutherford, *Selling Mrs. Consumer: Christine Frederick and the Rise of Household Efficiency* (Athens: University of Georgia Press, 2003).

38 Among a large list are Silvia Federici, *Revolution at Point Zero: Housework, Reproduction, and Feminist Struggle* (Oakland, CA: PM Press, 2012); Leopoldina Fortunati, *The Arcane of Reproduction: Housework, Prostitution, Labor and Capital* (New York: Autonomedia, 1995); Kylie Jarrett, *Feminism, Labour and Digital Media: The Digital Housewife* (London: Routledge, 2016).

39 Ellen Richards, *The Art of Right Living* (Boston: Whitcomb and Barrows, [1904] 1911).

40 This dynamic explains the outcry against TaskRabbit's "We Do Chores, You Live Life" advertising campaign from 2016, depicting various aspirational activities that could be enjoyed by users of the for-hire labor service. A woman doing yoga with the accompanying text "mopping the floor" directly referenced the housework that had been delegated for the benefit of the woman's health regime: see Michael Zelenko, "Ditch TaskRabbit and Do Your Own Laundry," *The Verge*, September 15, 2016, accessed September 16, 2017, https://www .theverge.com/tech/2016/9/15/12933074/taskrabbit-app-ads-chores-leisure -work-startups. On labor dissymmetry and intersectionality more broadly, see Marion Crain, Winifred Poster and Miriam Cherry, eds., *Invisible Labor: Hidden Work in the Contemporary World* (Oakland: University of California Press, 2016); Barbara Ehrenreich and Arlie Russell Hochschild, eds., *Global Woman: Nannies, Maids, and Sex Workers in the New Economy* (New York: Holt Paperback, 2002); Sharma, *In the Meantime*.

41 I make conjunctural analysis a method of accessing such moments in other writing on the workplace: see Gregg, "On Friday Night Drinks." For a description of conjunctural analysis in the history of cultural studies, see Melissa Gregg, *Cultural Studies' Affective Voices* (Houndmills, UK: Palgrave Macmillan, 2006), chap. 3.

42 Roland Barthes, *Mythologies*, trans. Annette Lavers (Frogmore, UK: Paladin, 1973).

43 Graeme Turner, *Film as Social Practice*, 4th ed. (London: Routledge, [1988] 2006).

44 Peter Sloterdijk, *You Must Change Your Life* (London: Polity, 2013).

45 Michel Foucault, *The Birth of Biopolitics: Lectures at the Collège de France, 1978–1979*, ed. Michael Senellart, trans. Graham Burchell (New York: Palgrave Macmillan, 2008); Nikolas Rose, *Inventing Ourselves: Psychology, Power, and*

Personhood (Cambridge: Cambridge University Press, 1998); Nikolas Rose, *The Politics of Life Itself: Biomedicine, Power, and Subjectivity in the Twenty-First Century* (Princeton, NJ: Princeton University Press, 2006). See also Anthony Giddens, *Modernity and Self-Identity: Self and Society in the Late Modern Age* (Stanford, CA: Stanford University Press, 1991).

46   Timon Beyes explains some of the many fruitful possibilities in Sloterdijk's thinking in "Peter Sloterdijk," in *The Oxford Handbook of Process Philosophy and Organization Studies*, ed. Jenny Helin et al. (Oxford: Oxford University Press, 2014), 567–84.

47   Sloterdijk, *You Must Change Your Life*, 292.

48   Here and elsewhere my thinking is heavily indebted to Illana Gershon, *Down and Out in the New Economy: How People Find (or Don't Find) Work Today* (Chicago: University of Chicago Press, 2017).

49   While not restricted to high-tech firms, mindfulness is certainly more established in Silicon Valley as a result of high-profile practitioners at Google, Facebook, Medium, and others: see David Gelles, *Mindful Work: How Meditation Is Changing Business from the Inside Out* (Boston: Mariner, 2016).

50   Vanessa Valenti, "Building a Culture of Care in Online Feminist Activism," paper presented at the Symposium on Social Media and Psychosocial Wellbeing, Rutgers University, New Brunswick, NJ, April 2014. Micki McGee outlines her excellent theory of the belabored self in *Self-Help, Inc.* I thank Ilana Gershon and Sverre Spoelstra for immediately noting this connection.

51   Eviatar Zerubavel, *Hidden Rhythms: Schedules and Calendars in Social Life* (Berkeley: University of California Press, [1981] 1985).

52   Adam Fish, "Technology Retreats and the Politics of Social Media," *Triple C: Communication, Capitalism and Critique* 15, no. 1 (2017): 355–69, accessed June 14, 2017, http://triple-c.at/index.php/tripleC/article/view/807/992; Fred Turner, "Burning Man at Google: A Cultural Infrastructure for New Media Production," *New Media and Society* 11, nos. 1–2 (February–March 2009): 73–94, accessed June 4, 2017, doi: 10.1177/1461444808099575; Fred Turner, *From Counterculture to Cyberculture: Stewart Brand, the Whole Earth Network, and the Rise of Digital Utopianism* (Chicago: University of Chicago Press, 2006); R. John Williams, "Technê-Zen and the Spiritual Quality of Global Capitalism," *Critical Inquiry* 37 (Autumn 2011): 17–70, accessed June 14, 2017, doi: 10.1086/661643.

53   Kathi Weeks, *The Problem with Work: Feminism, Marxism, Antiwork Politics, and Postwork Imaginaries* (Durham, NC: Duke University Press, 2011). See also Federici, *Revolution at Point Zero*; Fortunati, *The Arcane of Reproduction: Housework, Prostitution, Labor and Capital*; Jarrett, *Feminism, Labour and Digital Media*.

54   Peter Sloterdijk, *Bubbles—Spheres Volume 1: Microspherology*, trans. Wieland Hoban (Cambridge, MA: MIT Press, 2011); Peter Sloterdijk, *Foam—Spheres Volume III: Plural Spherology*, trans. Wieland Hoban (Cambridge, MA: MIT

Press, 2016); Peter Sloterdijk, *Globes—Spheres Volume II: Macrospherology*, trans. Wieland Hoban (Cambridge, MA: MIT Press, 2013).

55 Antonio García Martínez, *Chaos Monkeys: Obscene Fortune and Random Failure in Silicon Valley*, Kindle ed. (New York: HarperCollins, 2016), loc. 3582.

56 Mark Banks, *Creative Justice: Cultural Industries, Work and Inequality* (London: Rowman and Littlefield, 2017).

57 Trebor Scholz, *Platform Cooperativism: Challenging the Corporate Sharing Economy* (New York: Rosa Luxemburg, 2016), accessed August 30, 2016, http://www.rosalux-nyc.org/wp-content/files_mf/scholz_platformcoop_5.9.201650.pdf; Nick Srnicek, *Platform Capitalism* (Cambridge, UK: Polity, 2016).

1 A BRIEF HISTORY OF TIME MANAGEMENT

1 I include my own previous writing in this assessment. However, I remain chronically disappointed with analyses of work that continue to use heteronormative, nuclear-family parenting as a frame to lament the lost sanctity of the home—for example, Bridget Schulte, *Overwhelmed: Work, Love, and Play When No One Has the Time* (New York: Picador, 2004), which updates Arlie Russell Hochschild's groundbreaking *The Time Bind: When Work Becomes Home and Home Becomes Work* (New York: Henry Holt, 1997). These popular accounts can be reticent to acknowledge the empirical reality that women have *always* worked through and amid others' leisure, including their own: see Leopoldina Fortunati, "Gender and the Mobile Phone," in *Mobile Technologies: From Telecommunications to Media*, ed. Gerard Goggin and Larissa Hjorth (London: Routledge, 2009), 23–34; Larissa Hjorth, *Mobile Media in the Asia-Pacific: Gender and the Art of Being Mobile* (London: Routledge, 2009); Judy Wajcman, *Pressed for Time: The Acceleration of Life in Digital Capitalism* (Chicago: University of Chicago Press, 2015); Kathi Weeks, *The Problem with Work: Feminism, Marxism, Antiwork Politics, and Postwork Imaginaries* (Durham, NC: Duke University Press, 2011). In line with feminist and queer scholarship, I prefer to see women's work as the basis for another vocabulary of accomplishment that sustains more than just the individual. This is important in my later chapters, which describe the conditions of labor in cognitive capitalism and the growing experience of women's historically task-oriented relationship to time: see Cristina Morini, "The Feminization of Labour in Cognitive Capitalism," *Feminist Review* 87 (2007): 40–59, accessed May 5, 2017, doi: 10.1057/palgrave.fr.9400367.

2 Christine Frederick, *Household Engineering* (San Bernardino, CA: Ulan, [1915] 2014), 1–3.

3 There were similar appeals to housewives in Australia, as illustrated in advertisements analyzed in Ann Game and Rosemary Pringle, *Gender at Work*

(Sydney: Allen and Unwin, 1983). Sweden also had domestic science advocates and strong debate over the appropriate compensation for women's work. Later feminist scholars scorned these early practitioners of "housewife Taylorism." I thank Sune Sunesson for sharing this history with me.

4   Megan J. Elias, *Stir It Up: Home Economics in American Culture* (Philadelphia: University of Pennsylvania Press, 2008). The American Home Economics Association was founded in 1909 (the year before Brandeis coined the term "scientific management"), after some debate over whether the field should be called "home science."

5   "Bacteriology and sanitation were the foundational courses in most of the home economics programs that emerged around 1900": Elias, *Stir It Up*, 20.

6   Elias, *Stir It Up*, 11. Richards's attraction to notions of racial superiority is hinted at in the epigram she chooses from H. G. Wells's *Mankind in the Making*: "It is not birth rates that want raising, but Ideals."

7   Sarah A. Leavitt, *From Catharine Beecher to Martha Stewart: A Cultural History of Domestic Advice* (Chapel Hill: University of North Carolina Press), 9, 24.

8   Catharine Beecher and Harriet Beecher Stowe, *The American Woman's Home*, ed. Nicole Tonkovitch (Hartford, CT: Harriet Beecher Stowe Center, [1869] 2002), 17.

9   Beecher and Beecher Stowe, *The American Woman's Home*, 174.

10 Beecher and Beecher Stowe, *The American Woman's Home*, 164.

11 Beecher and Beecher Stowe, *The American Woman's Home*, 24.

12 Beecher and Beecher Stowe, *The American Woman's Home*, 23.

13 Beecher and Beecher Stowe, *The American Woman's Home*, 237.

14 Beecher and Beecher Stowe, *The American Woman's Home*, 236.

15 Beecher and Beecher Stowe, *The American Woman's Home*, 246. The attitude was shared by writers such as Christine Frederick, who offers a surfeit of detail. "While there are exceptions, it seems to be true that workers of these nationalities have the following characteristics: Irish (good hearted but often untidy, inefficient, little responsibility) Scotch-English (great dependability, sense of duty, well trained). German (thrifty, hard-working, capable of much manual work). Scandinavian (self-reliant, sometimes tricky, often extravagant, excellent as laundresses and cleaners). Polish-Lithuanian, etc. (emotional, little responsibility, inefficient, but frequently good cooks). French (very neat, thrifty cooks and sewers, sometimes unreliable or looking to their own interest, but excellent managers; not capable of heavy work)": Frederick, *Household Engineering*, 447.

16 Beecher and Beecher Stowe, *The American Woman's Home*, 170.

17 Beecher and Beecher Stowe, *The American Woman's Home*, 170.

18 Susan Buck-Morss, "Envisioning Capital: Political Economy on Display," *Critical Inquiry* 21, no. 2 (1995), 434–67, accessed June 13, 2017, doi 10.1086/448759.

19   The term "happiness minutes" comes from Lillian Gilbreth: see Jill Lepore, "Not So Fast," *New Yorker*, October 12, 2009, accessed July 25, 2016, http://www.newyorker.com/magazine/2009/10/12/not-so-fast#ixzz35hOEefI4.

20   Christine Frederick, *The New Housekeeping* (Philadelphia: Curtis Publishing, 1912).

21   I obtained my copy of the 1923 edition through Amazon's print-on-demand service.

22   Frederick, *Household Engineering*, 76.

23   Frederick, *Household Engineering*, 92.

24   Janice Williams Rutherford, *Selling Mrs. Consumer: Christine Frederick and the Rise of Household Efficiency* (Athens: University of Georgia Press, 2003), 93.

25   Frederick, *Household Engineering*, 82.

26   Jane Lancaster, *Making Time: Lillian Moller Gilbreth—A Life beyond "Cheaper by the Dozen"* (Boston: Northeastern University Press, 2004); this ad copy and an illustration of the desk appear in a gallery following page 172.

27   Gilbreth later received recognition for her work, becoming the first female member of the Society of Industrial Engineers in 1921. She and Frank (posthumously) were awarded the Gantt Gold Medal from the American Society of Mechanical Engineers and the American Management Association in 1944. In 1966, Gilbreth was the first woman to receive the Hoover Medal for distinguished public service by an engineer.

28   Rutherford, *Selling Mrs. Consumer*, 51.

29   Frederick, *Household Engineering*, 194–95.

30   Frederick, *Household Engineering*, 96.

31   Frederick W. Taylor, *The Principles of Scientific Management* (New York: Harper and Brothers, 1911).

32   Robert Kanigel, *The One Best Way: Frederick Winslow Taylor and the Enigma of Efficiency* (Cambridge, MA: MIT Press, 1997).

33   Lepore, "Not So Fast."

34   "Gilbreth Time and Motion Study in Bricklaying," film, accessed August 16, 2015, https://www.youtube.com/watch?v=lDg9REgkCQk.

35   "Original Films of Frank B. Gilbreth (Part I)," accessed August 16, 2015, https://archive.org/details/OriginalFilm.

36   Scott Curtis, "Images of Efficiency: The Films of Frank B. Gilbreth" in *Films That Work: The Productivity of Media*, ed. Vinzenz Hediger and Patrick Vonderau (Amsterdam: Amsterdam University Press, 2009), 85–99.

37   A selection of these films is available on YouTube, at https://www.youtube.com/watch?v=11lKItGNuiY.

38   "Gilbreth Reforms a Typist," film, accessed August 16, 2015, https://www.youtube.com/watch?v=8iTOSgAnJ54.

39   Curtis, "Images of Efficiency," 93. An earlier version of this section appears in Melissa Gregg, "The Athleticism of Accomplishment: Speed in the Work-

place," in *The Sociology of Speed: Digital, Organizational, and Social Tempo-ralities*, ed. Judy Wajcman and Nigel Dodd (Oxford: Oxford University Press, 2016), 102–14.

40   Lillian Gilbreth, *The Psychology of Management: The Function of the Mind in Determining, Teaching and Installing Methods of Least Waste* (New York: Sturgis and Walton, 1914), 33–34.

41   Gilbreth, *The Psychology of Management*, 36–37.

42   Gilbreth, *The Psychology of Management*, 36–37, emphasis added.

43   Gilbreth, *The Psychology of Management*, 36–37.

44   Laura Mulvey, "Visual Pleasure and Narrative Cinema," *Screen* 16, no. 3 (1975): 6–18.

45   Richard Lindstrom, "'They All Believe They Are Undiscovered Mary Pickfords': Workers, Photography, and Scientific Management," *Technology and Culture* 41, no. 4 (2000): 725–51, accessed June 4, 2017, doi: 10.1353/tech.2000 .0170.

46   Typing world championships were an annual event in the early 1900s, with press coverage often lamenting the limitations of human motion in relation to machine capacity. Robert Messenger's rich archive at OzTypewriter shows the stadium-size seating accommodating these spectacles of speed: "Last Days of Speed Typing Glory," *OzTypewriter: The Wonderful World of Typewriters*, November 15, 2014, accessed July 25, 2016, http://oztypewriter.blogspot. com/2014/11/last-days-of-speed-typing-glory.html.

47   An exception to dominant accounts of Hawthorne's significance was Mary Gilson's review of the Roethlisberger tome, which chastised the authors for "discovering the obvious." Adding to my point about women's absence from the management canon, her scathing critique attributed the study's unremarkable findings to the researchers' "inexperience in the field of industrial practice": see Charles D. Wrege and Ronald G. Greenwood, "Mary B. Gilson—A Historical Study of the Neglected Accomplishments of a Woman Who Pioneered in Personnel Management," unpublished paper, accessed June 13, 2017, https://www.thebhc.org/sites/default/files/beh/BEHprint/v011/p0035-p0042 .pdf, 40.

48   Augustine Brannigan, "Social Psychology Engineers Wealth and Intelligence: The Hawthorne and Pygmalion Effects," in *The Rise and Fall of Social Psychology: The Use and Misuse of the Experimental Method* (New York: Walter de Gruyter, 2004), 63–90.

49   Reproductions of the graphs can be seen in these samples from the Harvard Business School collection: http://www.library.hbs.edu/hc/hawthorne/03 .html#three.

50   Richard Gillespie, *Manufacturing Knowledge: A History of the Hawthorne Experiments* (Cambridge: Cambridge University Press, 1991), 55.

51   Gillespie, *Manufacturing Knowledge*, 51.

52 Gillespie, *Manufacturing Knowledge*, 51.

53 Elton Mayo, *Human Problems of Industrial Civilization* (New York: Macmillan, 1933), 35.

54 Richard C. S. Trahair, *Elton Mayo: The Humanist Temper* (New Brunswick, NJ: Transaction, [1984] 2005), 198.

55 Trahair, *Elton Mayo*, 199.

56 See Zaleznik's "Foreword" in Trahair, *Elton Mayo*, 3.

57 Trahair, *Elton Mayo*, 112, 117.

58 Trahair, *Elton Mayo*, 112.

59 Trahair, *Elton Mayo*, 114.

60 There is one edited collection dedicated solely to Mayo that I have been unable to access in the course of writing, because it is prohibitively expensive.

61 Jean Piaget, *Six Psychological Studies*, trans. Anita Tenzer (New York: Vintage, 1968), v.

62 Gillespie, *Manufacturing Knowledge*, 54–55. This context helps to explain one of Lillian Gilbreth's later projects proving that the menstrual cycle did not have any negative impact on women's productivity: see Jonathan Grudin and Gayna Williams, "Two Women Who Pioneered User-Centered Design," ACM *Interactions* 20, no. 6 (October 2013): 16, accessed June 4, 2017, doi: 10.1145/2530538.

63 Trahair, *Elton Mayo*, 229. In Alex Carey's reading of the archive, "this 'lack of attention to work and preference for conversing together for considerable periods' was judged to be reaching such proportions that the 'experiment was being jeopardized and something had to be done.' A variety of disciplinary procedures of increasing severity were applied, but with little effect. Finally, the leaders in talking (operators 1A and 2A) were dismissed from the test room 'for lack of cooperation which would have otherwise necessitated greatly increased disciplinary measures'": Alex Carey, "The Hawthorne Studies: A Radical Criticism," *American Sociological Review* 32, no. 3 (1967): 414.

64 Trahair, *Elton Mayo*, 230.

65 Mayo, *Human Problems of Industrial Civilization*, 114–15.

66 Gillespie, *Manufacturing Knowledge*, 73

67 Carey, "The Hawthorne Studies," 416.

68 As Friedrich Kittler notes about the typewriter, "It was precisely their marginal position in the power system of script that forced women to develop their manual dexterity": Friedrich A. Kittler, *Gramophone, Film, Typewriter* (Stanford, CA: Stanford University Press, 1999), 194. For a more contemporary view of women's dexterous work in manufacturing, see Leslie T. Chang, *Factory Girls: From Village to City in a Changing China* (New York: Spiegel and Grau, 2009).

69 Another complaint the girls raised was that researchers could see too much of their legs, leading to a small panel being installed on the shared workbench in the interests of modesty.

70 Gillespie, *Manufacturing Knowledge*, 59.

71   The Historical Collections at the Harvard Business School's Baker Library
     hold the raw data for the Hawthorne studies, selections from which are fea-
     tured on a special website, http://www.library.hbs.edu/hc/hawthorne/intro
     .html#i, describing the Human Relations Movement.

72   See Jenny Chan, "A Suicide Survivor: The Life of a Chinese Worker," *New Tech-
     nology, Work and Employment* 28, no. 2 (2013): 84–99, accessed June 13, 2017,
     doi: 10.1111/ntwe.12007; Jenny Chan, Pun Ngai and Mark Selden, "The Politics
     of Global Production: Apple, Foxconn and China's New Working Class," *New
     Technology, Work and Employment* 28, no. 2: (2013): 100–15, accessed June 13,
     2017, doi: 10.1111/ntwe.12008; Jack Linchuan Qiu, *Goodbye iSlave: A Manifesto
     for Digital Abolition* (Urbana-Champaign: University of Illinois Press, 2016).

73   Jeffrey A. Sonnenfeld, "Shedding Light on the Hawthorne Studies," *Journal
     of Occupational Behavior* 6 (1985): 124, accessed June 13, 2017, doi: 10.1002/job
     .4030060203.

74   Michel Foucault, *The History of Sexuality, Volume One: An Introduction*, trans.
     Robert Hurley (New York: Pantheon, 1978).

75   Walter Scott, *Increasing Human Efficiency in Business* (New York: Macmillan,
     1911).

2   EXECUTIVE ATHLETICISM

1   Nigel Thrift, *Knowing Capitalism* (London: Sage, 2005).

2   David Harvey, *A Brief History of Neoliberalism* (Oxford: Oxford University
    Press, 2005).

3   Stuart Crainer and Des Dearlove, *Gravy Training: Inside the Business of Busi-
    ness Schools* (San Francisco: Jossey-Bass, 1999); Andrzej Huczynski, *Manage-
    ment Gurus*, rev. ed. (London: Routledge, 2006).

4   Michel Foucault, "An Aesthetics of Existence," in *Politics, Philosophy, Culture:
    Interviews and Other Writings, 1977–1984*, ed. Lawrence D. Kritzman (New
    York: Routledge, 1988).

5   In cultural studies, it is characteristic to draw on popular texts to understand
    the reproduction of ideology, even if the field has shown reluctance to ap-
    ply this principle to popular genres of business: see Melissa Gregg, "The Ef-
    fective Academic Executive," *Cultural Studies* 29, no. 4 (2015): 590–608, doi:
    10.1080/09502386.2014.1000609.

6   A case in point is the tale of Charles Schwab, onetime president of Bethlehem
    Steel, whose tale of challenging a consultant to improve his company's pro-
    ductivity appears in, among others, John Adair, *Effective Time Management:
    How to Save Time and Spend It Wisely* (London: Pan, 1982), 61, and R. Alec
    Mackenzie, *The Time Trap: How to Get More Done In Less Time* (New York:
    McGraw-Hill, 1975): 38–39.

7   Adrian Mackenzie, "The Affect of Efficiency," 143.

8   Judith Butler, *Gender Trouble: Feminism and the Subversion of Identity* (New York: Routledge, 1999).

9   Like Butler, I am extending Simone de Beauvoir's foundational observation, "One is not born, but rather becomes (a) woman": Simone de Beauvoir, *The Second Sex*, trans. H. M. Parshley (Harmondsworth, UK: Penguin, [1949] 1972).

10   Gideon Haigh, *The Office: A Hardworking History* (Carlton, Australia: Miegunyah, 2012), 545.

11   William H. Whyte, *The Organization Man* (Harmondsworth, UK: Penguin, 1956).

12   As Whyte explained, in his account of *The Organization Man*, loyalty to the right company contributed to the worker's social status. As such, for U.S. commentators of the time, the principal anxiety raised by organization life was whether attachment to a large bureaucracy necessarily produced conformity. Both Whyte's account and C. Wright Mills's *White Collar* (New York: Oxford University Press, 1951) saw the organization as a threat to individual autonomy. In retrospect, we can see that such concerns over individual agency in many ways misrecognized the values espoused by management heavyweights who were often on the lookout for the "few wild ducks" that would keep the company machine from stagnating: Thomas J. Watson Sr., interviewed in Albert Maysles and David Maysles's film *IBM: A Self Portrait* (1964).

13   David Allen, *Getting Things Done* (New York: Viking, 2001), 8. The overlaps are striking between Allen's commonsense productivity guidance and Nikolas Rose's Foucauldian reading of the art of self-governance in *Powers of Freedom: Reframing Political Thought* (London: Cambridge University Press, 1999).

14   Cited in, among others, Adair, *Effective Time Management*, 27, 55.

15   System Company, *How to Systematize the Day's Work: 87 Plans and Shortcuts Used and Proved at the Desks of 43 Executives*, 9th ed. (Chicago: A. W. Shaw, 1911).

16   This combination of features populates other management classics, iterating on Peter Drucker, *The Effective Executive* (London: Warner, [1967] 1991).

17   System Company, *How to Systematize the Day's Work*, 8. The masculine pronoun adopted in this period reinforces the sense that a man's experience of time is representative of executive labor. Time-management manuals have dealt with this history in different ways over the years. James McCay's *The Management of Time* contains one of the few explicit acknowledgments of gender noted in this study. The 1995 Prentice Hall edition begins by noting that, at the original publishing date of 1959, "Women had not entered the work force in today's large numbers, and those in the work force had not yet been able to move into managerial and executive positions. While McCay's thoughts and advice are just as insightful today as they were then, sexism, in particular, unbiased language, in general, were not concerns of men and women in the '50s

work place": James McCay, *The Management of Time* (Englewood Cliffs, NJ: Prentice Hall, [1959] 1995), xii.

18 System Company, *How to Systematize the Day's Work*, 34.

19 System Company, *How to Systematize the Day's Work*, 20.

20 System Company, *How to Systematize the Day's Work*, 23.

21 System Company, *How to Systematize the Day's Work*, 41.

22 See, e.g., Tom Peters, *Thriving on Chaos: Handbook for a Management Revolution* (New York: Alfred A. Knopf, 1987); Anthony Robbins, *Awaken the Giant Within: How to Take Immediate Control of Your Mental, Emotional, Physical and Financial Destiny!* (New York: Simon and Schuster, 1991). Andrzej Huczynski is one of several writers to show how these gurus trade on the capacity "to transport readers symbolically from a world of everyday experience to a mythical realm": Huczynski, *Management Gurus*, 228.

23 Allyson Lewis, *The Seven Minute Difference: Small Steps to Big Changes* (Chicago: Kaplan, 2006); Laura Stack, *Leave the Office Earlier: The Productivity Pro® Shows You How to Do More in Less Time . . . and Feel Great about It* (New York: Broadway, 2004); Brian Tracy, *Eat That Frog! 21 Great Ways to Stop Procrastinating and Get More Done in Less Time* (San Francisco: Berrett-Koehler, 2006).

24 Stephen Arterburn, *Winning at Work without Losing at Love* (Nashville: Thomas Nelson, 1994).

25 Alan Lakein, *How to Get Control of Your Time and Your Life* (New York: Penguin, 1973), 117.

26 Richard Koch elaborates in *The 80-20 Principle* (New York: Crown Business, 1999).

27 Drucker, *The Effective Executive*, 36.

28 Edwin C. Bliss, *Getting Things Done: The ABCs of Time Management* (New York: Bantam, [1976] 1980).

29 Stephen Covey, *The 7 Habits of Highly Effective People* (New York: Simon and Schuster, 1989).

30 Bliss, *Getting Things Done*, 19.

31 Bliss, *Getting Things Done*, 20.

32 Bliss, *Getting Things Done*, 20.

33 Drucker, *The Effective Executive*, 37–38.

34 Adair, *Effective Time Management*, 27–34.

35 Adair, *Effective Time Management*, 27.

36 R. Alec Mackenzie, *The Time Trap: How to Get More Done in Less Time* (New York: McGraw-Hill, 1975).

37 Adair, *Effective Time Management*, 30.

38 Adair, *Effective Time Management*, 32; see also Mackenzie, *The Time Trap*, 24.

39 See chapter 14 of Lakein, *How to Get Control of Your Time and Your Life*.

40 Lakein, *How to Get Control of Your Time and Your Life*, 136.

41 See http://www.amazon.com/Eat-That-Frog-Great-Procrastinating/dp/1576754227 /ref=asap_bc?ie=UTF8, accessed July 24, 2016.

42 Bliss, *Getting Things Done*, 9. The term "wastebasketry" is elaborated in the glossary (115).

43 Bliss, *Getting Things Done*, 24. The counterproductive effects of multitasking in the workplace remain subject to debate. A representative overview from the field of psychology is Gloria Mark, "Multitasking in the Digital Age," *Synthesis Lectures on Human-Centered Informatics* 8, no. 3 (April 2015): 1–113, accessed July 24, 2016, doi: https://doi.org/10.2200/S00635ED1V01Y201503HCI029.

44 Bliss, *Getting Things Done*, 39.

45 "Five Things Your Emails Need to Include to Get People to Read and Respond," *Fast Company*, April 27, 2015, accessed July 24, 2016, http://www.fastcompany .com/3045439/work-smart/the-5-things-your-emails-need-to-include-to-get -people-to-read-and-respond.

46 Adair, *Effective Time Management*, 8.

47 Mackenzie, *The Time Trap*, 1.

48 Adair, *Effective Time Management*, 47.

49 Accommodating the privileged expectations of elite frequent flyers is the focus of critique in Sarah Sharma, *In the Meantime: Temporality and Cultural Politics* (Durham, NC: Duke University Press, 2014). The peculiar intimacy of the frequent flyer, specifically as it is portrayed in the film *Up in the Air*, is discussed in Melissa Gregg, "White Collar Intimacy," in *Digital Cultures and the Politics of Emotion*, ed. Athina Karatzogianni and Adi Kuntsman (London: Routledge, 2012),147–64.

50 Lakein, *How to Get Control of Your Time and Your Life*, 114.

51 R. Alec Mackenzie, *The Time Trap*, 68.

52 Lakein, *How to Get Control of Your Time and Your Life*, 6.

53 Lakein, *How to Get Control of Your Time and Your Life*, 9.

54 Allen, *Getting Things Done*, 18.

55 Allen, *Getting Things Done*, 15.

56 Allen, *Getting Things Done*, 181.

57 Allen, *Getting Things Done*, 35.

58 Merlin Mann, whose *43 Folders* blog took its title from the organizational system Allen's book outlines, became a minor celebrity on the Silicon Valley speaking circuit by espousing the values behind Allen's ideas. Mann's "Inbox Zero" talk to Google employees in 2007 marks a high point in enthusiasm for time management techniques before productivity became part of a more comprehensive interest in the quantified self. I discuss this both in chapter 3 in this volume and in Melissa Gregg, "Getting Things Done: Productivity, Self-Management and the Order of Things," in *Networked Affect*, ed. Ken Hillis, Susanna Paasonen and Michael Petit (Cambridge, MA: MIT Press, 2015), 187–202.

59　A number of these allusions appear in Allen's TED talk, "Getting Things Done: The Art of Stress-Free Productivity," accessed July 24, 2016, http://ed.ted.com/on /oqfsvelw. On flow, the definitive source that continues to influence the world of business and IT is Mihaly Csikszentmihalyi, *Finding Flow: The Psychology of Engagement with Everyday Life* (New York: Basic, 1997).

60　Allen, *Getting Things Done*, 11.

61　Ulrich Bröckling, "Gendering the Enterprising Self: Subjectification Programs and Gender Differences in Guides to Success," *Distinktion*, no. 11 (2005): 7–23, accessed June 13, 2017, doi: 10.1080/1600910X.2005.9672910.

62　Bröckling, "Gendering the Enterprising Self," 18.

63　Lakein, *How to Get Control of Your Time and Your Life*, 8.

64　Dale Carnegie, *How to Win Friends and Influence People*, rev. ed. (North Ryde, Australia: Eden, [1936] 1988), 26.

65　Recent publications reflect ongoing popular interest in habit formation in securing the conditions of success, updating the timeless appeal of Covey's *The Seven Habits of Highly Effective People*: see Charles Duhigg, *The Power of Habit: Why We Do What We Do in Life and Business* (New York: Random House, 2012).

66　Mackenzie, *The Time Trap*, 32–34.

67　Allen, *Getting Things Done*, xviii.

68　See Micki McGee, *Self-Help Inc.: Makeover Culture in American Life* (Oxford: Oxford University Press, 2005).

69　Stack, *Leave the Office Earlier*; Kris Cole, *Make Time: Practical Time Management that Really Works!* (Frenchs Forest, Australia: Pearson Education, 2001).

70　Barry Schwartz, *Queueing and Waiting: Studies in the Social Organization of Access and Delay* (Chicago: University of Chicago Press, 1975).

71　Bliss, *Getting Things Done*, 19.

72　Allen, *Getting Things Done*, 43.

73　Allen, *Getting Things Done*, 43.

74　Kenneth Burke, "Literature as Equipment for Living," in *The Critical Tradition: Classic Texts and Contemporary Trends*, 2d ed., ed. David H. Richter (Boston: Bedford, 1998), 593–95.

75　This responsible attitude culminates in rhetorical exercises. Following an activity that advises readers to rank time wasters in order of priority, Mackenzie asks, "Do you agree that in *you* lie both the major causes and the major solutions of your problems with wasted time?" For Mackenzie, "At the heart of time management is management of self": Mackenzie, *The Time Trap*, 7.

76　Burke, "Literature as Equipment for Living," 593.

77　Burke, "Literature as Equipment for Living," 596.

78　For more examples like these, see Ralph Keyes, *Timelock: How Life Got So Hectic and What You Can Do about It* (New York: HarperCollins, 1991).

79 Mark Banks, "Fit and Working Again? The Instrumental Leisure of the 'Creative Class,'" *Environment and Planning A* 41, no. 3 (2009): 668–81, accessed July 24, 2016, doi: 10.1068/a40333.

80 Pierre Bourdieu, "The Forms of Capital," in *Handbook of Theory and Research for the Sociology of Education*, ed. John Richardson (New York: Greenwood, 1986): 241–58.

81 Mackenzie, "The Affect of Efficiency," 137.

82 Becoming an entrepreneur of the self is "a desensitization program," according to Bröckling, "Gendering the Enterprising Self," 20. Collegial solidarity is limited in the contemporary workplace "to those who can foster one's own progress." Bröckling notes the social Darwinism of networking advice that tells women, "Surround yourself with people who are on the same path as you are and who want to win. . . . Avoid dealing with the self-proclaimed victims of this world. Do not feel bad about this, but rather respect the self-responsibility of these people, too. This behavior is not unsociable and it does not indicate a lack of philanthropy. You have the right to make an uncompromising selection of people who are good for you, who have left behind the comfortable zone of unassumingness like you": Bröckling, "Gendering the Enterprising Self," 20 (quoting Sonja A. Buholzer, *Frauen starten durch: Erfolgsstrategien für Gewinnerinnen* [Landsberg am Lech, Germany: MVG Verlag, 1999]: 173).

83 Peter Sloterdijk, *You Must Change Your Life* (London: Polity, 2013).

84 Sloterdijk, *You Must Change Your Life*, 26.

85 Sloterdijk, *You Must Change Your Life*, 26.

86 Bröckling, "Gendering the Enterprising Self," 18.

87 Drucker, *The Effective Executive*, 27.

88 Mackenzie, *The Time Trap*, 16.

89 Drucker, *The Effective Executive*, 37.

90 Sloterdijk, *You Must Change Your Life*, 217, 222.

3 THE AESTHETICS OF ACTIVITY

1 J. J. McCorvey, "Productivity Apps Are Booming," *Fast Company*, November 18, 2013, accessed July 25, 2016, http://www.fastcompany.com/3021565/productivity-apps-are-booming,

2 The analysis in this chapter was written in close conversation with Luke Stark, whose report on the empirical study advanced many of the arguments to do with design aesthetics. More of his writing on visceral design is on display in Luke Stark, "Come on Feel the Data (and Smell It)" *The Atlantic*, May 19, 2014, accessed July 25, 2016, http://www.theatlantic.com/technology/archive/2014/05/data-visceralization/370899, and in subsequent research explaining the impact of platform design on the experience of workers in the gig econ-

omy. See Alex Rosenblat and Luke Stark, "Algorithmic Labor and Information Asymmetries: A Case Study of Uber's Drivers," *International Journal of Communication* 10, no. 27 (2016): 3758–84, accessed June 4, 2017, https://ssrn.com /abstract=2686227.

3   This reflects industry trends that describe work-related technology use as enabling "productivity." By contrast, apps classified under Utilities and Business generally have both straightforward and flexible practical functions as tools (spreadsheet readers, scanning apps, flashlights), though it should be noted many of the productivity apps surveyed here are cross-listed in Business.

4   Defined as the two hundred most downloaded free and paid apps, respectively.

5   See https://www.tomorrow.do, accessed June 3, 2017.

6   See http://3030.binaryhammer.com and http://taskplayerapp.com, respectively, accessed June 3, 2017.

7   See https://en.todoist.com/windows, accessed June 3, 2017.

8   Donald A. Norman, *Emotional Design: Why We Love (or Hate) Everyday Things* (Cambridge, MA: Basic, 2004).

9   See http://www.taasky.com, accessed April 7, 2016.

10   Clear's website, originally at http://clearquot.es/clear, accessed June 3, 2017, was no longer loading at the time of revision.

11   See https://ifttt.com, accessed June 3, 2017.

12.   Ian Bogost, "Hyperemployment, or the Exhausting Work of the Technology User," *The Atlantic*, November 8, 2013, accessed June 3, 2017, http://www.the atlantic.com/technology/archive/2013/11/hyperemployment-or-the-exhausting -work-of-the-technology-user/281149.

13   Mynd is no longer operating at the time of writing. For Smart Day, see http:// www.mysmartday.com/, accessed June 3, 2017. Tempo Smart Calendar was acquired by Salesforce.com in 2015.

14   See https://swiftkey.com/en, accessed June 3, 2017.

15   See https://swiftkey.com/en/keyboard/android, accessed June 3, 2017.

16   Parts of this section previously appeared in Melissa Gregg, "Getting Things Done: Productivity, Self-Management and the Order of Things," in *Networked Affect*, ed. Ken Hillis, Susanna Paasonen, and Michael Petit (Cambridge, MA: MIT Press, 2015), 187–202.

17   The key protagonist in this domain is Sherry Turkle, in a sequence of cautionary publications: see Sherry Turkle, *Alone Together: Why We Expect More from Technology and Less from Each Other* (New York: Basic Books, 2011); Sherry Turkle, *Reclaiming Conversation: The Power of Talk in a Digital Age* (New York: Penguin, 2015).

18   See https://www.youtube.com/watch?v=z9UjeTMb3Yk, accessed July 25, 2016.

19   Jane Gallop, *Anecdotal Theory* (Durham, NC: Duke University Press, 2002); Meaghan Morris, *Identity Anecdotes: Translation and Media Culture* (London: Sage, 2006).

20 Dale Carnegie, *How to Win Friends and Influence People*, rev. ed. (North Ryde, Australia: Eden, [1936] 1988).

21 Michel Foucault, *The History of Sexuality, Volume One: An Introduction*, trans. Robert Hurley (New York: Pantheon, 1978).

22 See http://www.43folders.com, accessed June 3, 2017. The site was last updated on October 17, 2011.

23 Writing in *The Guardian*, Oliver Burkeman revisits this material and discovers that Mann failed to deliver his own productivity book to the publisher on time—effectively demonstrating the failure of his own system: see Oliver Burkeman, "Why Time Management Is Ruining Our Lives," 2016, accessed December 22, 2016, https://www.theguardian.com/technology/2016/dec/22/why-time-management-is-ruining-our-lives. Given this, it is no less fascinating to contemplate the effects of Mann's influence during this peak moment of GTD evangelism in the heart of Silicon Valley, since former Google employees now run their own companies according to productivity principles (see chapter 4). "Talks at Google" are regularly recorded for public consumption and have featured a number of time management evangelists over the years. A compelling example is Tim Ferriss's attributing to the Stoics the basic principles of his mindfulness practice, saying, "You fall to the level of your training": see Tim Ferriss, "How to Cage the Monkey Mind," accessed June 3, 2017, https://www.youtube.com/watch?v=I7Foam6oKPI.

24 See http://getcoldturkey.com.

25 See http://selfcontrolapp.com.

26 See http://visitsteve.com/made/selfcontrol. This explanation was offered by the developer in response to my blog post "The Territory of the Post-Professional," November 5, 2012, accessed May 9, 2017 http://homecookedtheory.com/archives/2012/11/05/the-territory-of-the-post-professional.

27 See http://pavlok.com/hello.php, accessed April 8, 2016.

28 See www.rescuetime.com, www.publicspace.net/Vitamin-R, and www.omnigroup.com/products/omnifocus, accessed June 3, 2017.

29 Michel Foucault, *The Order of Things: An Archaeology of the Human Sciences* (New York: Pantheon, 1970).

30 See Timothy Ferriss, *The Four-Hour Workweek: Escape 9-5, Live Anywhere, and Join the New Rich* (New York: Crown, 2007).

31 Such as Walter Scott's *Increasing Human Efficiency in Business* (New York: Macmillan, 1911).

32 The phrase is the working title for Lauren Berlant's forthcoming book, referenced in "The Commons: Infrastructures for Troubling Times," *Environment and Planning D: Society and Space* 34, no. 3 (2016): 393–419.

33 Alec Mackenzie, *The Time Trap* (New York: AMACOM, 1972), 69.

34 Lambert, comment on "The Territory of the Post-Professional."

35 Tom Streeter, *The Net Effect: Romanticism, Capitalism, and the Internet* (New York: New York University Press, 2011), 13.

36 Streeter, *The Net Effect*, 13.

37 Charles Duhigg elaborates, "Motivation is triggered by making choices that demonstrate to ourselves that we are in control. The specific choice we make matters less than the assertion of control. It's this feeling of self-determination that gets us going": Charles Duhigg, *Smarter, Faster, Better: The Secrets of Being Productive in Life and Business* (New York: Random House), 20.

38 Luc Boltanski and Ève Chiapello, *The New Spirit of Capitalism*, trans. Gregory Elliott (New York: Verso, 2005).

39 William H. Whyte, *The Organization Man* (Harmondsworth, UK: Penguin, 1956).

40 On the relationship between the Quantified Self subculture and productivity, see Gina Neff and Dawn Nafus, *Self-Tracking* (Cambridge: MIT Press, 2016). Also Phoebe Moore and Andrew Robinson, "The Quantified Self: What Counts in the Neoliberal Workplace," *New Media and Society* 18, no. 11 (2015): 2774–92, accessed May 9, 2017, doi: 10.1177/1461444815604328.

41 Mackenzie, "The Affect of Efficiency," 149. Mackenzie's analysis accentuates GTD's casual solipsism, which enables already privileged individuals "to differentiate themselves." GTD provides "a delusional and probably short-lived self-satisfaction to individuals keen to keep abreast of the waves created by their own careers and their own enthusiasm for more communication and more speed": Mackenzie, "The Affect of Efficiency," 138. It illustrates productivity's circular reward structure, which holds that it is always better to "do more." But such "enhanced efficiency only matters if some other people appear to be less mobile"—that is, if all agree to the same economy of activity: Mackenzie, "The Affect of Efficiency," 143.

42 Trebor Scholz, *Uberworked and Underpaid: How Workers Are Disrupting the Digital Economy* (Cambridge: Polity, 2017).

43 Ayn Rand, *Atlas Shrugged*, (New York: Penguin, [1957] 1992).

44 Morgan Ames, Daniela Rosner and Ingrid Erickson, "Worship, Faith, and Evangelism: Religion as an Ideological Lens for Engineering Worlds," in *Proceedings of CSCW 2015, ACM Conference on Computer-Supported Cooperative Work* (New York: ACM, 2015); Streeter, *The Net Effect*; Fred Turner, "Burning Man at Google: A Cultural Infrastructure for New Media Production," *New Media and Society* 11, nos. 1–2 (February–March 2009): 73–94, accessed May 9, 2017, doi: 10.1177/1461444808099575; Fred Turner, *From Counterculture to Cyberculture: Stewart Brand, the Whole Earth Network, and the Rise of Digital Utopianism* (Chicago: University of Chicago Press, 2006).

45 Miya Tokumitsu, *Do What You Love: And Other Lies About Success and Happiness* (New York: Regan Arts, 2015).

46 Michel Foucault, "An Aesthetics of Existence," in *Politics, Philosophy, Culture: Interviews and Other Writings, 1977–1984*, ed. Lawrence D. Kritzman (New York: Routledge, 1988).

4 MINDFUL LABOR

1 Ben Tarnoff, "The New Status Symbol: It's Not What You Spend—It's How Hard You Work," *The Guardian*, April 24, 2017, accessed May 9, 2017, https://www.theguardian.com/technology/2017/apr/24/new-status-symbol -hard-work-spending-ceos.

2 Mark Weiser and John Seely Brown published "Designing Calm Technology" from Xerox PARC as early as 1995: Mark Weiser and John Seely Brown, "Designing Calm Technology," Xerox PARC, December 21, 1995, accessed June 13, 2017, http://www.ubiq.com/weiser/calmtech/calmtech.htm. This background informs the more recent writing of Amber Case, who addresses practitioners in the now established field of User Experience Design: Amber Case, *Calm Technology: Principles and Patterns for Non-Intrusive Design* (Sebastapol, CA: O'Reilly Media, 2015). On the varieties of technology refusal and nonuse in scholarly work, see Eric Baumer, Jenna Burrell, Morgan Ames, Jed Brubaker and Paul Dourish, "On the Importance and Implications of Studying Technology Non-Use," *Interactions* 22, no. 2 (2015): 52–56, accessed May 9, 2017, doi: 10.1145/2723667.

3 As with Luke Stark in the previous chapter, at the time of this study Ellie was a doctoral student in the Intel Science and Technology Center for Social Computing that brought me to Intel. Her thesis was defended at the Department of Information and Computer Science, University of California, Irvine, in 2015.

4 See Thu-Huong Ha, "America's Obsession with Adult Coloring Is a Cry for Help," QZ, April 24, 2016, accessed April 26, 2016, http://qz.com/650378/the -sad-reason-american-adults-are-so-obsessed-with-coloring-books. Scholarship is limited on the success of mindfulness techniques in the management of stress and workload, although more is under way. An excellent overview is Lillian Eby et al., "Mindfulness-Based Training Interventions for Employees: A Qualitative Review of the Literature," *Human Resource Management Review* (April 2017), accessed May 10, 2017, doi: 10.1016/j.hrmr.2017.03.004. I thank Sam Ladner for the pointer.

5 Leslie A. Perlow illustrates the definitive benefits of predictable time off for high performance work cultures such as consulting in *Sleeping with Your Smartphone: How to Break the 24/7 Habit and Change the Way You Work* (Boston: Harvard Business Review Press, 2012). Lawrence F. Katz and Alan B. Krueger, "The Rise and Nature of Alternative Work Arrangements in the United States, 1995–2015," March 29, 2016, accessed May 10, 2017, http://krueger

.princeton.edu/sites/default/files/akrueger/files/katz_krueger_cws_-_march _29_20165.pdf.

6 See http://blog.trello.com/tools-for-remote-work-success-infographic, accessed May 10, 2017.

7 David Gelles, *Mindful Work: How Meditation Is Changing Business from the Inside Out* (Boston: First Mariner, 2016).

8 Arlie Russell Hochschild, *The Managed Heart: Commercialization of Human Feeling* (Berkeley: University of California Press, 1983).

9 See Eva Illouz, *Cold Intimacies* (Cambridge: Polity, 2007). Given the task-oriented nature of work performance outlined in chapter 3, this chapter furthers the case for an erasure of the distinction E. P. Thompson famously made between peasant societies—dependent on the season, focused on the task—and modern employment relations. "As soon as actual hands are employed the shift from task-orientation to timed labour is marked," Thompson wrote: E. P. Thompson, "Time, Work-Discipline, and Industrial Capitalism," *Past and Present* 38 (1967): 56–97. In the present conjuncture, when knowledge professions depend so heavily on the mind rather than the hand, a new attitude to time is also occasioned. It is not that women failed to follow the appropriate development to modern, factory-based experiences of time management as architected by the clock. As we know, women have been involved in factory labor from the very beginning. Rather, it is the experience of time management in relation to others—care labor— that has outlasted the stopwatch metrics of the Organization. Thompson even anticipates this in his landmark essay, writing, "The rhythms of women's work in the home are not wholly attuned to the measurement of a clock"; the mother of small children "attends to other human tides." Whether care of the self enabled through mindfulness practice can lead to selfless concern for other colleagues will be the basis of discussion in the next two chapters.

10 B. Joseph Pine II and James H. Gilmore, "Welcome to the Experience Economy," *Harvard Business Review*, July–August 1998, accessed May 10, 2017, https://hbr.org/1998/07/welcome-to-the-experience-economy.

11 Eric Newcomer and Olivia Zaleski, "When Their Shifts End, Uber Drivers Set Up Camp in Parking Lots across the U.S." *Bloomberg Technology*, January 23, 2017, accessed May 10, 2017, https://www.bloomberg.com/news/articles/2017 -01-23/when-their-shifts-end-uber-drivers-set-up-camp-in-parking-lots -across-the-u-s.

12 Lawrence Grossberg, *Dancing in Spite of Myself: Essays on Popular Culture* (Durham, NC: Duke University Press, 1997), 15. I make a similar argument about the nascent popularity of Facebook in Melissa Gregg, *Work's Intimacy* (London: Polity, 2011).

13 Evgeny Morozov, "The Mindfulness Racket," *New Republic*, February 23, 2014, accessed September 1, 2016, https://newrepublic.com/article/116618/technologys -mindfulness-racket.

14 Cristina Morini, "The Feminization of Labour in Cognitive Capitalism," *Feminist Review* 87 (2007): 40–59, accessed May 5, 2017, doi: 10.1057/palgrave.fr .9400367.

15 Maurizio Lazzarato, "Immaterial Labor," in *Radical Thought in Italy: A Potential Politics*, ed. Paolo Virno and Michael Hardt (Minneapolis: University of Minnesota Press, 1996), 132–46; Tiziana Terranova, "Free Labor: Producing Culture for the Digital Economy," *Social Text* 18, no. 2 (2000): 33–58, accessed May 9, 2017, doi:10.1215/01642472-18-2_63-33.

16 Ron Purser and David Loy, "Beyond McMindfulness," *Huffington Post*, August 31, 2013, accessed May 10, 2017, http://www.huffingtonpost.com/ron-purser /beyond-mcmindfulness_b_3519289.html.

17 Later in the chapter I use autoethnographic observations to establish this point. Seeking methodological solutions for the productivity pressures of life as a mobile knowledge worker is a feature I continue from my previous writing. In naming part III "Anthropotechnics," I acknowledge both Sloterdijk's influence and my own implication in processes of management that promote a simultaneously bankrupt and archly personalizing discourse of corporate career aspiration.

18 Eve Kosofsky Sedgwick, "Pedagogy of Buddhism," in *Touching Feeling: Affect, Pedagogy, Performativity* (Durham, NC: Duke University Press, 2003), 153–82.

19 R. John Williams, "Technê-Zen and the Spiritual Quality of Global Capitalism," *Critical Inquiry* 37 (Autumn 2011): 17–70, accessed June 14, 2017, doi: 10.1086/661643.

20 Gelles, *Mindful Work*, 1–3. The cliché of the guru at the workplace was both confirmed and lampooned in the first season of HBO's *Silicon Valley* (2014).

21 Eckhart Tolle, *The Power of Now: A Guide to Spiritual Enlightenment* (Vancouver: Namaste, 1997).

22 Jon Kabat-Zinn, *Full Catastrophe Living: Using the Wisdom of Your Body and Mind to Face Stress, Pain, and Illness*, 15th anniversary ed. (New York: Delta Trade Paperbacks, [1990] 2005).

23 The clinic had been operating for more than thirty-five years at the time of writing. In the early imprints of the book, the number of patients graduating from the program worked as a form of evidence to improve the legitimacy of MBSR in the mainstream view.

24 Jon Kabat-Zinn, *Wherever You Go, There You Are: Mindfulness Meditation in Everyday Life* (New York: Hyperion, 1994).

25 Kabat-Zinn, *Full Catastrophe Living*, 12–13.

26 The signature iconography of Craig Jarrow, the "Time Management Ninja"—a masked head—carries odd connotations, given Jarrow's ethnic status and stated goal "to win the battle against wasted time, disorganization and all other things evil": see https://timemanagementninja.com, accessed June 4, 2017. David Allen's 2012 TED talk explains the art of stress-free productivity as

a judo move: see David Allen, "The Art of Stress-Free Productivity," accessed June 4, 2017, https://www.youtube.com/watch?v=CHxhjDPKfbY. These examples illustrate what Jane Chi Hyun Park terms "oriental style," or the ways in which East Asian cultures bear the false privilege of conveying technological superiority: Jane Chi Hyun Park, *Yellow Future: Oriental Style in Hollywood Cinema* (Minneapolis: University of Minnesota Press, 2010).

27   Cheng Yi, *Tao of Organization: The I Ching for Group Dynamics*, trans. Thomas Cleary (Boston: Shambala, 1988).

28   Williams, "Technê-Zen and the Spiritual Quality of Global Capitalism."

29   Kabat-Zinn, *Full Catastrophe Living*, 33.

30   Facebook's motto, "Move fast and break things," and the more pervasive creed of the software engineer, "Done is better than perfect," are contemporary updates of this long-standing business maxim.

31   Kabat-Zinn, *Full Catastrophe Living*, 60.

32   Kabat-Zinn, *Full Catastrophe Living*, 56.

33   Kabat-Zinn, *Full Catastrophe Living*, 60.

34   For instance, the "V" in Laura Stack's PRODUCTIVE rubric recommends quarantining part of your calendar for "vitality"—attention to physiology and self-care: Laura Stack, *Leave the Office Earlier: The Productivity Pro® Shows You How to Do More in Less Time . . . and Feel Great about It* (New York: Broadway, 2004), 243–69. Alan Lakein advises readers to "always reserve at least an hour a day of uncommitted time. Leave holes in your schedule for recovery": Alan Lakein, *How to Get Control of Your Time and Your Life* (New York: Penguin, 1973), 57.

35   See Thich Nhat Hanh, "Mindfulness as a Foundation for Health," accessed February 24, 2018, https://www.youtube.com/watch?v=Ijnt-eXukwk.

36   Intel's Awake@Work program is another example. This employee-led initiative was officially adopted as part of the company's workplace wellness programs only after a concerted effort to prove the value of the training by advocates who taught the classes on their own time. Meditation circles continue to operate at lunchtime on some campuses. Following the layoff that occurred at Intel in 2016, the program was listed as one of a range of support services available to workers in the interests of easing what one manager described as "survivor remorse."

37   An example from Wisdom 2.0 2013 is when Evan Williams, co-founder of Blogger and Twitter, and Jonathan Rosenstein, creator of Facebook's Like button and founder of collaboration software platform Asana, discuss "Mindfully Building a Company from the Ground Up" with the event organizer, Soren Gordhamer, accessed May 10, 2017, http://new.livestream.com/accounts/2635433 /events/1887199/videos/12290783.

38   There are overlaps between the quasi-spiritual aspects of Wisdom 2.0 and the Conscious Business ideals associated with the Esalen Institute at Big Sur.

(Esalen hosted the 2014 Wisdom 2.0 conference.) Conscious Business conferences are comparatively removed from the technology emphasis of Wisdom 2.0, instead encouraging companies to operate in accordance with four key principles: Higher Purpose, Conscious Leadership, Stakeholder Orientation, and Conscious Culture: see http://www.consciouscapitalism.org.

39 Screengrab from http://choosemuse.com, March 2014.

40 Nick Scott, "The App That Can Read Your Mind," CNN, September 25, 2013, accessed May 15, 2017, http://www.cnn.com/2013/09/25/tech/muse-brain-training -orig-ideas/index.html#. Subsequent quotes are from the video.

41 It is not incidental to my argument that EXOS consults directly to sports teams, the military, and big companies to provide wellness programs targeting both physical exercise and diet/meal guidelines (see https://en.wikipedia .org/wiki/EXOS). My own workplace at Intel offers appointments with EXOS trainers as part of its annual health benefits for full-time employees.

42 All quotes are from bLife website screengrabs, March 2014, http://blog.myblife .com/about. At the time of this writing, the bLife website is no longer updating.

43 Paul Campbell, "The Science of Mind Fitness," TEDx Venice Beach, published December 26, 2013, accessed June 4, 2017, https://www.youtube.com /watch?v=ZfoErA-ReeE.

44 Direct e-mail, May 24, 2016.

45 Thync Anthem Video, accessed June 4, 2017, https://www.youtube.com /watch?v=FydvBG6S1hE.

46 At the time of writing, Thync has released a "Relax Pro" version for the business professional trying to control anxiety and sleep. It is featured on the splash page at http://www.thync.com, accessed June 4, 2017.

47 See Megan Rose Dickey, "This Headband Reads Your Brainwaves and Creates a Chart Showing How 'Zen' You Are," *Business Insider*, January 13, 2014, accessed June 4, 2017. http://www.businessinsider.com/muse-brain-sensing-headband -2014-1.

48 Ellie Harmon, presentation to the Social Media and Psycho/Social Well Being Symposium, Rutgers University, New Brunswick, NJ, 2014.

49 In an internal report on wellness apps for Intel, Harmon raises a number of observations pertinent to theories of affective labor. With brain-sensing technologies, the performance of appropriate affect moves beyond the emotional labor of service with a smile. Instead of keeping a "poker face" in professional settings, Harmon writes, the "systems prompt us to ask, how do you keep a poker brain? In what ways can our brain waves betray our emotions? How do you hide your feeling of success or failure from the computer?" Wearable technologies like these challenge us to train our bodies to impress our hidden selves as much as other people, to control our brain's performance as registered by a continually updated and tweaked algorithm.

50 Ron Purser and David Forbes, "Search outside Yourself: Google Misses a Lesson

in Wisdom 101," *Huffington Post*, May 5, 2014, accessed June 4, 2017, http://www
.huffingtonpost.com/ron-purser/google-misses-a-lesson_b_4900285.html

51   Kabat-Zinn, *Full Catastrophe Living*, 101.

52   The speech, like all Wisdom 2.0 videos, is available for conference delegates
at the event website with a paid login: http://livestream.com/accounts/2635433
/events/1887199/videos/12435560.

53   "The Rise of Mindfulness in Society: Arianna Huffington, Jon Kabat-Zinn,"
accessed June 4, 2017, https://www.youtube.com/watch?v=2jtOY2mpHdg.

54   Noah Shachtman, "In Silicon Valley, Meditation Is No Fad. It Could Make Your
Career," *Wired*, June 18, 2013, accessed June 13, 2017, http://www.wired.com
/2013/06/meditation-mindfulness-silicon-valley.

55   A characteristic aside mentioned by Patricia Clough in her keynote at the Apps
and Affect conference, Western University, Ontario, 2013.

56   Wendy Chun, *Updating to Remain the Same: Habitual New Media* (Cambridge, MA: MIT Press, 2016).

57   Emily Tess Katz, "Arianna Huffington Reveals How Fainting Changed Her
Whole Life," *Huffington Post*, March 25, 2014, accessed June 4, 2017, http://www
.huffingtonpost.com/2014/03/25/arianna-huffington-fainting_n_5030365.html.

58   Levi Felix, "I HAVE A BRAIN TUMOR—WeGotThis!" e-mail sent April 14,
2016. I thank Ellie Harmon for remaining a loyal research informant and forwarding the e-mail to me long after her own project was completed.

59   Lauren Berlant, *Cruel Optimism* (Durham, NC: Duke University Press, 2011).

60   Sarah Sharma, *In the Meantime: Temporality and Cultural Politics* (Durham,
NC: Duke University Press, 2014). On the productive role of negative affects in
the emotional armory of contemporary capitalism, see Sianne Ngai, *Ugly Feelings* (Cambridge. MA: Harvard University Press, 2007).

61   This blog entry at http://www.goodtherapy.org/blog/overcoming-fomo-what
-fuels-your-fear-of-missing-out-0418167, accessed September 2, 2016, is an
example. On the need to politicize detox efforts and hold technology companies accountable for device dependence, see Adam Fish, "Technology Retreats and the Politics of Social Media," *Triple C: Communication, Capitalism and Critique* 15, no. 1 (2017): 355–69, accessed June 4, 2017, http://triple-c
.at/index.php/tripleC/article/view/807/992. Alex Madrigal was an early skeptic
of technology refusal: see Alex Madrigal, "'Camp Grounded,' 'Digital Detox,'
and the Age of Techno-Anxiety," *The Atlantic*, July 9, 2013, accessed May 10, 2017,
https://www.theatlantic.com/technology/archive/2013/07/camp-grounded
-digital-detox-and-the-age-of-techno-anxiety/277600.

62   Julia Ticona studies contingent workers and the essential role of mobile devices in juggling multiple jobs: Julie Ticona, "Left to Our Own Devices: Navigating the Risks of Work and Love with Personal Technologies," Ph.D. diss.,
University of Virginia, Charlottesville, VA, 2016. Meanwhile, Melissa Mazmanian and Ingrid Erickson show the impact of professional availability expec-

tations on professionals in "The Product of Availability: Understanding the Economic Underpinnings of Constant Connectivity," *Proceedings of the ACM SIGCHI Conference on Human Factors in Computing Systems* (2014): 763–72.

63   Kabat-Zinn, *Full Catastrophe Living*, 96.

64   Kabat-Zinn, *Full Catastrophe Living*, 13.

65   Harmon's repeated visits to Wisdom 2.0 revealed the importance of daily meditation at Obvious/Medium and of the companywide yoga classes started by Gopi Kallayil at Google, among other mindful business initiatives.

66   Thich Nhat Hanh, *Being Peace* (Berkeley, CA: Parallax, [1987] 1996).

67   See Kathi Weeks, *The Problem with Work: Feminism, Marxism, Antiwork Politics, and Postwork Imaginaries* (Durham, NC: Duke University Press, 2011), and the work of the artists Richard Ibghy and Marilou Lemmens, whose consistent thematic interest in questioning the productivity imperative inspired me to solicit their work for this book's cover. See http://www.ibghylemmens.com.

68   As the previous chapter noted, Ferris outlined this practice in a talk he gave at Google on May 26: Tim Ferriss, "How to Cage the Monkey Mind," accessed May 15, 2017, https://www.youtube.com/watch?v=I7Foam6oKPI.

69   Sloterdijk, *You Must Change*, 268.

70   Slavoj Žižek, "From Western Marxism to Western Buddhism," *Cabinet Magazine*, no. 2 (Spring 2011), accessed June 4, 2017, http://www.cabinetmagazine.org/issues/2/western.php.

71   Morozov, "The Mindfulness Racket."

CONCLUSION

1   Ulrich Bröckling, "Gendering the Enterprising Self: Subjectification Programs and Gender Differences in Guides to Success," *Distinktion*, no. 11 (2005): 18, accessed June 13, 2017, doi: 10.1080/1600910X.2005.9672910. Sianne Ngai observes a similar trend of subjective reconfiguration, drawing on Paul Virno: Sianne Ngai, *Ugly Feelings* (Cambridge, MA: Harvard University Press, 2007), 4.

2   Bröckling, "Gendering the Enterprising Self," 18.

3   Ahmed's larger point is imperative. She writes, "Black women and women of color; working-class women; migrant women, women who have worked in the factories, in the fields, at home, women who care for their own children as well as other children, such women have become the arms for other women whose time and energy has been freed. . . . If the freeing up of time and energy depends on other people's labor, we are simply passing our exhaustion on to others": Sara Ahmed, *Living a Feminist Life* (Durham, NC: Duke University Press, 2017), 85.

4   Sarah Sharma, *In the Meantime: Temporality and Cultural Politics* (Durham, NC: Duke University Press, 2014), 149.

5   Stephen Barley and Gideon Kunda explain that scientific management "oc-curred in conjunction with mechanical engineering's emergence as a dis-tinct occupation" just as a new wave of management theory accompanied the growth of electrical engineering and the broad adoption of the mainframe computer: Stephen R. Barley and Gideon Kunda, "Design and Devotion: Surges of Rational and Normative Ideologies of Control in Managerial Dis-course," *Administrative Science Quarterly* 37, no. 3 (1992): 370, 376, accessed March 19, 2017, doi: 10.2307/2393449. The fields of engineering and manage-ment share an equally fluctuating interest in the humane and social elements of workplace design.

6   Orit Halpern, *Beautiful Data: A History of Vision and Reason since 1945* (Dur-ham, NC: Duke University Press, 2015). I expand on this point in Melissa Gregg, "Inside the Data Spectacle," *Television and New Media* 16, no. 1 (2015): 37–51, doi: 10.1177/1527476414547774.

7   Elizabeth Freeman, *Time Binds: Queer Temporalities, Queer Histories* (Durham, NC: Duke University Press, 2010); Aileen Moreton-Robertson, *The White Pos-sessive: Property, Power, and Indigenous Sovereignty* (Minneapolis: Minnesota University Press, 2015); Judy Wajcman, *Feminism Confronts Technology* (Uni-versity Park: Pennsylvania State University Press, 1991).

8   Lilly Irani, "Difference and Dependence among Digital Workers: The Case of Amazon Mechanical Turk," *South Atlantic Quarterly* 114, no. 1 (2015): 225–34, accessed June 13, 2017, doi: 10.1215/00382876-2831665. See also *In the Crowd*, which documents Mary L. Gray and Siddharth Suri's year-long study of online crowd workers in the United States and India, accessed May 17, 2017, http://www.inthecrowd.org.

9   Neha Thirani Bagri, "Startups in the Gig Economy Will Go to Great Lengths to Avoid Calling Their Employees Employees," *Quartz*, April 6, 2017, accessed May 17, 2017, https://qz.com/952034/startups-in-the-gig-economy-like-uber-and-deliveroo-will-go-to-great-lengths-to-avoid-calling-their-employees-employees. For a full discussion, see Arun Sandararajan, *The Sharing Economy: The End of Employment and the Rise of Crowd-Based Capitalism* (Cambridge, MA: MIT Press, 2016).

10   Nick Srnicek, *Platform Capitalism* (Cambridge: Polity, 2016).

11   A clopen is a rostered shift which requires the worker to close and then reopen the store the following day, often without sufficient time to rest and return; see Daniel Beekman, "Seattle Council May Tackle 'Livable' Schedules for Area Workers," *Seattle Times*, February 4, 2016, accessed May 17, 2017, http://www.seattletimes.com/seattle-news/politics/panel-discussion-calls-for-consistent-service-industry-job-scheduling.

12   The corporate coworking trend is often regarded as an affront to the collectiv-ist origins of community coworking, as well as an assault on the traditional serviced office real estate market. One way to think about the role of cowork-

ing in the current intersection of high tech and real estate investment is that it provides an outlet for critique of the dominant paradigm for arranging work in the enterprise. In her influential study of gay family life, Kath Weston argues that alternatives to a norm often serve to reinforce the dominance of the established model. Even a strong and vocal appreciation of deviations from tradition can underscore the significance of the socially sanctioned version of the practice. In exercising a new opportunity to work alongside *colleagues* that they choose, coworkers display some of the elective affinities that are central to sustaining queer life, even while they rely on the normative idea of the company office to differentiate their choice: Kath Weston, *Families We Choose* (New York: Columbia University Press, 1991).

13   The fact that Slack offers an enterprise version of its product does not disprove my point. I see this tension daily at Intel: the technology and work preferences of users and the bureaucratic IT departments that are struggling to keep up with short-term product turnover and the sophisticated demands of so-called agile workers.

14   Here I follow the example of Timon Beyes and other critical management theorists who introduce the philosophy of aesthetics to provide the contours of a reimagined, and more socially just organization: see Timon Beyes, "Art, Aesthetics and Organization," in *A Research Agenda for Management and Organization Studies,* ed. Barbara Czarniawska (Cheltenham, UK: Edward Elgar, 2016): 115–25. My reading of Daybreaker is also informed by ongoing conversations with Mark Banks, who describes the politics of class, labor, and transcendence in "Being in the Zone of Cultural Work," *Culture Unbound* 6 (2014): 241–62, accessed June 14, 2017, doi: 10.3384/cu.2000.1525.146241.

15   Like Ellie Harmon and Luke Stark, who worked on previous chapters, Lodato was a doctoral student in the Intel Science and Technology Center for Social Computing until 2015, graduating to a postdoctoral position at the Georgia Institute of Technology in 2016–17. Before conducting our research on coworking, we collaborated on projects that focused on the politics of civic hacking in the context of austerity: see Carl DiSalvo, Melissa Gregg, and Thomas Lodato, "Building Belonging," *Interactions* 21, no. 4 (2014): 58–61. I am extremely grateful for Lodato's generosity in teaching me about these new work worlds, which have proved so rewarding to explore in and around our own employment circumstances.

16   This and the following quotation appear in Melissa Gregg and Thomas Lodato, "Managing Community: Coworking, Hospitality and the Future of Work," in *Affect in Relation,* ed. Birgitt Röttger-Rössler and Jan Slaby (New York: Routledge, 2018): 175–96.

17   Seb Olma, *In Defence of Serendipity* (London: Repeater, 2016).

18   Small Business Labs admits the difficulties in tracking a booming market with the non-standard data available internationally in their otherwise compel-

ling forecast at http://www.smallbizlabs.com/2016/08/coworking-forecast-44 -million-members-in-2020.html, accessed May 22, 2017.

19 Gregg and Lodato, "Managing Community," 177.

20 Stephen R. Barley and Gideon Kunda, *Gurus, Hired Guns, and Warm Bodies: Itinerant Experts in a Knowledge Economy* (Princeton, NJ: Princeton University Press, 2004).

21 My profound thanks to Benjamin Dyett for his generous tour of Grind spaces in New York, the closest I will ever get to Wall Street.

22 To the best of my knowledge, MBO Partners first introduced the term "solopreneur" in its annual "State of Independence in America" report: https://www. mbopartners.com/state-of-independence, accessed June 4, 2017.

23 As the website's tagline states, "You need more than a 9–5. We get it": https:// beunsettled.co/, accessed June 4, 2017.

24 See https://www.nomadcruise.com/, accessed May 22, 2017. Stephanie Walden provides a realistic take on the nomad work/vacation in "My Life as a Remote Year Guinea Pig," *Mashable*, accessed June 4, 2017, http://mashable.com/2016/08/13 /remote-year/?utm_cid=mash-com-Tw-main-link#4WtvhBfPo8qz.

25 Colleen Shalby, "Weekday Morning Dance Parties Are Now a Thing," July 13, 2015, accessed June 4, 2017, http://www.pbs.org/newshour/art/start-your -morning-by-going-to-a-7am-sober-rave. There is irony in this objective, given that Rhada and her twin sister, Miki, admit in an interview that they are essentially unemployable. The pair have avoided any typical career path through a run of successful start-up businesses of which Daybreaker is but one. In the portfolio of ventures the twins manage, a line of sustainable underwear designed to rid the world of menstrual shame is another. The twins cite their athletic background as crucial to their business acumen: see Courtney Iseman, "Williamsburg Adventures with the Twin Sisters behind Thinx and Daybreaker," *Racked*, May 23, 2016, accessed June 4, 2017, http://ny.racked.com/2016/5/23/11717668 /miki-radha-agrawal-thinx-daybreaker-williamsburg-nyc.

26 Maggie McCracken, "Four Booze-Free, Mindful Events to Check Out This Summer," *Care 2*, June 7, 2016, accessed June 4, 2017, http://www.care2.com/green living/4-booze-free-mindful-events-to-check-out-this-summer.html.

27 In one email advertisement, the Thync patch discussed in chapter 4 was featured by instructors attending Daybreaker NYC, showing an overlap in the demographics assumed of day dancers and mindfulness technologists.

28 Shalby, "Weekday Morning Weekday Morning Dance Parties Are Now a Thing."

29 SoulCycle's generous IPO valuation attracted multiple write-ups in business media outlets, including Josh Barro's profile "SoulCycle: You Say 'Cult,' I Say 'Loyal Customer Base,'" August 7, 2015, accessed June 4, 2017, http://www .nytimes.com/2015/08/09/upshot/soulcycle-you-say-cult-i-say-loyal-customer -base.html. Michelle Obama's passion for SoulCycle is outlined in a subse-

quent *New York Times* article: Julie Hirschfeld Davis, "A Beat and a Bike: The First Lady's Candlelit Habit," January 10, 2016, accessed May 22, 2017, https://www.nytimes.com/2016/01/11/us/politics/a-beat-and-a-bike-michelle-obamas-candlelit-habit.html?_r=0.

30 Peter Sloterdijk, *Bubbles—Spheres Volume 1: Microspherology*, trans. Wieland Hoban (Cambridge, MA: MIT Press, 2011).

31 "At 'Daybreaker,' a Dance Party to Start the Day," CBS Los Angeles, December 16, 2015, accessed May 22, 2017, http://losangeles.cbslocal.com/2015/12/16/at-daybreaker-a-dance-party-to-start-the-day.

32 "At 'Daybreaker.'" On the productive networking potential and creative frisson of Burning Man in the West Coast tech aristocracy, see Fred Turner, "Burning Man at Google: A Cultural Infrastructure for New Media Production," *New Media and Society* 11, nos. 1–2 (February–March 2009): 73–94, accessed May 9, 2017, doi: 10.1177/1461444808099575.

33 This is an evolution from the dominant form of professional affect and work-related socializing I described in Melissa Gregg, "On Friday Night Drinks: Workplace Affects in the Age of the Cubicle." In *The Affect Theory Reader*, ed. Melissa Gregg and Gregory J. Seigworth, 250–68 (Durham, NC: Duke University Press, 2010).

34 Jen Wieczner, "This Huge Millennial Dance Party Is Literally Taking over Macy's," *Fortune*, April 13, 2016, accessed June 4, 2017, http://fortune.com/2016/04/13/macys-daybreaker-dance-party.

35 Clive Hamilton, *Growth Fetish* (London: Pluto, 2004).

36 Peter Sloterdijk, *You Must Change Your Life* (London: Polity, 2013), 450.

37 Here I am inspired by conversations with Katherine Gibson and especially by the discussion of work that appears in J. K. Gibson-Graham, Jenny Cameron, and Stephen Healy, *Take Back the Economy: An Ethical Guide for Transforming Our Communities* (Minneapolis: University of Minnesota Press, 2013).

Bibliography

Adair, John. *Effective Time Management: How to Save Time and Spend It Wisely.* London: Pan, 1982.

Adkins, Lisa, and Maryanne Dever, eds. *The Post-Fordist Sexual Contract: Working and Living in Contingency.* Houndmills, UK: Palgrave Macmillan, 2016.

Ahmed, Sara. *Living a Feminist Life.* Durham, NC: Duke University Press, 2017.

Ahmed, Sara. *On Being Included: Racism and Diversity in Institutional Life.* Durham, NC: Duke University Press, 2012.

Allen, David. *Getting Things Done.* New York: Viking, 2001.

Alvesson, Mats, Yiannis Gabriel, and Roland Paulsen. *Return to Meaning: A Social Science with Something to Say.* Oxford: Oxford University Press, 2017.

Ames, Morgan, Daniela Rosner, and Ingrid Erickson. "Worship, Faith, and Evangelism: Religion as an Ideological Lens for Engineering Worlds." In *Proceedings of CSCW 2015, ACM Conference on Computer-Supported Cooperative Work.* New York: ACM, 2015.

Aneesh, A. *Virtual Migration: The Programming of Globalization.* Durham, NC: Duke University Press, 2006.

Arterburn, Stephen. *Winning at Work without Losing at Love.* Nashville, TN: Thomas Nelson, 1994.

Balderston, Lydia Ray. *Housewifery: A Manual and Text Book of Practical Housekeeping.* Philadelphia: Lippincott, 1919.

Banks, Mark. "Being in the Zone of Cultural Work." *Culture Unbound* 6 (2014): 241–62. Accessed June 14, 2017. doi: 10.3384/cu.2000.1525.146241.

Banks, Mark. *Creative Justice: Cultural Industries, Work and Inequality.* London: Rowman and Littlefield, 2017.

Banks, Mark. "Fit and Working Again? The Instrumental Leisure of the 'Creative Class.'" *Environment and Planning A* 41, no. 3 (2009): 668–81. Accessed July 24, 2016. doi: 10.1068/a40333.

Barley, Stephen R., and Gideon Kunda. "Design and Devotion: Surges of Rational and Normative Ideologies of Control in Managerial Discourse." *Administrative Science Quarterly* 37, no. 3 (1992): 363–99. Accessed March 19, 2017. doi: 10.2307/2393449.

Barley, Stephen R., and Gideon Kunda. *Gurus, Hired Guns, and Warm Bodies: Itinerant Experts in a Knowledge Economy.* Princeton, NJ: Princeton University Press, 2004.

Barthes, Roland. *Mythologies,* trans. Annette Lavers. Frogmore, UK: Paladin, 1973.

Baumer, Eric, Jenna Burrell, Morgan Ames, Jed Brubaker, and Paul Dourish. "On the Importance and Implications of Studying Technology Non-Use." *Interactions* 22, no. 2 (February 2015): 52–56. Accessed May 9, 2017. doi: 10.1145/2723667.

Beauvoir, Simone de. *The Second Sex,* trans. H. M. Parshley. Harmondsworth, UK: Penguin, [1949] 1972.

Beecher, Catharine. *A Treatise on Domestic Economy, for the Use of Young Ladies at Home, and at School.* Boston: March, Capen, Lyon and Webb, 1841.

Beecher, Catharine, and Harriet Beecher Stowe. *The American Woman's Home,* ed. Nicole Tonkovitch. Hartford, CT: Harriet Beecher Stowe Center, [1869] 2002.

Berlant, Lauren. *Cruel Optimism.* Durham, NC: Duke University Press, 2011.

Beyes, Timon. "Art, Aesthetics and Organization." In *A Research Agenda for Management and Organization Studies,* ed. Barbara Czarniawska, 115–25. Cheltenham, UK: Edward Elgar Publishing, 2016.

Beyes, Timon. "Peter Sloterdijk." In *The Oxford Handbook of Process Philosophy and Organization Studies,* ed. Jenny Helin, Tor Hernes, Daniel Hjorth, and Robin Holt, 567–84. Oxford: Oxford University Press, 2014.

Biggart, Nicole. *Charismatic Capitalism: Direct Selling Organizations in America.* Chicago: University of Chicago Press, 1989.

Bliss, Edwin C. *Getting Things Done: The ABCs of Time Management.* New York: Bantam, [1976] 1980.

Boltanski, Luc, and Ève Chiapello. *The New Spirit of Capitalism,* trans. Gregory Elliott. New York: Verso, 2005.

Bourdieu, Pierre. "The Forms of Capital." In *Handbook of Theory and Research for the Sociology of Education,* ed. John Richardson, 241–58. New York: Greenwood, 1986.

Brannigan, Augustine. "Social Psychology Engineers Wealth and Intelligence: The Hawthorne and Pygmalion Effects." In *The Rise and Fall of Social Psychology: The Use and Misuse of the Experimental Method,* 63–90. New York: Walter de Gruyter, 2004.

Bröckling, Ulrich. "Gendering the Enterprising Self: Subjectification Programs and Gender Differences in Guides to Success." *Distinktion,* no. 11 (2005): 7–25. Accessed June 13, 2017. doi: 10.1080/1600910X.2005.9672910.

Buck-Morss, Susan. "Envisioning Capital: Political Economy on Display." *Critical Inquiry* 21, no. 2 (1995): 434–67. Accessed June 13, 2017. doi 10.1086/448759.

Buholzer, Sonja A. *Frauen starten durch: Erfolgsstrategien für Gewinnerinnen.* Landsberg am Lech, Germany: MVG Verlag, 1999.

Burawoy, Michael. *Manufacturing Consent: Changes in the Labor Process under Monopoly Capitalism.* Chicago: University of Chicago Press, 1979.

Burke, Kenneth. "Literature as Equipment for Living." In *The Critical Tradition: Classic Texts and Contemporary Trends*, 2d ed., ed. David H. Richter, 593–98. Boston: Bedford, 1998.

Butler, Judith. *Gender Trouble: Feminism and the Subversion of Identity.* New York: Routledge, 1999.

Carey, Alex. "The Hawthorne Studies: A Radical Criticism." *American Sociological Review* 32, no. 3 (1967): 403–16.

Carnegie, Dale. *How to Win Friends and Influence People.* Rev. ed. North Ryde, Australia: Eden, [1936] 1988.

Case, Amber. *Calm Technology: Principles and Patterns for Non-Intrusive Design.* Sebastapol, CA: O'Reilly Media, 2015.

Chan, Jenny. "A Suicide Survivor: The Life of a Chinese Worker." *New Technology, Work and Employment* 28, no. 2 (2013): 84–99. Accessed June 13, 2017. doi: 10.1111/ntwe.12007.

Chan, Jenny, Pun Ngai, and Mark Selden. "The Politics of Global Production: Apple, Foxconn and China's New Working Class." *New Technology, Work and Employment* 28, no. 2 (2013): 100–15. Accessed June 13, 2017. doi: 10.1111/ntwe.12008.

Chang, Leslie T. *Factory Girls: From Village to City in a Changing China.* New York: Spiegel and Grau, 2009.

Cheng, Yi. *Tao of Organization: The I Ching for Group Dynamics*, trans. Thomas Cleary. Boston: Shambala, 1988.

Chun, Wendy. *Updating to Remain the Same: Habitual New Media.* Cambridge, MA: MIT Press, 2016.

Cole, Kris. *Make Time: Practical Time Management That Really Works!* Frenchs Forest, Australia: Pearson Education, 2001.

Cooper, Melinda, and Catherine Waldby. *Clinical Labor: Tissue Donors and Research Subjects in the Global Bioeconomy.* Durham, NC: Duke University Press, 2014.

Covey, Stephen. *The Seven Habits of Highly Effective People.* New York: Simon and Schuster, 1989.

Crain, Marion, Winifred Poster, and Miriam Cherry, eds. *Invisible Labor: Hidden Work in the Contemporary World.* Oakland: University of California Press, 2016.

Crainer, Stuart, and Des Dearlove. *Gravy Training: Inside the Business of Business Schools.* San Francisco: Jossey-Bass, 1999.

Csikszentmihalyi, Mihaly. *Finding Flow: The Psychology of Engagement with Everyday Life.* New York: Basic, 1997.

Curtis, Scott. "Images of Efficiency: The Films of Frank B. Gilbreth." In *Films That Work: The Productivity of Media*, ed. Vinzenz Hediger and Patrick Vonderau, 85–99. Amsterdam: Amsterdam University Press, 2009.

Davies, William. *The Happiness Industry: How the Government and Big Business Sold Us Well-Being*. London: Verso, 2015.

DiSalvo, Carl, Melissa Gregg, and Thomas Lodato. "Building Belonging." *Interactions* 21, no. 4 (2014): 58–61. doi: 10.1145/2628685.

Drucker, Peter. *The Effective Executive*. London: Warner, [1967] 1991.

Duhigg, Charles. *The Power of Habit: Why We Do What We Do in Life and Business*. New York: Random House, 2012.

Duhigg, Charles. *Smarter, Faster, Better: The Secrets of Being Productive in Life and in Business*. New York: Random House, 2016.

Eby, Lillian, Tammy D. Allen, Kate M. Conley, Rachel L. Williamson, Tyler G. Henderson, and Victor S. Mancini. "Mindfulness-Based Training Interventions for Employees: A Qualitative Review of the Literature." *Human Resource Management Review* (April 2017). Accessed May 10, 2017. doi: 10.1016/j.hrmr.2017.03.004.

Ehrenreich, Barbara, and Arlie Russell Hochschild, eds. *Global Woman: Nannies, Maids, and Sex Workers in the New Economy*. New York: Holt Paperback, 2002.

Elias, Megan J. *Stir It Up: Home Economics in American Culture*. Philadelphia: University of Pennsylvania Press, 2008.

Ely, Robin J., Pamela Stone, and Colleen Ammerman. "Rethink What You 'Know' about High-Achieving Women." *Harvard Business Review* (December 2014). Accessed July 25, 2016. https://hbr.org/2014/12/rethink-what-you-know-about-high-achieving-women.

Federici, Silvia. *Revolution at Point Zero: Housework, Reproduction, and Feminist Struggle*. Oakland, CA: PM Press, 2012.

Ferriss, Timothy. *The Four-Hour Workweek: Escape 9–5, Live Anywhere, and Join the New Rich*. New York: Crown, 2007.

Fish, Adam. "Technology Retreats and the Politics of Social Media." *Triple C: Communication, Capitalism and Critique* 15, no. 1 (2017): 355–69. Accessed June 4, 2017. http://triple-c.at/index.php/tripleC/article/view/807/992.

Fortunati, Leopoldina. *The Arcane of Reproduction: Housework, Prostitution, Labor and Capital*. New York: Autonomedia, 1995.

Fortunati, Leopoldina. "Gender and the Mobile Phone." In *Mobile Technologies: From Telecommunications to Media*, ed. Gerard Goggin and Larissa Hjorth, 23–24. London: Routledge, 2009.

Foucault, Michel. "An Aesthetics of Existence." In *Politics, Philosophy, Culture: Interviews and Other Writings, 1977–1984*, ed. Lawrence D. Kritzman. New York: Routledge, 1988.

Foucault, Michel. *The Birth of Biopolitics: Lectures at the Collège de France, 1978–1979*. Edited by Michel Senellart, trans. Graham Burchell. New York: Palgrave Macmillan, 2008.

Foucault, Michel. *The History of Sexuality, Volume One: An Introduction*, trans. Robert Hurley. New York: Pantheon, 1978.

Foucault, Michel. *The Order of Things: An Archaeology of the Human Sciences*. New York: Pantheon, 1970.

Frederick, Christine. *Household Engineering*. San Bernadino, CA: Ulan, [1915] 2014.

Frederick, Christine. *The New Housekeeping*. Philadelphia, PA: Curtis Publishing, 1912.

Freeman, Elizabeth. *Time Binds: Queer Temporalities, Queer Histories*. Durham, NC: Duke University Press, 2010.

Gallop, Jane. *Anecdotal Theory*. Durham, NC: Duke University Press, 2002.

Game, Ann, and Rosemary Pringle. *Gender at Work*. Sydney: Allen and Unwin, 1983.

Gelles, David. *Mindful Work: How Meditation Is Changing Business from the Inside Out*. Boston: Mariner, 2016.

Gershon, Illana. *Down and Out in the New Economy: How People Find (or Don't Find) Work Today*. Chicago: University of Chicago Press, 2017.

Gibson-Graham, J. K., Jenny Cameron, and Stephen Healy. *Take Back the Economy: An Ethical Guide for Transforming our Communities*. Minneapolis: University of Minnesota Press, 2013.

Giddens, Anthony, *Modernity and Self-Identity: Self and Society in the Late Modern Age*. Stanford, CA: Stanford University Press, 1991.

Gilbreth, Lillian. *The Psychology of Management: The Function of the Mind in Determining, Teaching, and Installing Methods of Least Waste*. New York: Sturgis and Walton, 1914.

Gill, Rosalind, and Andy Pratt. "In the Social Factory? Immaterial Labour, Precariousness and Cultural Work." *Theory, Culture and Society* 25, nos. 7–8 (2008): 1–30.

Gillespie, Richard. *Manufacturing Knowledge: A History of the Hawthorne Experiments*. Cambridge: Cambridge University Press, 1991.

Graham, Laurel D. "Domesticating Efficiency: Lillian Gilbreth's Scientific Management of Homemakers, 1924–1930." *Signs* 24, no. 31 (1999): 633–74. Accessed June 14, 2017. doi 10.1086/495368.

Gregg, Melissa. "The Athleticism of Accomplishment: Speed in the Workplace." In *The Sociology of Speed: Digital, Organizational, and Social Temporalities*, ed. Judy Wajcman and Nigel Dodd, 102–14. Oxford: Oxford University Press, 2016.

Gregg, Melissa. *Cultural Studies' Affective Voices*. Houndmills, UK: Palgrave Macmillan, 2006.

Gregg, Melissa. "The Effective Academic Executive." *Cultural Studies* 29, no. 4 (2015): 590–608. doi: 10.1080/09502386.2014.1000609.

Gregg, Melissa. "Getting Things Done: Productivity, Self-Management and the Order of Things." In *Networked Affect*, ed. Ken Hillis, Susanna Paasonen, and Michael Petit, 187–202. Cambridge, MA: MIT Press, 2015.

Gregg, Melissa. "Inside the Data Spectacle." *Television and New Media* 16, no. 1 (2015): 37–51. doi: 10.1177/1527476414547774.

Gregg, Melissa. "On Friday Night Drinks: Workplace Affects in the Age of the Cubicle." In *The Affect Theory Reader*, ed. Melissa Gregg and Gregory J. Seigworth, 250–68. Durham, NC: Duke University Press, 2010.

Gregg, Melissa. "Presence Bleed: Performing Professionalism Online." In *Theorizing Cultural Work: Labour, Continuity and Change in the Creative Industries*, ed. Mark Banks, Rosalind Gill, and Stephanie Taylor, 122–34. London: Routledge, 2013.

Gregg, Melissa. "The Return of Organisation Man: Commuter Narratives and Suburban Critique." *Cultural Studies Review* 18, no. 2 (September 2012): 242–61. doi: 10.5130/csr.v18i2.2767.

Gregg, Melissa. "White Collar Intimacy." In *Digital Cultures and the Politics of Emotion*, ed. Athina Karatzogianni and Adi Kuntsman, 147–64. London: Routledge, 2012.

Gregg, Melissa. *Work's Intimacy*. London: Polity, 2011.

Gregg, Melissa, and Thomas Lodato. "Managing Community: Coworking, Hospitality and the Future of Work." In *Affect in Relation*, ed. Birgitt Röttger-Rössler and Jan Slaby. Forthcoming, 175–96. New York: Routledge, 2018.

Grossberg, Lawrence. *Dancing in Spite of Myself: Essays on Popular Culture*. Durham, NC: Duke University Press, 1997.

Grudin, Jonathan, and Gayna Williams. "Two Women Who Pioneered User-Centered Design," *ACM Interactions* 20, no. 6 (October 2013): 15–20. Accessed June 4, 2017. doi: 10.1145/2530538.

Haigh, Gideon. *The Office: A Hardworking History*. Carlton, Australia: Miegunyah, 2012.

Halpern, Orit. *Beautiful Data: A History of Vision and Reason since 1945*. Durham, NC: Duke University Press, 2015.

Hamilton, Clive. *Growth Fetish*. London: Pluto, 2004.

Hanh, Thich Nhat. *Being Peace*. Berkeley, CA: Parallax, [1987] 1996.

Harvey, David. *A Brief History of Neoliberalism*. Oxford: Oxford University Press, 2005.

Hatton, Erin. *The Temp Economy: From Kelly Girls to Permatemps in Postwar America*. Philadelphia: Temple University Press, 2011.

Hester, Helen. "Technically Female: Women, Machines, and Hyperemployment." Paper presented at the Inhuman Symposium, Fridericianum, Kassel, Germany, 2015. Accessed June 12, 2017. https://www.youtube.com/watch?v=ZSBefHq7C_0&feature=youtu.be.

Hjorth, Larissa. *Mobile Media in the Asia-Pacific: Gender and the Art of Being Mobile*. London: Routledge, 2009.

Hochschild, Arlie Russell. *The Managed Heart: Commercialization of Human Feeling*. Berkeley: University of California Press, 1983.

Hochschild, Arlie Russell. *The Time Bind: When Work Becomes Home and Home Becomes Work*. New York: Henry Holt, 1997.

Huczynski, Andrzej. *Management Gurus*, rev. ed. London: Routledge, 2006.

Illouz, Eva. *Cold Intimacies*. Cambridge: Polity, 2007.

Irani, Lilly. "Difference and Dependence among Digital Workers: The Case of Amazon Mechanical Turk." *South Atlantic Quarterly* 114, no. 1 (2015): 225–34. Accessed June 13, 2017. doi: 10.1215/00382876-2831665.

Jarrett, Kylie. *Feminism, Labour and Digital Media: The Digital Housewife*. London: Routledge, 2016.

Kabat-Zinn, Jon. *Full Catastrophe Living: Using the Wisdom of Your Body and Mind to Face Stress, Pain, and Illness*, 15th anniversary ed. New York: Delta Trade Paperbacks, [1990] 2005.

Kabat-Zinn, Jon. *Wherever You Go, There You Are: Mindfulness Meditation in Everyday Life*. New York: Hyperion, 1994.

Kanigel, Robert. *The One Best Way: Frederick Winslow Taylor and the Enigma of Efficiency*. Cambridge, MA: MIT Press, 1997.

Kanter, Rosabeth Moss. *Men and Women of the Corporation*. New York: Basic, 1977.

Keyes, Ralph. *Timelock: How Life Got So Hectic and What You Can Do about It*. New York: HarperCollins, 1991.

Kittler, Friedrich A. *Gramophone, Film, Typewriter*. Stanford, CA: Stanford University Press, 1999.

Koch, Richard. *The 80-20 Principle*. New York: Crown Business, 1999.

Lakein, Alan. *How to Get Control of Your Time and Your Life*. New York: Penguin, 1973.

Lancaster, Jane. *Making Time: Lillian Moller Gilbreth—A Life beyond "Cheaper by the Dozen."* Boston: Northeastern University Press, 2004.

Lazzarato, Maurizio. "Immaterial Labor." In *Radical Thought in Italy: A Potential Politics*, ed. Paolo Virno and Michael Hardt, 132–46. Minneapolis: University of Minnesota Press, 1996.

Leavitt, Sarah A. *From Catharine Beecher to Martha Stewart: A Cultural History of Domestic Advice*. Chapel Hill: University of North Carolina Press.

Lewis, Allyson. *The Seven Minute Difference: Small Steps to Big Changes*. Chicago: Kaplan, 2006.

Lindstrom, Richard. "'They All Believe They Are Undiscovered Mary Pickfords': Workers, Photography, and Scientific Management." *Technology and Culture* 41, no. 4 (October 2000): 725–51. Accessed June 4, 2017. doi: 10.1353/tech.2000.0170.

Lovink, Geert. "Indifference of the Networked Presence: On Time Management of the Self." In *24/7: Time and Temporality in the Network Society*, ed. Robert Hassan and Ronald E. Purser, 161–72. Stanford, CA: Stanford Business Books, 2007.

Lutz, Tom. *Doing Nothing: A History of Loafers, Loungers, Slackers, and Bums in America*. New York: Farrar, Straus and Giroux, 2006.

MacIntyre, Alasdair. *After Virtue: A Study in Moral Theory*, 2d ed. Notre Dame, IN: University of Notre Dame Press, 1984.

Mackenzie, Adrian. "The Affect of Efficiency: Personal Productivity Equipment Encounters the Multiple." *Ephemera: Theory and Politics in Organization* 8, no. 2 (2008): 137–56. Accessed March 19, 2017. http://www.ephemerajournal .org/sites/default/files/8-2mackenzie.pdf.

Mackenzie, R. Alec. *The Time Trap: How to Get More Done in Less Time*. New York: McGraw-Hill, 1975.

Maier, Corinne. *Hello Laziness: Why Hard Work Doesn't Pay*, trans. David Watson. London: Orion, 2005.

Mark, Gloria. *Multitasking in the Digital Age: Synthesis Lectures on Human-Centered Informatics* 8, no. 3 (April 2015): 1–113. Accessed July 24, 2016. doi: 10.2200 /S00635ED1V01Y201503HCI029.

Martínez, Antonio García. *Chaos Monkeys: Obscene Fortune and Random Failure in Silicon Valley*, Kindle ed. New York: HarperCollins, 2016.

Mayo, Elton. *Human Problems of Industrial Civilization*. New York: Macmillan, 1933.

Mazmanian, Melissa, and Ingrid Erickson. "The Product of Availability: Understanding the Economic Underpinnings of Constant Connectivity." In *Proceedings of the ACM SIGCHI Conference on Human Factors in Computing Systems* (2014): 763–72.

Mazmanian, Melissa, Wanda J. Orlikowski, and JoAnne Yates. "The Autonomy Paradox: The Implications of Mobile Email Devices for Knowledge Professionals." *Organization Science* 24 (2013): 1337–57. Accessed March 19, 2017. doi: 10.1287 /orsc.1120.0806.

McCay, James. *The Management of Time*. Englewood Cliffs, NJ: Prentice Hall, [1959] 1995.

McGee, Micki. *Self-Help, Inc.: Makeover Culture in American Life*. Oxford: Oxford University Press, 2005.

McRobbie, Angela. *The Aftermath of Feminism: Gender, Culture and Social Change*. London: Sage, 2009.

Mills, C. Wright. *White Collar*. New York: Oxford University Press, 1951.

Moore, Phoebe, and Andrew Robinson. "The Quantified Self: What Counts in the Neoliberal Workplace." *New Media and Society* 18, no. 11 (2015): 2774–92. Accessed May 9, 2017. doi: 10.1177/1461444815604328.

Moreton-Robertson, Aileen. *The White Possessive: Property, Power, and Indigenous Sovereignty*. Minneapolis: University of Minnesota Press, 2015.

Moretti, Enrico. *The New Geography of Jobs*. New York: Mariner, 2013.

Morini, Cristina. "The Feminization of Labour in Cognitive Capitalism." *Feminist Review* 87 (2007): 40–59. Accessed May 5, 2017. doi: 10.1057/palgrave.fr .9400367.

Morris, Meaghan. *Identity Anecdotes: Translation and Media Culture*. London: Sage, 2006.

Mulvey, Laura. "Visual Pleasure and Narrative Cinema." *Screen* 16, no. 3 (1975): 6–18.

Mumford, Lewis. *Technics and Civilization*. New York: Harcourt, Brace, 1934.

Neff, Gina, and Dawn Nafus. *Self-Tracking*. Cambridge, MA: MIT Press, 2016.

Neilson, Brett, and Ned Rossiter. "From Precarity to Precariousness and Back Again: Labour, Life and Unstable Networks." *Fibreculture Journal* 5 (2005). Accessed March 19, 2017. http://five.fibreculturejournal.org/fcj-022-from-precarity-to -precariousness-and-back-again-labour-life-and-unstable-networks.

Ngai, Sianne. *Ugly Feelings*. Cambridge, MA: Harvard University Press, 2007.

Norman, Donald A. *Emotional Design: Why We Love (or Hate) Everyday Things.* Cambridge, MA: Basic, 2004.

Olma, Seb. *In Defence of Serendipity*. London: Repeater, 2016.

Park, Jane Chi Hyun. *Yellow Future: Oriental Style in Hollywood Cinema*. Minneapolis: University of Minnesota Press, 2010.

Partnoy, Frank. *Wait: The Useful Art of Procrastination*. London: Profile, 2012.

Pateman, Carole. *The Sexual Contract*. Stanford, CA: Stanford University Press, 1988.

Perlow, Leslie A. *Sleeping with Your Smartphone: How to Break the 24/7 Habit and Change the Way You Work*. Boston: Harvard Business Review Press, 2012.

Peters, Tom. *Thriving on Chaos: Handbook for a Management Revolution*. New York: Alfred A. Knopf, 1987.

Piaget, Jean. *Six Psychological Studies*, trans. Anita Tenzer. New York: Vintage, 1968.

Qiu, Jack Linchuan. *Goodbye iSlave: A Manifesto for Digital Abolition*. Urbana-Champaign: University of Illinois Press, 2016.

Rand, Ayn. *Atlas Shrugged*, 35th anniversary ed. New York: Penguin, [1957] 1992.

Richards, Ellen. *The Art of Right Living*. Boston: Whitcomb and Barrows, [1904] 1911.

Robbins, Anthony. *Awaken the Giant Within: How to Take Immediate Control of Your Mental, Emotional, Physical and Financial Destiny!* New York: Simon and Schuster, 1991.

Rose, Nikolas. *Inventing Ourselves: Psychology, Power, and Personhood*. Cambridge: Cambridge University Press, 1998.

Rose, Nikolas. *The Politics of Life Itself: Biomedicine, Power, and Subjectivity in the Twenty-First Century*. Princeton, NJ: Princeton University Press, 2006.

Rose, Nikolas. *Powers of Freedom: Reframing Political Thought*. London: Cambridge University Press, 1999.

Rosenblat, Alex, and Luke Stark. "Algorithmic Labor and Information Asymmetries: A Case Study of Uber's Drivers." *International Journal of Communication* 10, no. 27 (2016): 3758–84. Accessed June 4, 2017. https://ssrn.com/abstract =2686227.

Ross, Andrew. *Fast Boat to China: High-Tech Outsourcing and the Consequences of Free Trade—Lessons from Shanghai*. New York: Vintage, 2007.

Rossiter, Ned. *Software, Infrastructure, Labor: A Media Theory of Logistical Nightmares*. London: Routledge, 2016.

Rutherford, Janice Williams. *Selling Mrs. Consumer: Christine Frederick and the Rise of Household Efficiency*. Athens: University of Georgia Press, 2003.

Sandararajan, Arun. *The Sharing Economy: The End of Employment and the Rise of Crowd-Based Capitalism*. Cambridge, MA: MIT Press, 2016.

Scholz, Trebor. *Platform Cooperativism: Challenging the Corporate Sharing Economy*. New York: Rosa Luxemburg, 2016. Retrieved August 30, 2016 from http://www .rosalux-nyc.org/wp-content/files_mf/scholz_platformcoop_5.9.201650.pdf.

Scholz, Trebor. *Uberworked and Underpaid: How Workers Are Disrupting the Digital Economy*. Cambridge: Polity, 2017.

Schulte, Bridget. *Overwhelmed: Work, Love, and Play When No One Has the Time*. New York: Picador, 2004.

Schwartz, Barry. *Queueing and Waiting: Studies in the Social Organization of Access and Delay*. Chicago: University of Chicago Press, 1975.

Schwartz, Barry. *Why We Work*. London: Simon and Schuster, 2015.

Scott, Walter. *Increasing Human Efficiency in Business*. New York: Macmillan, 1911.

Sedgwick, Eve Kosofsky. "Pedagogy of Buddhism." In *Touching Feeling: Affect, Pedagogy, Performativity*, 153–82. Durham, NC: Duke University Press, 2003.

Sennett, Richard. *The Corrosion of Character: The Personal Consequences of Work in the New Capitalism*. New York: W. W. Norton, 1998.

Sharma, Sarah. *In the Meantime: Temporality and Cultural Politics*. Durham, NC: Duke University Press, 2014.

Sharma, Sarah. "Speed Traps and the Temporal: Of Taxis, Truck Stops, and Task-Rabbits." In *The Sociology of Speed: Digital, Organizational, and Social Temporalities*, ed. Judy Wajcman and Nigel Dodd, 131–51. Oxford: Oxford University Press, 2017.

Sloterdijk, Peter. *Bubbles—Spheres Volume 1: Microspherology*, trans. Wieland Hoban. Cambridge, MA: MIT Press, 2011.

Sloterdijk, Peter. *Foam—Spheres Volume III: Plural Spherology*, trans. Wieland Hoban. Cambridge, MA: MIT Press, 2016.

Sloterdijk, Peter. *Globes—Spheres Volume II: Macrospherology*, trans. Wieland Hoban. Cambridge, MA: MIT Press, 2013.

Sloterdijk, Peter. *You Must Change Your Life*. London: Polity, 2013.

Smart, Andrew. *Auto-Pilot: The Art and Science of Doing Nothing*. New York: OR Books, 2013.

Sonnenfeld, Jeffrey A. "Shedding Light on the Hawthorne Studies." *Journal of Occupational Behavior* 6 (1985): 111–30. Accessed June 13, 2017, doi: 10.1002 /job.4030060203.

Srnicek, Nick. *Platform Capitalism*. Cambridge: Polity, 2016.

Stack, Laura. *Leave the Office Earlier: The Productivity Pro® Shows You How to Do More in Less Time . . . and Feel Great about It*. New York: Broadway, 2004.

Standing, Guy. *The Precariat: The New Dangerous Class*. London: Bloomsbury Academic, 2011.

Steyaert, Chris, Timon Beyes, and Martin Parker, eds. *The Routledge Companion to the Humanities and Social Sciences in Management Education.* London: Routledge, 2016.

Streeter, Tom. *The Net Effect: Romanticism, Capitalism, and the Internet.* New York: New York University Press, 2011.

System Company. *How to Systematize the Day's Work: 87 Plans and Shortcuts Used and Proved at the Desks of 43 Executives,* 9th ed. Chicago: A. W. Shaw, 1911.

Taylor, Frederick W. *The Principles of Scientific Management.* New York: Harper and Brothers, 1911.

Terranova, Tiziana. "Free Labor: Producing Culture for the Digital Economy." *Social Text* 18, no. 2 (2000): 33–58. Accessed May 9, 2017. doi:10.1215/01642472–18–2 _63–33.

Thompson, E. P. "Time, Work-Discipline, and Industrial Capitalism." *Past and Present* 38 (December 1967): 56–97.

Thrift, Nigel. *Knowing Capitalism.* London: Sage, 2005.

Ticona, Julia. "Left to Our Own Devices: Navigating the Risks of Work and Love with Personal Technologies." Ph.D. diss., University of Virginia, Charlottesville, VA, 2016.

Tokumitsu, Miya. *Do What You Love: And Other Lies about Success and Happiness.* New York: Regan Arts, 2015.

Tolle, Eckhart. *The Power of Now: A Guide to Spiritual Enlightenment.* Vancouver: Namaste, 1997.

Tracy, Brian. *Eat That Frog! 21 Great Ways to Stop Procrastinating and Get More Done in Less Time.* San Francisco: Berrett-Koehler, 2006.

Trahair, Richard C. S. *Elton Mayo: The Humanist Temper.* New Brunswick, NJ: Transaction, [1984] 2005.

Turkle, Sherry. *Alone Together: Why We Expect More from Technology and Less from Each Other.* New York: Basic, 2011.

Turkle, Sherry. *Reclaiming Conversation: The Power of Talk in a Digital Age.* New York: Penguin, 2015.

Turner, Fred. "Burning Man at Google: A Cultural Infrastructure for New Media Production." *New Media and Society* 11, nos. 1–2 (February–March 2009): 73–94. Accessed May 9, 2017. doi: 10.1177/1461444808099575.

Turner, Fred. *From Counterculture to Cyberculture: Stewart Brand, the Whole Earth Network, and the Rise of Digital Utopianism.* Chicago: University of Chicago Press, 2006.

Turner, Graeme. *Film as Social Practice,* 4th ed. London: Routledge, [1988] 2006.

Valenti, Vanessa. "Building a Culture of Care in Online Feminist Activism." Paper presented at the Symposium on Social Media and Psychosocial Wellbeing, Rutgers University, New Brunswick, NJ, April 2014.

Wajcman, Judy. *Feminism Confronts Technology.* University Park: Pennsylvania State University Press, 1991.

Wajcman, Judy. *Pressed for Time: The Acceleration of Life in Digital Capitalism*. Chicago: University of Chicago Press, 2015.

Weber, Max. *The Protestant Ethic and the Spirit of Capitalism*, trans. Talcott Parsons. London: George Allen and Unwin, 1930.

Weeks, Kathi. *The Problem with Work: Feminism, Marxism, Antiwork Politics, and Postwork Imaginaries*. Durham, NC: Duke University Press, 2011.

Weston, Kath. *Families We Choose*. New York: Columbia University Press, 1991.

Whyte, William H. *The Organization Man*. Harmondsworth, UK: Penguin, 1956.

Williams, R. John. "Technê-Zen and the Spiritual Quality of Global Capitalism." *Critical Inquiry* 37 (Autumn 2011): 17–70. Accessed June 14, 2017. doi: 10.1086/661643.

Wrege, Charles D., and Ronald G. Greenwood. "Mary B. Gilson—A Historical Study of the Neglected Accomplishments of a Woman Who Pioneered in Personnel Management." Unpublished ms. Accessed June 13, 2017. https://www .thebhc.org/sites/default/files/beh/BEHprint/v011/p0035-p0042.pdf.

Zerubavel, Eviatar. *Hidden Rhythms: Schedules and Calendars in Social Life*. Berkeley: University of California Press, [1981] 1985.

Žižek, Slavoj. "From Western Marxism to Western Buddhism." *Cabinet Magazine* 2 (Spring 2011). Accessed June 4, 2017. http://www.cabinetmagazine.org/issues/2 /western.php.

Index

at the Desks of 43 Executives (System
  Company), 57–59, 65, 68
How to Win Friends and Influence People
  (Carnegie), 70
Hsieh, Tony, 111
Huffington, Arianna, 111, 118–19
human factors engineering, 11–12
humanization of workplace, 55–56
Human Problems of Industrial Civilization
  (Mayo), 41–42
human relations movement, 46–47
Humin app, 5
hybrid conversations, 20–21
hyperemployment, 84

IBM, 32, 55, 149n21
"ideal man," 35
ideals, life of, 26
IFTTT (If This Then That) app, 84
immateriality, 105
"important but not urgent" tasks, 61–62
"Inbox Zero" technique, 87, 162n58
individual, 14, 39–40, 48, 95–96, 129–30; as
  failure, 87–88, 90; heroic, 4, 16, 97–98,
  103; privileged over collective, 91, 130;
  psychological self-surveillance, 76
information technology (IT), 10, 13, 78.
  See also productivity apps
instant tasks, 64
instrumental leisure, 75
Intel, 78, 104, 124, 171n36
InteraXon, 112
interdependence, collegial, 54
interview techniques, 42–44, 47
"intuitive" design, 81–82
isolation: diminished awareness of others,
  54, 67, 93; executive athleticism, 53–54;
  mindfulness and, 107, 119–20; normal-
  ization of, 5, 15; as spiritual transcendence, 97; of workers, x, 4–5, 49

James, William, 70
Japanese management techniques, 56, 108

job security, 55–56
Jobs, Steve, 107

Kabat-Zinn, Jon, 107–10, 116–21, 116, 117,
  124
Kickstarter, 131, 132
knowing capitalism, 53
"Know thyself," 77
"Know Thy Time," 77

labor-saving theories, 11
Ladies' Home Journal, 30
Lakein, Alan, 53, 60–61, 64, 67, 70
Lambert, Steve, 89
Lancaster, Jane, 34
Leavitt, Sarah, 25
legacies, 8, 11
life coaching, 48
life-hacking websites, 66
linear progression, notions of, 16, 130
Lippincott's Home Manuals series, 28
lists and rules, 65–67; deferral lists, 71–73
literary self-production, 69–70, 76
"Literature as Equipment for Living"
  (Burke), 73–74
Lodato, Thomas, 132–33
logistical work, 68, 78–79, 93–99, 128–30,
  129–30
loyalty, 56
lunch, as factor in productivity, 40

Mackenzie, R. Alec, 63, 66, 70, 91, 147n3
Mad Men (television series), 107
Management of Time, The (McKay), 53
Manhattan's Efficiency Society, 23
Mann, Merlin, 87–88, 89, 162n58
Marey, Etienne Jules, 36
marketing, 78
Martinez, Antonio Garcia, 18–19
mass-market management thinking, 60
masters and slaves, language of, 19
maxims, 60
Mayo, Barbara, 42–43

Mayo, Dorothea, 42
Mayo, Elton, 40–47, 128, 158n63
McCay, James, 53, 160–61n17
McKinsey Institute, 3
meaning, 9, 98–99, 121, 138–39
Mechanical Turk, 129
medical interrogation, 44–47
mentoring: Mayo's influence on, 47
micro-movements, 35–37
middle management, 74–75
migrant women, 41, 47
mindful labor, 105–6, 119–20; as organized resistance, 106
mindfulness, 15–17, 69, 103–26, 142; as
  activity, 108–9; apps, 85; being over doing, 110; body-mind gap reified, 116–17;
  "body scan," 109, 116; chronic self-
  analysis, 110; commodified, 105–6, 116;
  connection to others and cosmos, 110,
  117; corporate wellness programs, 70,
  105; detox programs, 120–21; devices,
  111–14; fear of missing out on your
  next job, 120–23; flawed execution, 122;
  hopelessness, rise of, 120–21; isolation
  and, 107, 119–20; judgment suspended,
  108–9; meditation circles, 171n36; from
  me to we, 117–20; mindful workplaces,
  123–26; as "non-doing," 110, 119, 121; optimism for, 125–26; popularity and need
  for, 104–5; populist neuroscience and,
  88; power of now, 106–10; as tactical
  response, 107; technology for, 111–17;
  universalism, casual, 117–19, 122–23.
  See also asceticism
mindfulness apps, 104
"Mindfulness as a Foundation for Health"
  (Thich Nhat Hanh)
mindfulness-based stress reduction
  (MBSR), 107, 109, 114, 116, 120
mobile apps, 12–13
mobile devices, 10
modernity, 8
Moon, Lauren, 104

morality: time-management studies and,
  9, 11, 19, 26–27, 39, 44, 49
Morozov, Evgeny, 105, 126
multitasking, 7
Muse (intelligent headband), 111–13, 121
mythology of time management, 13, 98

National Academy of Engineering, 34
neoliberalism, 54, 96, 127; individualizing
  discourses of, 14
neuroscience, populist, 88
New Age approaches, 119, 123
New England families, 25, 28
New Housekeeping, The (Frederick),
  30–31
"no layoffs, ever" slogan (IBM), 55
Nomad Cruise, 134
non-Western cultural traditions, 69
Norman, Donald, 81
now, concept of, 106–10, 124

Obama, Michelle, 136
occupational insecurity, 5
Olma, Seb, 133
Omnifocus app, 90
omniscience, 90–91
ontological bearing, 66
order, politics of, 91
ordering work, 79
order of things, 79, 82, 86, 90
O'Reilly Media Next Economy conference, 131
Organization, 3, 8, 53, 94–95, 99; organization outside, 48
Organization Man, 56, 160n12
Orientalism as "Oriental culture," 108
other-oriented ethics, 18
outputs of labor, 4, 10–11, 21, 105;
  athleticism and, 56, 61, 75–76; time-
  management studies, 35, 37, 39–41,
  45–46
outsourcing, 4, 12; by homemakers, 24
Ovsepyan, Argine, 136

questionnaires, 71

racial and cultural issues, 6, 9–10, 27, 174n3
recognition for work, 37–49
recordings, making, 70
record-keeping pursuits, 128
Relay Room study (Western Electric), 40–46
repetition, 70, 75, 80
Rescue Time app, 90
responsibility: freedom and, 56; interiorized, 106, 129–30, 163n75
Richards, Ellen, 11, 12, 24–25
Rilke, Rainer Maria, 14
"Rise of Mindfulness in Society, The" (Huffington), 118
ritualization, 15, 60, 95, 138; mindfulness and, 114, 124–25
Roden, Ted, 5
Roethlisberger, Fritz, 40–46, 157n47
Rose, Nikolas, 14
Rosenstein, Justin, 117–18
Rutherford, Janice Williams, 32
Rybacki, Irene, 44–46

salaried workers, 3, 6, 8, 56, 74–75, 130–31, 149n20
scaffolding, 36
schedules, 4, 6, 79, 86, 94, 129–30
scientific management, 10, 21, 175n5; cinematic vision, 36–40, 76, 85, 114. See also domestic science/home economy
second person singular, 76
secretary, 5, 91–93, 157n46, 158n68
Sedgwick, Eve Kosofsky, 106
self-actualization, quantified, 96, 167n49
self-appraisal, 47, 60–62, 72–73; confession tradition, 87–88
self-care, 73–77; "not urgent," 71–73
Self Control app, 88–89
self-discipline, 88–90
self-help guides, ix–x, 12–13, 53; as

codified practice, 54; domestic science, 24–32; personal address characteristic, 70; for women in business, 70. See also time management genres
self-improvement, 11, 14, 76
self-management, 13–14
self-scrutiny, 4
Sennett, Richard, 8
servant question, 12, 27–29, 31, 155n15
service economy, 129
sexual contract, 93
Shachtman, Noah, 119
shared office operators, 131
sharing economy platforms, 17, 130–31
Sharma, Sarah, 7–8, 128
Shell, 66
Silicon Valley, 18–19, 98, 107, 109
Slack (software), 131–32
Sloterdijk, Peter, 13–14, 17–18, 54, 76–77, 96, 125
smartphones, 82
social ethic, 96
social security, 6
Socrates, 77
software, 5–6, 12, 78–79; for personal use, 78–82. See also mindfulness apps; productivity apps
software engineers/programmers, 19
solopreneurs, 134
SoulCycle, 116, 136, 177–78n29
spiritual/religious dimensions of productivity, 9, 12, 14, 21, 25–26, 55, 75, 93; confession tradition, 87–88; ethical dimension of capitalism, 98–99; mindfulness, spiritual legacies at heart of, 105; omniscience and omnipotence, 90–91; others' belief systems adapted, 108; outsourcing and delegating as, 99; in productivity apps, 86–87; ritualization, 15, 60, 95, 114, 125, 138; transcendence, 97
spreadsheets, 63
Stack, Laura, 70